THE COMPLETE
GUIDE TO
WRITING
YOUR
DISSERTATION

Other study skills titles from How To Books:

THE COMPLETE STUDY SKILLS GUIDE
A practical guide for all students who want to know how to learn
Dr Catherine Dawson

WRITING A UCAS PERSONAL STATEMENT IN SEVEN EASY STEPS
A really useful guide to creating a successful personal statement
Julia Dolowicz

HOW TO PASS YOUR EXAMS
Proven techniques for any exam that will guarantee success
Mike Evans

THE JOY OF ENGLISH
100 Illuminating conversations about the English language
Jesse Karjalainen

Write or phone for a catalogue to:

How To Books
Spring Hill House
Spring Hill Road
Begbroke
Oxford
OX5 1RX
Tel. 01865 375794

Or email: info@howtobooks.co.uk

Visit our website www.howtobooks.co.uk to find out more about us and our books.

Like our Facebook page **How To Books & Spring Hill**

Follow us on **Twitter@Howtobooksltd**

Read our books online www.howto.co.uk

THE COMPLETE GUIDE TO
WRITING
YOUR
DISSERTATION

ADVICE, TECHNIQUES AND
INSIGHTS TO HELP YOU
ENHANCE YOUR GRADES

STEVE BALL

howtobooks

Published by How To Books Ltd,
Spring Hill House, Spring Hill Road,
Begbroke, Oxford OX5 1RX, United Kingdom
Tel: (01865) 375794, Fax: (01865) 379162
info@howtobooks.co.uk
www.howtobooks.co.uk

How To Books greatly reduce the carbon footprint of their books by sourcing their typesetting and printing in the UK.

British Library Cataloguing in Publication Data
A catalogue record for this book is available from the British Library

ISBN 978 1 84528 454 1

Produced for How To Books by Deer Park Productions, Tavistock
Typeset by Pantek Media, Maidstone, Kent.
Printed and bound in Great Britain by Bell & Bain Ltd, Glasgow

NOTE: The material contained in this book is set out in good faith for general guidance and no liability can be accepted for loss or expense incurred as a result of relying in particular circumstances on statements made in the book. Laws and regulation are complex and liable to change, and readers should check the current position with the relevant authorities before making personal arrangements.

For Ann, Matt, Tom, James and Will

Contents

Preface

When I was first invited to write this guide I dutifully worked out a structure and pondered the main elements or the content, but I didn't foresee how long the book would need to be or how much time it would eventually take me to write. Not only am I trying to offer something of value to as wide a range of subjects and disciplines as possible, but graduate and postgraduate studies exist in a rapidly changing higher education environment that defies easy generalizations. Many of these changes (though certainly not all) are for the better. One positive consequence is that ever larger numbers of students are encouraged to undertake research as part of their academic studies, a change that is even more marked at undergraduate than at postgraduate level, where research has long had a central role. At risk of repeating what I say in the Introduction, my principal aim here is to help students to make the best of all that hard thinking by turning it into an effective written document – the dissertation itself.

Because of the extra gestation time and labour this book required I have more than the usual need to make an author's plea for forgiveness to family and friends for being unavailable or in hiding at times. This applies particularly to my family. In spite of trying to find as much time as I could around the edges of the 'day job' and many other commitments, I had to take myself off on two separate trips to Staithes, North Yorks – one in 2010 to get the serious business of writing under way and another in the summer of 2011 to finish it. (I was born and brought up by the sea so that's a method that works for me.)

Some of an academic's understanding and expertise in the area of student research come from his or her own studies and training, but the majority of it grows over many years during the supervision and teaching of students themselves. I therefore offer my grateful thanks to all of those undergraduate and postgraduate dissertation students who – unknown to themselves – have helped me to write this book by working with me in either of my roles as supervisor or research methods teacher. Their questions, interests and insights have contributed greatly to my choice of content and my awareness of what students often find difficult or mysterious. It's always a privilege to work with students and we academics learn a great deal in the process.

I'd also like to thank our subject librarian Chris Fowler for her comments on some parts of the draft. Naturally, I am entirely responsible for any shortcomings that remain.

Steve Ball, Oxfordshire and North Yorkshire, 2010–11

Introduction

The target readers of this book are dissertation (or 'major project', 'extended essay', etc.) students in their final undergraduate year or at Masters level who want to showcase their research, thinking, analysis and hard work in the best possible way.

A secondary objective of this book is to help readers understand and apply the tone and character of academic writing in general, so it should be useful to non-dissertation students on other higher education courses. For example, I hope that many parts of the book will be of value to PhD students planning and writing up their theses. Although those students are working on a more extended timescale and creating a longer and more complex document from deeper research, many of the principles of organizing and writing up research, ideas and analysis remain the same.

I also hope that the book will be valuable to another group of students – those who have come to higher education after a long period away from formal education, or who otherwise have relatively little experience of academic writing. People in this position may also be studying part time while holding down a job or bringing up a family and have very limited time even for their main topic of study, let alone for working on extra areas such as study or writing skills. If you are one of these intrepid people, it's likely that you are studying in an environment where students are assumed to have the right kind of writing experience already, so you may feel nervous about what you don't know. There could be additional writing guidance and support services at your university, in which case you must investigate them, but this book will provide you with much of what you may have missed in your time away from formal education.

The idea behind this book

When I was asked to write this book I had to think about what would be most useful to the widest possible range of dissertation students at undergraduate or Masters level. I reflected on the kinds of things that distinguish successful dissertation students – those who thrived on dissertation work as opposed to those who merely plodded through it as a kind of chore, and of course those who got the best marks as opposed to those who didn't. One obvious difference was in the quality of the research that they undertook; another, equally obvious, was how students engaged with the business of working on and writing their dissertations – did they manage their time well, were they diligent or 'disengaged'? Another vital factor was whether they had developed into self-directed researchers who could conduct their own independent inquiry, in contrast to those who expected the dissertation to function like a taught course in which their 'teachers' point them towards 'the answers' or provide a set of ready-made material that contains 'the answers' within it. A dissertation tests the organization, diligence and independence of students far more than any taught course.

The third 'independent learner' factor may become even more significant in the coming years. The depressing price increases that students face in higher education in the UK and elsewhere could reinforce a damaging view that degree level education is some kind of 'product'. People contemplating university may be tempted to think 'I'm paying more so I want better service', rather as somebody expects better service in a more expensive hotel, and demands to be waited on like a king or queen in a vastly expensive one. The problem is that the core purpose and approach of higher education cannot be abandoned without destroying its value, so for example a dissertation has to test independent study and research regardless of what students have to pay to enter the building, as it were. It can't be meaningfully changed into something else where 'servants' bring you what you need. That would simply destroy it and make it pointless.

But another and very variable factor that I noted was the quality of the written dissertation itself, the 'publication' that conveyed all the evidence of what people had done over the preceding months and years. Very often I had seen students choose a good topic, approach it with enthusiasm, do all the right things and undertake good research, and then hand in a fairly ordinary or even poor dissertation that undermined everything they had done.

The long and complex process of actually writing the dissertation – turning your ideas, research, reading, interpretations into a structured document that is fluent and clear and also maximizes your chance of good marks – attracts relatively little attention in some research methods texts and is the subject of fewer books on its own. But the dissertation itself, this final document, is the only visible output of a process that has continued over many months or a year or more – and *it's all that the marker sees*.

So these considerations convinced me that I should write about creating the dissertation itself rather than add yet another example to the number of research methods texts out there, some of which are excellent. This book will be bought by unknown readers across all possible disciplines, so I can't do much about your choice of topic, your general level of diligence and interest, the policies of your university or department, or the particular educational environment in which you find yourself – though I can add some reminders that occur to me along the way. But it seemed to me that a concentration on writing the document would be the most useful approach for most students, if used in conjunction with research methods texts and classes. As I say, I have seen many good pieces of research fail to produce good dissertations.

You as author, you as publisher

Traditional research training can sometimes appear to take your writing ability and mastery of expressive techniques for granted. It's as if they assume you learn all there is to know about writing at school, with perhaps a bit of extra training in the first year of university to help with academic writing in your subject area. Hence when you come to do your final undergraduate year or start at Masters level all you need to think about is the research content and process in your chosen topic plus some appropriate methods of research. Well yes, you certainly do need to think hard about those things, but they're not enough to produce a good dissertation. You must also integrate all of this expertise and research into appropriate ways and channels of expression. You need to publish your research and analysis effectively. My perspective in this book is that your dissertation is very much a publication, albeit one with a peculiarly small and rather fussy readership centred on the people who are going to mark it. Many research methods books dip in and out of that publishing aspect, but this one deals with it head on in every chapter.

So that is where this book differs from many study guides and research methods texts. All the way through, it concentrates on planning, structuring and writing the dissertation, to make the best of all that work you are doing. It is a deceptively ambitious thing for me to try to do, because there is such a huge variety of dissertation-like study and examination across the higher education world. For example, I say on several occasions in this book that a dissertation is not really an essay, but in some arts disciplines a dissertation has a great many essay-like characteristics, and may even be called something like an 'extended essay' rather than a dissertation. In other disciplines, by contrast, typically in science and technology subjects, students may undertake projects and produce reports and other technical documents that are radically different from any kind of essay. In this book I have to try to say something of value for *all* of these kinds of study, and when I talk of the 'dissertation' you should accept that as a shorthand term that covers them all.

Inevitably, anybody writing a wide-ranging book like this has to draw on their own academic and other experience and then find out as much as they can about other areas of study. A law academic may struggle to write something meaningful about, say, engineering, health care or drama, and an engineer may be in a similar position with regard to history or sociology. My own background is that I studied as an undergraduate in engineering, in psychology for a while, and then in philosophy, and as a postgraduate in philosophy. Also, for many years I have been teaching and researching in an academic discipline (publishing) that incorporates diverse research elements from across the arts and humanities, the social sciences and business studies. I'm also linked with politics publishing and political studies, and for a great many years have been an academic editor in many roles and at several levels from commissioning to copy-editing, meaning that I have spent a large part of my life working with academic writing as acquirer, analyst, developer, critic, author's help-mate and more. Thinking through, and about, academic writing is second nature to me. I hope this breadth helps me to see widely enough to make a good job of understanding the range of studies covered by dissertation students, even though I have a relatively full view of some subjects and a much less complete view of others. This is true of anybody writing any kind of study guide or research methods text too.

To help generalize the value of this book I have tried to concentrate on the common elements of what makes up a dissertation or report or extended essay – those things that apply across all such studies, what-ever the discipline. Once you are sure of these, then you can bring some of the more subject-specific detail from your 'local' circumstances: your course documentation, your prior studies in the subject, your research methods classes, and of course by talking to your supervisor and other staff. As far as possible, therefore, I look at what is generalizable – the academic 'best practice' that showcases your own endeavours.

My approach throughout is that the dissertation is a piece of rational evidence-based inquiry that you undertake largely on your own, and that you should aim for structural effectiveness, clarity of expression, and cogency of argument from evidence through to conclusions. I am assuming, in other words, that a dissertation is not just a rambling, opin-ionated lump of text that you dash off in the last few weeks or (even worse) days of the course.

But, as I say, this is not a research methods book, whether general or subject-specific, though I have to allude to research methods and approaches quite often. Nor is it a creative writing text in disguise, or a book based on everyday self-help homilies and platitudes. Although I try to include as much as possible for a large and varied range of students with different backgrounds, at the same time I must avoid reminding you too often of what you already know – which would be annoying.

So you won't find a lot of advice about, say, how it is a good idea to turn on your desk light if it's dark, or that it's unwise to throw your laptop off a tall building, or that drinking a bottle of vodka before you start writing is unlikely to improve the quality of what you write. Duh! As far as methods and rituals are concerned you probably have your own strong ideas and settled customs already. By now you must know which ones work for you. I don't mean that there aren't more sensible and less sensible things to do, and indeed I do mention those where I think they're germane and generally applicable.

There is one proviso, though, and I mention it here at the risk of sounding platitudinous. It is that writing a dissertation is a big deal. It's different from shaped, taught courses, and you should treat it differently. Expect it to take a lot of time, a lot of energy, a lot of work – be prepared for all of that. It may be the only time you do something like it in your life. However, the fact that you're reading this book suggests that you do care enough to want to do it properly.

As far as your own writing is concerned, by the time you have reached the later stages of an undergraduate course, or postgraduate studies, you'll have developed your own settled style and habits of writing. Over several years of essays, reports and exams at school and college, you have evolved your own way of saying things and of writing them down to please people in an academic setting. One of the themes in this book is that you should take time to stand back from all this, and actually look at your writing and how effective it is as another person might see it – in particular those significant 'other people' who are going to mark it. Your developed styles and habits of writing may be fantastic for the purpose, or they may not: I provide some guidelines to help you see which. I'll say more about this in Chapter 6 and also Chapter 10, but I hope you see what I'm getting at. So I hope my advice about style, structure and similar topics is not the equivalent of saying that you should find a nice chair and remember to turn on the light.

Ideally, your dissertation takes your ideas, your research, your work, and showcases them, so it makes sense to do that effectively. It is no good hoping that your markers are willing to hack their way through a jungle of awful disorganized prose to find the treasure hidden within. Don't they know that you're brilliant? Well, they may do, but when they come to mark your dissertation they must take what they find – what you actually say. Your printed dissertation is the only outward evidence of what you've been doing for the past months or years. They have nothing else to go on. You should not expect them to try to second guess what they think you might have wanted to say: 'Hmm', a marker might say. 'Here's an ambiguous sentence that could be interpreted in one of two ways. Did Alex mean this rather brilliant thing or that rather stupid thing? Ah, but we know Alex is brilliant so he/she must have meant the brilliant thing . . .'

No, I'm afraid it doesn't work like that. Besides, brilliant people do say stupid things just like everybody else, and sometimes gifted students make a real mess of a dissertation. When that happens we as markers can feel sad about it, but we are obliged to mark the mess and not the gift. Also, in many marking regimes dissertations are now marked blind – that is, in theory the markers do not know the identity of the students who wrote them, so there is even less chance that the marker will have an unprofessional weak moment and give you the benefit of the doubt.

Under the influence

By the time you start work on your dissertation you will already have read a lot of academic writing in your discipline, and will have written a fair amount too. But there are two particular areas of influence that I'll mention now and return to at times later in the book because they may have a harmful effect on the character and quality of your own academic writing.

The first influence for good or ill is professional academic writing itself, the kind of thing you find in academic monographs and particularly in journals. Most of what gets written is technically excellent – or at least it is technically adequate, or we trust it would not have been published. But professional academic writing can also be stylistically abysmal and involve formulaic text that resembles a kind of insider code. It's easy to confuse the academic voice, the appropriate medium for rational discourse of the kind that you want to use for your dissertation, with this crabbed, sterile formula-speak, which is a kind of writing that can so easily become a habit early in an academic's career. And because you're behaving as a kind of apprentice academic when you write a dissertation – whether or not you actually go on to take further degrees and look for an academic career – it is easy to copy that approach, to think that, ah yes, this is the way you are actually supposed to write in academic environments. Be assured that it is not: there is no necessary connection between rational discourse and hideous prose.

Alas, there are many pressures on poor old academics these days that mean that this kind of language is unlikely to go away. But *you* don't have to write like that. You can write good academic prose without adopting that awful language, which is something I say more about in Chapter 6.

The second very important influence is the language of public communication, of the media and the online world, which perhaps has a more insidious effect than the stylistic formulas of bad academic writing. The reason why this may be worse is that here we are not simply talking about a matter of style but about content too. News media now appear dominated by comment rather than reportage, or the forced excitement of 24 hour 'breaking news'. Broadcasters and journalists routinely contrive simplistic narratives that constrain complex events into sensational or dramatic forms; everything becomes a kind of soap opera.

Also ubiquitous is the related language of websites, blogs, endless comments on articles and stories (by the usually anonymous 'commentards' strung out beneath), of Facebook and Twitter – that vast noise 'out there' in what gets called cyberspace, a constant babel of voices that simply assert and declare. Canon cameras are the best in the world; Carlos Tevez is better than Wayne Rooney; the Hotel Splendide in Anytown is crap; global warming is a conspiracy and a fiction; *everybody knows* that the US government covered up an alien landing at Roswell; each one of us has a guardian angel; cats are better than dogs. Some of it may be informative and interesting, but much of it is negative, whining, pompous, sneering, mocking and ludicrously self-important, and a great deal of the tone is casually aggressive. Cyberspace just opens its mouth, as it were, and lets it all come pouring out.

This relentlessly declarative writing and speaking – largely unreflective and unargued in any rational sense – is impossible to avoid. It surrounds us and we hear and read it every day, so much so that it may seem 'normal' and have become accepted as the *lingua franca* of information and ideas. Whether you agree with that verdict or not, this kind of language is not appropriate for academic discourse. Yet it is so familiar that we may sometimes not be aware that we are using it. It is also close to the way we talk in everyday situations, so in many senses declarative language is 'normal'. If we are standing at the bus stop and somebody asks whether a number 12 will come soon, we say things like 'Yep. Should be one in ten minutes.' We don't say 'Based on the following evidence [which you then list], I judge that the number 12 will come past this spot in nine minutes, and here is the reasoning and analysis that I used to come to that judgement, together with a brief critical summary of previous occasions on which I and others have assessed the likely appearance of a bus at stops such as this . . .'

Look, I know you are aware of this; you probably actively and deliberately engage with the 'e-world' through social media, or perhaps your own blog, and are not just a passive, unthinking recipient. You may have critiqued all this at school or later as part of your studies. So when you stop and think about it, you are most unlikely to think this ubiquitous loud noise is the right kind of language to use in your dissertation; but the danger is that when you are off your guard, perhaps tired or writing in a hurry to meet a deadline, you may unwittingly lapse into it. Because it is such a natural-seeming, familiar form of language it will probably survive your checking stages too, and pass under your quality-control radar to end up in your final dissertation. As I say, this is not just about the style and structure of writing (Chapter 6) but also about how that connects with what you say (see e.g. Chapter 4).

How to use this book

I hope that you will use the book in any way that suits you. One idea would be to read the whole thing through first, perhaps early in your dissertation year or during the term before, or during your research methods course. But you don't have to do it this way. If you prefer, you can dip into chapters or sections of it when you want to look up particular things and use it as a kind of guidebook. And of course you can combine these two approaches. There is a kind of progression from the earlier to the later chapters, but if you want to read the book in reverse chapter order, or just read some chapters and ignore others, it should still be perfectly intelligible and I hope useful. Perhaps the one exception to this is Chapter 10, which contains a great many hints for self-checking but targets the later stages of your dissertation work when you have produced a draft. But even there you may want to read it early in your dissertation work, as a guide to what you can expect to do later.

Here is a note of caution, one that I return to at different points in the book. If your research methods teaching, course documentation and other guidelines and instructions differ from what I say, then you should probably follow what *they* say – because they're the ones awarding the marks, not me. If you're worried about deciding something like this, go and talk to your supervisor. They know what practices prevail in your institution and your department. I have to work at a much more general level. Hence, if in this book I suggest – even strongly suggest – that you do X, but your department or research course says you must do the very different Y, then other things being equal you should do Y. Perhaps my necessarily general account missed something important about your discipline or topic. (But you can still reflect on why I suggested that you do X, and the relative merits of X and Y.)

And one other note of caution. You may wonder whether reading this book, or sleeping with it under your pillow, will guarantee that you'll get top marks – rather like popping a magic 'distinction' pill? No, that's entirely unrealistic, and to think it would be is to miss the point about dissertation work – because in a dissertation what happens is almost entirely down to you. You set the targets, you decide how to reach them, and you create the text that informs the world about it all. This book is a tool, and I earnestly hope a valuable one, but the rest is down to you. Remember that the dissertation or project puts you in charge. More than for any other type of course, it depends on how you plan and execute your project. You can view this book as another resource that you draw on to help you with aspects of your dissertation, and I certainly do hope that it helps you to focus what you're doing and produce a better result.

A dissertation puts your independence at a premium, with you as research director, like no other part of your studies. You'll find that the more you assume this independent role and the more energy you put into your dissertation work, the more your staff will respond with time and interest and help. That's what they're there for, and it's how higher education normally works. A student who stays passive and expects their supervisor to set everything out for them merely reduces the dissertation to a feeble kind of taught course of little value. You'll find a lot about organizing and shaping your research in research methods books, and no doubt in your research methods courses too.

A dissertation or major project is a little scary to start with, as you contemplate all that empty space you have to fill. But you're off the leash, so the first thing to do is to run around and get used to the freedom to do your own thing. Celebrate it, and dive into the process willingly. Or, to use that cliché that waiters often adopt when they bring you your food, 'enjoy'!

1 RTFM

RTFM? Just in case you don't know, this is an acronym that started out in the world of computer technical support. The R, T and M stand for 'Read the manual!', and the F is a well-known word that makes the message a lot more forceful.

Computer support staff know from bitter experience that vastly many of the problems that users bring to them would not have arisen had the user read the manual – the instructions – before they started using the equipment. And that is my message in this chapter. Read the instructions before you start work on your dissertation,[1] then again at intervals while you are writing it, and once more before you hand in the finished work.

When I was first an undergraduate, students did not receive many detailed instructions and guidelines before writing dissertations or other major research or project-based work. There may have been a single page of notes outlining the requirements, and sometimes there were verbal instructions only. You were given a deadline, a word limit, and not much else. A lot depended on your supervisor (and your supervisor remains a very important person today).

Now things are very different. Nearly all universities and colleges produce detailed and carefully constructed documents and guidelines for work of this kind. Often these take the form of handbooks or similar multi-page documents, distributed before you start your planning and research – sometimes during the previous term or year. You will almost certainly be required to take research methods courses that should provide general techniques as well as information specific to research in

---

[1] In the following chapters I use the term 'dissertation' to refer to the kind of independent, research based inquiry and its written outcome that is the subject of this book. There are other variations that draw on the same approaches but go under different names, such as 'project' or 'major project' (with associated reflective reports), 'study' and 'extended essay', which I will mention at suitable times – but always in the sense of their being high level inquiries undertaken towards the end of university courses, not in the sense that you can do a 'project' at school. This saves me from having to say 'your dissertation, project, study or extended essay' all the time.

your subject area. Or the courses may be optional – in which case, take them if you can. If you can't find other information that you need in this 'official' documentation you will have to ask tutors and supervisors for it.

In this book I can only give general advice, general guidelines, and widely applicable writing methods and techniques that will work in most cases. What I cannot do is cover all of the particular requirements of your university, staff or subject area, which you can only discover by reading your subject's dissertation guide. In some cases, what your subject[2] or university requires may be different from what I say.

As you read this book, if you discover a clash between what I suggest you do and what your university or department tells you to do via research methods courses or their official documents, then do what they say rather than what I say!

Of course, you can always reflect on the difference and try and work out the reasons for it, which would be a useful exercise, and if you are still in doubt ask your supervisor.

Here's a fairly trivial example of what I mean: I like the use of the first person, though only where this is appropriate and correct in the context. I hate silly expressions like 'the present writer' or other pseudo-objective constructions (I'll come back to this in Chapter 6, so don't worry if you're not sure what I mean here). So I would say:

I interviewed ten social work staff from the medical centre.

and definitely not

The present writer interviewed ten social work staff . . .

or, even more tediously

Ten social work staff were interviewed by the present writer . . .

---

[2]   I use 'subject' in this book to cover what can go by other names, such as 'discipline' or 'field', in different universities and departments. So a 'subject' in this sense means philosophy, or physics, or English, or modern languages, or civil engineering, or law, or estate management . . . and so on. I use the terms 'subject', 'discipline' and 'field' interchangeably throughout this book unless I say otherwise for some special purpose.

And so on. But – and this is the point of this example – if your dissertation manual, or your tutor or supervisor, tells you to use impersonal constructions or 'the present writer', then *do what they say, not what I say*. They are the people who have set up the criteria for your dissertation, and they are the people who are going to mark it.

This is an important point: subject areas develop particular 'cultures' of research and writing, and beyond that different universities and even departments will have evolved 'right' and 'wrong' ways of doing things – perhaps following the preferences of the people who first set up the standards of writing and submitting course materials. Academic staff in these disciplines have grown up in these traditions and follow these practices; they use that kind of language themselves. Like it or not, you are not going to change this (and neither am I), so do please follow their required structures, methods and use of language.

Now that we've established that you really must RTFM, what kinds of information and what details can you expect to find in your subject-specific handbooks, guides or manuals?[3]

The basics: when, how long, what to include
What's the deadline?

The timescale for a dissertation from first activity to the point of delivery can vary. Much depends on the type and level of degree or study you are engaged in, but it is unlikely that a dissertation will take less than one term or semester to complete, and usually the time is longer – say a year (or a year's-worth of semester or terms) for an undergraduate final year or taught MA, and perhaps over two years for research Masters courses or MPhil degrees. You may also be studying part time, in which case you need to make sure you know how this affects the timing of your dissertation work.

Your handbook will tell you when the completed dissertation must be delivered. It is a very strange handbook if it doesn't, and in that case you must ask your dissertation course tutor or supervisor for that information. As soon as you have the date, write it in your diary – by this stage of your studies you must keep some kind of diary. In the next chapter I

---

[3] In this book I normally use the term 'handbook' to cover the manual or instructions for your dissertation, partly to avoid having to talk about the 'documentation' all the time. Handbook, manual, course instructions, module guide are all common names for it, though it may have a different name at your university or college.

examine in detail how to manage the time aspects of your dissertation, but here I'm just pointing out the key aspects of the instructions. Treat the deadline as something immovable and unchangeable, an end date that you may not change for any reason.

That gives you the end date, but when does your dissertation begin? It is sometimes harder to think of a precise starting date for your project. Here's a suggestion: it starts *now*, or, more precisely, as soon as you decide you will choose to take the dissertation (if it is optional), or as soon as you have finished the previous year's work (say, after you finish your second-year coursework, if the dissertation is a third-year course). The sooner you think your way into your dissertation, the more prepared you are and the better it will be. For an undergraduate dissertation that runs over the third year, for example, this early start means that you can be thinking, planning, scheming all the way through the preceding summer – even when you're lying on the beach or in a muddy field at a festival or selling T-shirts in a high-street outlet. To turn the same example round, it is not wise to regard a third-year dissertation as something that only affects the last term or semester of the year. I have known many students do that, and it is a recipe for a poor grade or even a fail. Remember: your dissertation starts now. Start thinking!

How many words?

This sounds fairly obvious, doesn't it? And it is, though students can sometimes create problems for themselves by not reading the small print associated with the stipulated word length. All dissertations must have some kind of word limit, and the total will be in the handbook somewhere. But what is included in that word limit? The abstract? The bibliography?

The number of words is restricted for several reasons. One reason is that the dissertation is the end product of a course at your institution, and that means there will be a tariff for how much students can fairly be expected to write for that course. Another reason is that a fixed word count means all students are writing broadly the same amount of material, which is useful on grounds of fairness but also when making comparisons and judgements at marking.

A third and key reason is that the word limit requires that you shape and concentrate your ideas into a fixed space. In other words, it helps to form part of the discipline (in the sense of order and control) of this category of academic writing – you can't simply 'go off on one' and write enough material for a college textbook or a three-decker novel. You may have done some brilliant research but it won't help you or the rest of the world if you express it in a sprawling and chaotic way. That brings us back to the main reason for this book: it helps you to take the ideas you have, the reading you have done, and the new and independent research you have undertaken and express it all in a controlled, orderly and appropriate way. (Incidentally, this does not mean you have to write in a dry, tedious, plodding, formulaic or pretentious manner, but more on that in Chapter 6.)

So, find out what the word limit is and write it down at the start of your research notebook. Also write down what is included in that word limit – bibliographies and reference lists are a common source of confusion here; are they included in the total or excluded? And what about the 'tolerance' band for that word count? If the limit is 10,000, or 15,000, or 30,000, say, how far on either side of those totals are you allowed to stray? Are 29,000 or 31,000 acceptable for a 30,000 word limit, for example? If you don't know the answer and can't find it in the handbook, go and ask somebody who can tell you, and then write that down too.

Another 'small print' factor is whether you are required to show your final word count on the finished dissertation. Very commonly you are, and because almost all students now create their written work using word-processors it is an easy thing to find out; modern software calculates the total for you. If the handbook says put your total somewhere on the dissertation (usually on the title page or on an official cover sheet that you must attach), then do it. If you don't, you may lose a mark or two – irritating enough – but you may also annoy your marker, who will then have to find out what the total is and may also be suspicious that you didn't include it because you have not followed the word limit requirements. It is very unwise to do things that annoy the markers.

Format, covers and binding

Your dissertation must be presented in a suitable form, which means that you are not allowed to hand in a sheaf of papers casually stapled at one corner, or thrown together into a plastic sleeve, or fashioned into a paper dart. Even if these methods of submission have been acceptable for other kinds of coursework during your university or college career (possibly not the dart option), they won't be enough for a dissertation.

I am unable to tell you precisely what these special requirements are, because they will be clearly set out in your dissertation handbook or university regulations, but I can review the main factors that these rules cover. They are usually concerned with paper size, design and typeface (font), line spacing, margins, title pages, appendices, cover sheets and binding. I'll deal with electronic submission separately.

In European universities the required paper size is likely to be the familiar A4 rather than the standard letter size in use in the USA, but all word-processors can output to either. A frequent stipulation is that you must print out on one side of the paper using double line spacing and leaving large margins. This is rather like the traditional publisher requirements for the submission of book typescripts, and the reason is not so much for readability but to allow space between the lines and in the margin for others to add changes, comments and notes; however, not all universities encourage markers to write on dissertations now, so these spaces may not be used at all. Whether or not these details are functional or a mere relic of ancient rules, if the instructions say A4, double spaced with wide margins, then make sure you print out on A4 with double spacing and wide margins. There may also be requirements for particular typefaces and type sizes (now universally but loosely called 'fonts') – such as the dull but ubiquitous 12 point Times New Roman. If there are typeface requirements, write them down and follow them.

Most dissertation specifications allow, or even encourage, appendices, which are normally not included in the word limits. Make sure you know what the rules are for your dissertation before you start, and ask your tutor or supervisor if you can't find the answer in the handbook.

Your dissertation will have a title page as a formal requirement, and also as part of the very important navigation system that helps your readers (and the markers) find their way round your work, but you will almost certainly be asked to include an official cover page too. This is normally an institutionally produced form on which you add obvious identifying details such as your name or number and the title, and perhaps the word count too, but increasingly you will also be asked to sign your name after a formal declaration about the nature of the dissertation and its originality – such as that it obeys the university regulations and is your own unaided work. Naturally, it would be foolish not to include the cover sheet (say, because you are desperately short of time at the deadline) because your work will probably be rejected and returned to you, after which you will have to resubmit it late. But you should also take very seriously your signing of the declaration: you are signing that it is your own unaided work, so you must be absolutely sure that it is (more on this in Chapter 9).

And the binding? Normally, this is specified by your institution, not just by type of binding (such as spiral bound) but also in requiring you to use your university's official cover boards. If you want to use another kind of binding, do make sure that it is allowed first. Perhaps you are overseas when you have to deliver the dissertation and are therefore unable to use the recommended binding services. If so, you can prepare for this by taking cover sheets and boards with you before you travel.

Nor should you assume that something very extravagant and expensive is better than the standard binding and will therefore impress your marker – it certainly won't gain you any marks. A quarter-leather craft-bound dissertation with gold blocking, head and tail bands, a silk bookmark and a gilded clasp may be very pretty, but far from impressing the markers it may even be thrown back at you because it breaks the submission rules. If you really want to do something like this, get explicit permission from the course leader first. (Of course, there's nothing to stop you arranging for specially bound copies to give to friends or family, or to keep at home as a reward for all your hard work. Just don't hand them in for marking.)

And – one more 'of course' comment – if you are asked for two copies, then submit two copies. You can ask your tutor or supervisor for advice if this means you are facing high printing costs – say, because you are including a lot of expensive full colour artwork and don't want to pay for two versions of it. They may allow you to hand in a cheaper version for the second copy – in our example, it would be black and white only.

Electronic submission

In some subjects, you may be asked to submit your dissertation in electronic form only (say, as a word-processed file or as a PDF), but this is unusual unless the field is one in which digital forms are being studied. In most cases, you must provide the traditional paper version as two bound copies, but increasingly you are asked to submit the electronic version at the same time, or at least to keep an electronic copy and be prepared to submit it if asked. Another common requirement is that you must also upload an electronic version to a file comparison and checking system such as Turnitin (see Chapter 9). These systems have various uses but a key reason for their use is to prevent plagiarism.

I talk more about IT issues in Chapter 5, but here's another important reminder before we move on. If you are asked to submit or retain an electronic version of your dissertation as well as your bound paper copies, make absolutely certain that the file is the one used to produce the printed version and is exactly the same in all ways. If there are any differences between them this will cause the markers to be suspicious. Unfortunately, a very small minority of villainous students have been known to submit altered files to try to conceal plagiarism or other offences, and in so doing confirm their guilt and intent to cheat: I will come back to this sad topic in Chapter 9.

Just do it

Even if you find these mundane requirements irritating – word counts, fonts, bindings and so on – just follow them. Do what they ask, and don't risk having your dissertation returned for revision.

■ Read the instructions.

■ Write down the key points.

■ Follow them.

Deciphering educational and academic jargon

Some of the items in the handbook will refer to the course of study that lies behind the dissertation rather than the end-product. Over time, the delivery of courses to students in higher education has grown more complex and formal, but at the same time you should have access to more and better information in terms of what you can expect from the course and what is required of you when you study it. When academics design a new course we don't just dream up a course title and then come in and read weekly lectures from a dais. We now have to set out at length its objectives and learning outcomes and how the assessment works, as well as the more obvious elements such as the content of the course, the intended weekly programme and the reading list. These courses then have to go through a lengthy approval and quality-assurance process. What follows are a few of the terms you may encounter.

Learning outcomes

Although a dissertation is a functional piece of writing that is designed for an academic audience – particularly with the examiners in mind – the thinking behind it, and all of those hours spent planning it, researching it, writing and revising it, are extremely important. Its principal value to you during your time at college and in the years beyond is the learning and understanding you gained, and it is these that will help you to develop as a person as well as a scholar in your future studies or career. It is easy to forget this when you put so much effort in to creating the dissertation as an end-product, an object of the highest quality to impress the marker. It is also why cheats who buy dissertations off the internet gain nothing and why their degrees are worthless.

One of the formal ways in which this kind of gain is expressed is the 'learning outcome'. A formal description of a course such as the one leading to your dissertation often contains a list of these. The following list sets out some examples that I have adapted from a series of learning outcomes from a dissertation course. The student is told 'You will have:

- applied the skills, knowledge and understanding acquired during the course to the process of undertaking a major research project leading to an extended piece of writing

- described and commented on aspects of current research that relate to the selected topic

- made use of published materials (which will include both refereed research articles and non-refereed articles) and primary research sources as appropriate to the selected topic

- applied critical, analytical and evaluative skills to information and evidence accumulated during the investigation of the subject.'

Notice the way they are written and set out, and the kind of language they use. Learning outcomes are addressed to you, the student, and state what you will have achieved and where you will be, intellectually speaking, after you complete the course (which in our case means after you have handed in the dissertation).

The achievement terms are often written on the basis of a theoretical hierarchy of understanding known as Bloom's taxonomy. To put it simply, the higher the level of understanding and achievement, the more the language of the learning outcomes changes to talk of reflection, critical evaluation and other terms that emphasize sophisticated levels of inquiry and the ability to review and question what you confront as a person who knows, understands and learns.

It's easy to gloss over the learning outcomes for your dissertation when you read through the handbook. They may appear to be just random bits of bureaucracy that have to be there for formal reasons but that you can ignore. I suggest you stop and read them. If you think about the language they use it can help you understand the level at which your work on the dissertation must operate. They will remind you that working on a dissertation is an advanced mode of study. Producing a dissertation is a difficult and demanding exercise, and it is meant to be; it is not something straightforward like GCSE coursework. Remembering this may help you to feel better during times of difficulty when perhaps you have failed to make the progress you had hoped, or when some of your research plans hit problems. Yes, a dissertation is challenging: that is why it's worth doing and why you will feel a real sense of achievement when you've completed it.

'Descriptive', 'analytic', 'critical', 'reflective' . . .

These are all terms you have probably found in the descriptions of your dissertation course and in your handbook. I am not going to deal with them at length here because they reappear frequently later on when we examine the nature of the discussion and argument in your project (Chapter 4), but it's a good idea to be thinking about them right from the start. The learning outcomes (see above) may already have given you a clue.

When you earn a degree and take it into a workplace or further study, it stands as evidence that you have not just learnt a series of official 'facts', however complicated they may be, or that you have simply picked up a quantity of standard information that is appropriate to your subject area. That is a very crude and outmoded model of learning, and although it has some residual currency – you do need to know the appropriate 'stuff' – it is not by any means all that we do when we learn. We do not simply go to a university with empty minds and have them filled up by 'experts', like cars taking on fuel; the kind of 'knowledge' we would gain by those means might make us useful at pub quizzes but wouldn't get us very far in our dissertation writing. A dissertation is something that comes either at the end of a first degree – as a culmination of our degree studies – or as a core component of a higher degree, and it must confront the world of 'facts' in a much more critical and sceptical[4] way.

Incidentally, in this book I am not following some postmodern path that rejects the idea of 'facts' altogether, or that denies there are things that we need to know in order just to survive, let alone innovate and progress. But what we know and understand is subject to different degrees of confidence and justifiability, and we rely on both evidence and theory to inform and shape our views of the world and events. Whether their activities are part of the (usually) incremental and (always) collaborative enterprise of science or not, those involved in rational inquiry make and break theories, look for and investigate evidence, interrogate data, examine methods – both theirs and others' – and question received opinion.

---

[4] I am using the traditional and honourable sense of 'sceptical' here – that is, scepticism is that stance of systematic doubt, always looking beyond the surface and seeking evidence, that informs most styles of rational inquiry. At the very least it means 'not credulous'.
This is in contradistinction to the contemporary populist and politicized sense of scepticism in such expressions as 'climate sceptic', for which 'denial' is a much more suitable term than 'scepticism' as it refers to strong views against a proposition, not an open and inquiring mind about it.

How does this affect your dissertation work? For the purposes of this chapter, I will just say that these approaches underlie what you need to do when researching and writing your dissertation. For example, it means that in order to find out what others have said about your chosen topic, whether in the past or in the present, it is not enough to search on the topic, find some articles, and simply to repeat that 'Haverstock said A is the case, Grunwald and Snape said B is the case, and that Munnings said C is the case', perhaps by including quotes from these worthy researchers' writings (no, they're not real researchers – I made them up).

If, simply on the basis of these findings, you parroted the information that A, B and C are true, you would not be acting like a sophisticated researcher. You would be uncritically repeating what others had said. Not an inspiring foundation. Quite apart from the possibility of there being another researcher that you haven't yet read, Pollexfen, saying that A, B and C are mistaken and that instead D is the case (it is always possible for us to miss things), what about the claims of Haverstock and the others? Are they right, and how do you tell? Should you be taking what they say at face value, and hence uncritically? An example: what do you do if Jennifer knocks at your door and tells you there is a unicorn in the local supermarket car park? . . . Yes, all right. Let's make the example a bit less obvious: what if Jennifer tells you that there is a boa constrictor in the supermarket car park? Do you simply say to your friends that there is a boa in the car park? You may well say that it depends on how reliable Jennifer is: if Jennifer is an old friend of yours and has been reliable and truthful in the past, then you may be inclined to believe it (though you may visit the supermarket yourself just to check the story for yourself). But if you don't know Jennifer and she is a stranger you will be much less inclined to believe what she says; she may even turn out to be Lying Jennifer, a well-known and totally untrustworthy local character.

What we should think about Jennifer applies even more urgently to the vast amount of undifferentiated material on the Web. So much of what is out there in the array of blogs and websites and even supposedly respectable sources like repositories is largely unvalidated, to use a semi-technical term. And we are all only too aware of the way in which ideas and 'memes' can take hold and find a large audience via the internet. It should be clear from this that merely citing material from these sources is not in itself of any worth, and you have to critique it or justify its inclusion before it can find a place in your dissertation. For example, you might be citing Lying Jennifer's blog.

Back to Haverstock, Munnings and friends: is what they say true, or even usable? Are they like Jennifer your good friend or are they like Jennifer the liar? If they are *bona fide* academics, does that mean you can accept everything they say? Is what they say, in whole or in part, something that can serve as a basis for your own inquiry? In order to answer these questions you need to read what they say *critically*. As far as you are able, you must evaluate what they say in the light of their own reasoning, the evidence they adduce, the theories they produce or adapt and so on. You may well have to unpick the methods they used when they conducted their experiments, interviews or whatever other actions they took in order to draw their conclusions. This is part of the everyday process of academic inquiry: you can't make sense of anybody's conclusions without knowing how they reached them, and you can't do that unless you approach their work critically.

One more example before leaving this area for a while: let's assume that as well as reading other people's views and possible discoveries about your topic you decide to conduct some new investigations of your own. (As you probably know, this is called primary research.) Let's imagine you decide to interview ten people – perhaps the social work staff mentioned at the beginning of this chapter. You record what they say, and then simply list it all in your dissertation – ten transcripts, one after the other – with a subheading at the top 'Results'. Yes, this is a silly example in that few people would do something that crude – listing them in that way wouldn't even produce a good appendix, let alone a results section. But imagine a slightly higher degree of sophistication, where you chop up the interviews with some of your own text in between, still without commenting much on what they said, or analysing it in any way, or linking it to what other researchers have discovered or claimed. This is still merely descriptive – in this case, 'She said A and he said B and she said C . . .' – and unfortunately this is close to what some students do.

It may seem odd to have to remind people not to believe everything that they are told or – in particular, in the academic environment – everything that they read, but some students seem to write dissertations in just that spirit: 'These people said this, and these other people said that . . .' – so let's assume it's all true? Anyway, enough of this for now. Just remember that we are thoughtful, inquiring minds, not simply absorbers of other people's claims or putative 'facts'. We will come back to these themes many times in the following chapters.

Don't just read it and forget it

Before I finish with RTFM, let's just return to a point I made right at the beginning of this chapter. I said that you should read the handbook or instructions before you start the dissertation (well, 'Duh', you might say), but also that you should refer to them at intervals during the course of your work to check on some of the details such as the submission date and other formal requirements; and certainly you should read them again at the time of your final run-through, at the point at which you take your last full look at your whole dissertation before you hand it in. Double check the word limits and what these cover. Double check the delivery requirements, and so on. This is in part because we only remember a certain portion of instruction books and lists of rules – probably the ones we refer to all the time – and we tend to forget the rest.

Oh yes: I said much earlier in this chapter that you should write the key details in your research notebook. This presupposes you have such a thing. But this is a theme that I'll revisit in later chapters.

2 Planning, scheduling and resources

I said in the previous chapter that it is a good idea to think of your dissertation as starting now – that is, as soon as you sign up to do it or add it to your programme if it is optional, or as soon as you have finished your work for the previous year if it is not. If you are studying for a Masters degree then it is a good idea to make 'now' the start of your course – especially if it is a standard one-year taught MA or MSc of the kind offered in UK universities – and some (a minority of) people have a strong idea of what they'd like to work on even before they come. You may not be working on the dissertation at the start of your MA/MSc but you can certainly be thinking about it, following up interesting leads and ideas for reading. Incidentally, planning and scheduling are areas covered in research methods courses too, and although I'm concentrating on the dissertation itself in this book rather than research methods, here is an example of a topic that I can't talk about without bringing in the research methods aspects too.

At the risk of panicking you by saying 'start now', I'm also aware that many students do not have a clear idea of their dissertation area until the beginning of the course itself. Don't worry if this profile fits you – you still have plenty of time. However, if you are an undergraduate you should take advantage of the summer vacation before your final year: it's a wonderful time for reflecting on your dissertation or project topic and for reading around the subject. If you are a taught Masters student you may want a term or semester to orientate yourself and see what's interesting, especially where your degree subject is very different from your undergraduate studies.

Whatever kind of student you are, you have the raw materials to start planning your schedule. You know when you are starting and you also know the end date – the delivery date on which you have to submit the final work. So now you have the two ruling dates for the dissertation and can start to plan what will happen in the time between them. At the centre of this plan will be your schedule, where you fill in key dates and events along the way – some of them fairly definite and others more conjectural. Your tutor or teaching team may also provide guidance for the timing of your work – there could be a timeline or outline schedule in your course handbook, for instance, or they will discuss the possibilities in research methods classes. And your supervisor will no doubt offer advice along the way.

The plan and schedule will probably be the first work you do on the dissertation, and it is wise to set it down early. If you do it *now* (that word again) it will make you feel you've started. You can alter it later as changing circumstances and better information permit, so you can feel confident about getting something down on paper. If (as I recommend you should) you carry around a research notebook at all times, then the draft schedule or timeline can go in at the start, after the salient information you added when you read the course handbook (see Chapter 1). Even if you are bristling with gadgets, a real cyber-student, I still think it is a good idea to carry an old-fashioned paper notebook too – not because I'm a Luddite but because it gives you an instantly accessible resource at all times, regardless of time, place or available power sources. By all means keep information in your other favourite places – on your smartphone, your netbook, your laptop, various websites and online storage etc. – provided you back it up (more on this in Chapter 5).

Building a schedule

What can you put on your schedule in the early stages, when perhaps you only have a very general idea of what you're going to research and no hard information? I'm going to suggest that you approach it like a publishing schedule, which is not outlandish if you think that in many ways your dissertation *is* a kind of publication. When a publisher plans a book, say, they will normally start as you are starting, with only an end date – when do we want to publish? – and a start date – when will the author deliver the raw materials? You too have an end date and a starting date, so you can start sketching in events or phases of work between these two points. As to which end to start from, the beginning or the end, we can again borrow from publishers and work from both ends.

There are also two sets of timings to incorporate on your plan: one is the sequence of calendar months – January, February and so on – and the other is the sequence of academic terms or semesters at your institution, because this sequence has several potential effects. It may influence access to supervision and resources (such as the library) and also relates to classes, the formal timing of the dissertation course and so on. It also affects the amount of time you have to devote to the dissertation, but can pull in two different directions. Once lectures, seminars, course-work and exams are out of the way you have so much more time for the dissertation; on the other hand, there is a risk that you will lose what I can call academic momentum. When the vacation comes, especially after a hard term, it's tempting just to stop for a while – and of course you deserve a break– but the longer you're in stop mode the harder it is to get going again, and before you know it the next semester has arrived.

The institutional sequence

Let's look at the academic and teaching framework first. Here (Figures 2.1 and 2.2) are a couple of typical 'institutional' timelines for dissertations, one for an undergraduate dissertation in an institution with a three-term academic year, and the other for an MA dissertation where there is a two-semester year. They are not actual timelines from real universities and are only examples to show important points and events, including possible timings for research methods classes, which are sometimes scheduled before your dissertation period but may have to be taken concurrently. There are any number of possibilities; you can work out your own based on your circumstances and your university's timings.

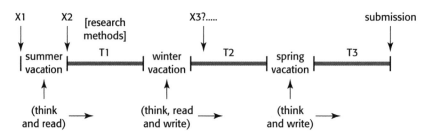

Figure 2.1 A dissertation course in a typical three-term final undergraduate year

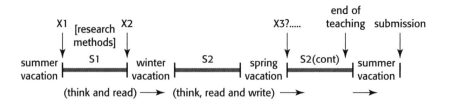

Figure 2.2 A two-semester MA dissertation course that continues beyond the end of formal teaching

KEY   T1 term 1 etc   X1 'now' point   X3 starting point for
       S1 semester 1 etc   X2 official start   some unwise students

These timelines show slightly different sequences but the elements are broadly the same and the implications for your study and planning are the same. First, note that there are large blocks of time in vacations. These have two types of implication: one, the upside, is that you can work through these periods without being distracted by formal classes, so that you can give your dissertation uninterrupted attention; the other kind of implication, the downside, is that your supervisor and other key staff may be away and that libraries, IT resources and laboratories may be less accessible or are open for shorter times, but of course this depends on your college or university. If you are studying at a resource-rich institution they may be able to afford to keep facilities open for 24 hours a day throughout much of the year.

Another factor is that a dissertation, especially at MA/MSc level, may extend beyond the formal teaching period so that students are working after they have finished their class-based courses. This is what happens at my university: students may finish their classes at the end of May but deliver their dissertations at the beginning of September. One implication of this is that students often need to find jobs or internships as soon as the teaching stops; if this applies to you then you must factor this in to your time planning. Having a job, even a part time one, will eat in to your dissertation time and your available energy, so you must make allowances for that in your schedule. Remember that you are doing the job to sustain yourself during your studies, so don't let the job take over. Your studies are your priority.

Notice that there are areas of what I've called 'thinking time' outside of the formal start and stop times for the dissertation course. You'll also see that I've added points X1, X2 and X3 in each case. The point X1 is the 'now' point, the place where I've already recommended you think of your dissertation as starting. The point X2 is the formal course start point, where 'officially' the dissertation part of your degree course begins.

And the point X3 is the place where many students actually start their dissertation work, very unwisely. For example, a student may regard a one-year dissertation running in a two-semester university as effectively a second-semester course only. We're very good at deluding ourselves with comforting rationalizations about such things: 'Well, I'm leaving my dissertation until the final semester, so that I can concentrate on my semester 1 courses and really give them a lot of attention.' This is dangerous and reckless: the dissertation is the one course you study that will benefit most from the maximum time for reading and reflection.

In the words of that corny expression, it is not rocket science. Just look at the difference between the various X points on the timelines. See how much you gain by starting at X1, and how much you risk by starting at X3.

The dissertation sequence

Now let's look at scheduling from the dissertation's vantage point rather than your university's timetable. What do you need to do and when?

To start with, we can plot this using a monthly timeline that extends from our 'now' point to the final submission date. I've already said that as 'publishers' we can work from both the start and finishing points at the same time so let's add a few general events and necessary activities. They will normally be general and vague when you start planning; you can make them more precise later. You can also add the institution detail from the previous section if you like, but for now let's concentrate on the dissertation month by month.

Working forwards from the starting point, what kinds of events will you need to build in? Keeping the crude kinds of categories that may be the only ideas you have at the 'now' point, you will perhaps start with things like 'researching' or 'reading', or if you have a clearer idea of the kind of study you'll undertake, perhaps you could add 'experiments' or 'interviews' or 'surveys', and perhaps to match these you would need something like 'data analysis' or 'results analysis' afterwards. Naturally, you'll be thinking about writing it all down too, so will you add an entry for 'writing up' or similar? Figure 2.3 is a simple timeline produced along these lines.

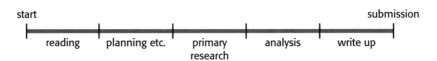

Figure 2.3 First thoughts on a dissertation sequence? No, not really – it isn't a simple succession of discrete processes

Crude, isn't it, and it pretends that everything fits into a single linear sequence. But already you have had to think about where these elements will fit into the months ahead. The blocks of activity you add will also start to suggest relationships, links and overlaps between the phases. For example, you can't suddenly start an experiment or a major survey or interview sequence without first planning and then (ideally) trialling it, so that means you need to add a block for 'design and trial' or something before your experiment or survey block, and perhaps you need to do some investigative reading before that, and so on.

Also, is it really the case that 'writing up' is a discrete block of activity that comes at the end of everything else? Do you really do all your reading and finish it, then all of your primary research and finish that, then all of your analysis and finish that, and only then start writing anything down? Of course not. In fact, I'm going to say many times in this book that you should start writing early to get words on to the page. You may hear research students say 'I'm writing up now', but that doesn't mean they haven't written a word before they entered that phase. Although towards the end of your dissertation work you will predominantly be writing rather than anything else, the writing phase is something that runs across a large part – most – of the dissertation sequence. A timeline is not very good at showing overlapping elements in this way, so I'm going to suggest another way of presenting your schedule using a Gantt chart, but before that let's look at what shows up when we examine the reverse direction.

What kinds of factors suggest themselves when working backwards from the end date instead of forwards from the start? You may feel that this is safely far away and hence that planning at this distance is not going to be a valuable activity; but it is very important. Here's one obvious, mundane event: printing and binding your dissertation. This is not something that can be achieved in zero time so you have to allow time for it. Is there an official thesis-binding firm or university facility that you have to use? How long will it take? When must you get hold of cover sheets and cover boards, where these are needed? Is the bindery going to be busy when you need to use their services? What happens if it's the end of the summer and everything is closed and people are away? And so on. The point of all of this – again, not rocket science – is that all of these trivial-seeming things take time that you must add to your schedule before the end date. Immediately you'll see them cut into your final writing and checking time.

And do you simply stop keying at the end of the bibliography or final appendix (with 'The End' underneath it?), instantly print it out, and then immediately walk to the binder to have it all put together? Of course not. You'll want to produce drafts and have people read them, and also undertake some final quality-control processes yourself. These will include proofreading and reference cross-checks, and I say more about all this in Chapter 10. But again, you need to add these processes before the binding phase – and, lo, another piece of time is bitten off the end of your schedule. Hence you must take the two directions of scheduling together to produce a combined draft schedule. Let's have one more look at our revised schedule, this time with both ends considered, before looking at a more sophisticated way of recording it (Figure 2.4).

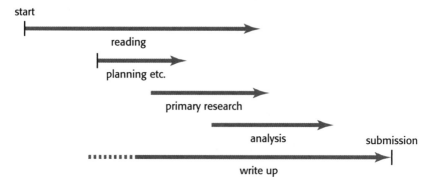

Figure 2.4 A slightly more realistic dissertation sequence, showing the same processes overlapping and running in parallel

Gantt charts

There are better ways of showing schedules with overlapping elements than a simple timeline. The one I'm going to recommend is the Gantt chart, named after the US engineer and consultant Henry Gantt, hence the unusual spelling.[1] It is not the only kind of time planning system available – there are loads of different ones, some showing all kinds of dependencies between tasks and other extra details. But Gantt charts are not hard to understand or create, and have been a staple of project planning for almost a century. It is likely that you already know about and have used them; also, you can buy software (or download shareware) that maintains such charts, as well as other project details, but this isn't necessary unless you really like to use such things. You can simply draw them up for yourself, either on paper or using a spreadsheet, or you can even key them line by line into a word-processor. Their principal advantage is that they give you an instant visual reminder of the stages of your project and their interrelationships – and here I mean 'project' in the more general sense, rather than as an alternative to a dissertation. This reflects the fact that whatever kind of dissertation you undertake, part of your role is as a project manager, planning and overseeing the whole sequence and the elements that make it up.

---

[1]   If you want to find out more about Gantt charts just search on 'Gantt' or 'Gantt charts'. Also, most research methods texts deal with project planning and scheduling to a greater or lesser extent. You may be required to use specific project management methods and software in your institution, in which case RTFM and make sure you use the right ones.

The charts use a time axis, usually horizontally, and stack the processes or tasks as a series of bars on the other axis, normally with the earliest-starting ones at the top and the later-starting ones sequenced underneath. Most Gantt charts therefore look something like a kind of horizontal bar chart (Figure 2.5).

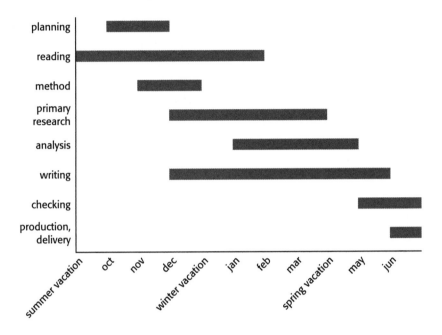

Figure 2.5 Simplified view of the dissertation sequence using a GANTT chart to show that processes are parallel and overlap

To create one, all you need to do is decide the overall timescale (from the 'now' point to final submission), all of the key tasks and events, and how long these take, and plot them. For the crude timeline a monthly sequence was probably adequate, but for your Gantt chart you'll probably want to take a more detailed view and use weekly blocks along the horizontal line. You'll be able to assign some of the blocks fairly accurately, but others will have more approximate extents and perhaps fuzzy edges. Don't worry – it's a map of your best available information at the time, and you can update it with better information as you go.

Notice how a Gantt chart lets you see at a glance where tasks and events fall, and also where they overlap. Some events will be short and sweet, and others may run for more or less the whole programme time.

So why not produce and print out a large Gantt chart of your dissertation now, and perhaps stick it on the wall in your study area, over your bed, in the kitchen or somewhere equally intrusive? I'm sorry if this suggestion sounds a bit Blue Peterish. If you do make a chart you may feel that it is a bit overpowering at times, and that it seems to be telling you that the dissertation will be a major part of your life for some months to come. But, hey – it is. If you don't treat the dissertation as a dominant part of your studies, something that's going to take a lot of your time and energy, then you will not be able to write a good one.

Contingencies, critical paths and change

Before leaving this discussion of time planning, let's look at a couple of the things that may cause you to revise your plans and hence your schedule. I refer to these factors again in Chapter 8, the troubleshooting chapter.

The first thing to note is that all professionally produced project plans and schedules build in contingency time – small periods of slack time or extra allowances that cater for things going wrong or not working out as planned. You should do this too. For example, ask yourself 'What do I do if this doesn't happen?' about things like people agreeing to interviews, or a key person not being available. Or ask yourself 'What happens if the timing goes wrong here?' about time-sensitive or time-consuming events. Imagine that crucial to a bioscience dissertation is an experiment that takes three weeks to run, but that it's not unknown for something to cause it to fail. Let's say that contamination of one of the inputs can invalidate the results. If you schedule this experiment right up to the last point at which you could run it, so that the end point is squashed against the next phase of your dissertation, what happens if it goes wrong? You have built in no contingency time, so you won't be able to run it again.

What you need to do is schedule the event earlier, to build in a 'What if?' possibility that creates a reserve time slot in which you could rerun this experiment if you had to. You would hope not to have to use it, and of course the experiment could always fail again, but there are always ultimate time limits. Your second schedule, the one with the failure contingency built in, is much safer, wiser and more flexible than the first high-risk version.

Quite often, you need to be aware not only of overlapping events when you create schedules but also those that are interdependent. In other words, you are only able to perform task B once you have completed task A. Obviously, there is no point scheduling task B to start until you have reached the end date for task A – and you may decide to build in a little bit of slack too as a contingency, in case task A takes a little longer than you'd hoped. Operations like task A are said to fall on the critical path through your project,[2] and it is that path that determines the overall timing of your project and the creation of your dissertation. This means that as far as possible you should discover the critical path and build your dissertation schedule around that.

One more thing before we look at resources: you now have a schedule, and I have said that you may need to amend this as you go along, but how much should you change it? How flexible should your schedule be? Clearly, it should not be rigid and immutable, particularly if it is a schedule that you created very early when you lack detailed information, such as at the 'now' point as I have suggested. It would be idiotic to adhere to this mindlessly, regardless of what happens.

On the other hand, if you allow yourself to change the schedule on a regular basis whenever any tiny problem arises, you could be heading for trouble. What will happen is that you will keep easing deadlines for yourself, and all of the tasks and processes will start to pile up at later and later points. All your contingency time will disappear and you will be under extreme pressure during the later parts of your dissertation work. Every problem becomes a major disaster because there is no possibility of putting it right, and you start to become a nervous wreck. Eventually you find yourself nervously approaching your supervisor or course leader to ask for an extension – which they will refuse because you have no legitimate grounds for extra time. Your problems are self-inflicted, and the result of poor project management.

So what should you do to prevent this? One wise precaution is to try and make any major schedule revisions early in the process as you obtain better information and firm up your plans, and confine any later revisions to smaller changes and adjustments. Of course, if there is a major problem later on you may need to adopt a serious change of plan deeper into the sequence (see Chapter 8), but I strongly suggest you talk to your supervisor first if you find yourself in this position. Whenever you plan tasks and processes, be realistic. In part, this is to do with contingencies again. Don't plan tight timings for tasks simply because you've done similar things in the past in very rapid times. Perhaps in the past you enjoyed a following wind and fair weather, whereas storms may lie ahead now. Also, a dissertation is likely to be a far bigger challenge than some of your earlier coursework: the short cuts and last-minute approaches that you got away with in the past may fail you in this more demanding task.

---

[2] This falls under a topic known as critical path analysis or the critical path method, whose details are beyond the scope of this short book. However, if you are interested in finding out more, a quick web search will provide more than enough information.

> Think carefully about timings. Unrealistic scheduling builds in failure right from the start. It will demoralize you.

As you firm up your schedule, complete with contingencies, identify firm dates that you are prepared to treat as strong deadlines, and mark these in some way so that they scream at you from the schedule. Don't move or change them except in dire emergencies, and preferably not without your supervisor's advice. You are setting deadlines for yourself, so be prepared to keep them, otherwise the whole exercise of scheduling becomes pointless and you risk becoming the desperate extension-craving student I mentioned above. You can manage deadlines, otherwise you would not have got this far. After you have set these hard dates, you can identify other, softer, dates or tasks that could be moved around if circumstances permit.

Identifying and managing resources

We've talked about time planning, but the other key aspect of project planning is resource management. Remember that this is something else that you are doing when you undertake a dissertation: you are a project manager. It's worth pausing to consider the range of tasks you are undertaking. You are all of the following:

- a researcher
- an analyst and critical thinker
- a publisher
- a project planner and manager
- a learner –
  - of research approaches and techniques
  - about your topic and field
  - about yourself.

It is no wonder that dissertations are demanding.

Key resources

So what exactly are the resources at your disposal? Some of them are fairly obvious and will vary according to the subject area you are working in. The main items that you will probably suggest for your list will include:

- your own institution's library and its staff

- other libraries, archives and repositories

- laboratories, workshops and other experimental sites

- the internet (of course)

- your supervisor

- your course tutors (dissertation course, research methods, etc.)

- your personal tutor

- IT provision, both personal and institutional.

You may have other types of resource that apply in your particular case, in which case just add them to your list. All of these sources need to be evaluated and explicitly incorporated in your dissertation plan. Most dissertations require some kind of formal proposal from you before you are added to the course, and it is common for you to have to list any resources that you will need before you start. For example, if you need special IT hardware or software, expensive video equipment or studio time, access to a hospital, the use of a particular lab and its equipment, and so on, you should work this out in advance and apply for the facilities or access, taking advice from your course team as necessary. Your university or college will almost certainly have regulations or at least guidelines about what you may and may not ask for. For example, if you are writing an undergraduate dissertation you will not be allowed to run an experiment on the Large Hadron Collider or have a week on a major telescope in Hawaii.

Try and anticipate resource problems early. If you are going to work with patients in a hospital, for example, you will not only need permission to gain access but you will have to fulfil all sorts of ethical, hygiene, and health and safety requirements too. The same applies to research that you might want to undertake in relation to, say, physically dangerous or politically sensitive environments. Needless to say, these are exactly the kinds of issues that you need to sort out at the beginning – or more properly before the beginning, at the risk of sounding nonsensical. It is likely that you will have received advice from tutors before you start, of course, and if you are working in a subject or department that frequently works with hospitals or individuals in other treatment environments, then they will have established methods of working and experience, so these problems are reduced.

I'll talk about using and managing IT later in the book (Chapter 5), but want to look at two other deceptively familiar resources before leaving these principal examples: your library and your supervisor.

The library

By the time you arrive on your dissertation course you will be very familiar with your college or university library, the parts of it that you need to visit for your subject area's resources, where you can go for study space, meeting space for group work and so on, and of course you will also know how to use the catalogues and access all of the electronic resources that increasingly dominate what the modern academic library offers. If you haven't already done so (surely you have?), you should immediately find out how to access all of those electronic resources when off-campus, because you must not expect to work on your dissertation only when in college buildings during 'office hours' – your dissertation or project is not a 'nine to five' activity.

Library organization varies from one institution to another, but you probably already know or at least have approached a member of the library staff whose job it is to look after your subject area. Some libraries have dedicated subject librarians. These staff members, as well as the library itself, make up a key resource that you will certainly use time and time again.

If your library hasn't got what you're looking for you can probably find it elsewhere. One long-established way is to use the inter-library loan system, though there may be a small charge for this. Your library may have special arrangements with other centres. Some university libraries run vacation schemes that allow students vacation access, and you can fill in an online form to apply to use the British Library. For archives and specialist libraries you will probably need to apply for access through your own library, though most archives provide useful information about their holdings and access in their online pages.

Even better, if you are studying at a UK institution it is likely that your library is affiliated to SCONUL (the Society of College, National and University Libraries), in which case you can apply to use the SCONUL Access Scheme. This allows you to use any other academic library that is also a Scheme member. Full-time undergraduates have reference access; part-time undergraduates, taught postgraduates, and certain sandwich course students have both reference access and lending rights. You apply for the Scheme at your own institution's library. And it is an excellent scheme: for example, if you go home or travel during the vacations you can use the local or nearest university library while you're away from base – particularly useful in those 'thinking' times before you officially start the course.

Talk to supervisors and library staff before launching quests for more unusual or specialist information or data to see whether it actually exists. What you want may be out there somewhere – if you're lucky in one place, but more probably to be collated from many different sources – or it may not, in which case you can waste a lot of time searching for something that isn't there.

Your supervisor

I am assuming that you have at least one supervisor assigned to you as part of your dissertation course. It would be very unusual if you did not. Having an experienced member of staff to call upon is invaluable because you can sometimes feel very exposed and lost when first taking on a dissertation. After the familiar framework of most university teaching, with its set pattern of prescribed reading, regular lectures or presentations and seminars or laboratory work, and clearly defined examinations or coursework, you're suddenly on your own. You choose what you study, what you are going to research, and though this is an inspiring and enlivening experience it can sometimes feel formless and insubstantial – as if you are surrounded by empty space with no clear idea of where to go next. This feeling is stronger still if you are having problems or going through a difficult patch.

I am unable to tell you how often you should see your supervisor, partly because rules and advice vary from one institution to the next and partly because it depends on the student, the supervisor and the topic. Some courses stipulate that you must see your supervisor on a minimum number of occasions as a condition of passing, whereas others impose no requirements at all. Supervisors are normally allocated on the basis of their specialist knowledge and experience in the subject area you have chosen – or as close to it as staff and student numbers allow.

Some students like to talk over ideas on a regular basis or appreciate the regular contact for guidance and reassurance that they're on the right track, whereas others are confident that they don't need help. This confidence is probably misplaced, and I think often stems from parallel attitudes towards tutors for pastoral support. If you regard going to talk to a tutor as uncool, or as a sign of being insufficiently self-reliant, then you might be tempted to think of supervisors in the same light. Please don't. The supervisor is there to support and enhance your self-reliance, not to threaten it (and see 'I'm so brilliant' below).

My own view is that you should see your supervisor on *at least* three occasions over the time of your dissertation, and ideally a lot more often. This is a very strong recommendation: not seeing your supervisor is foolish. After all, if the dissertation runs over the best part of a year, seeing the supervisor on three occasions probably means no more than a visit every two or three months – hardly arduous or threatening. Quite apart from their obvious inputs of technical detail and scholarship, a dissertation has many pitfalls that lie in wait for the unwary. Your supervisor has seen them many times before, but almost certainly you have not.

Once again, we can find so many ways to convince ourselves that we're doing the right thing by not turning up. Here are some familiar stances and rationalizations.

- 'Oh dear. Time is getting on and I haven't done much work for this dissertation so far. If I go to my supervisor she'll just tell me off – and I don't need that.' Well, you may receive a frown or two when you first turn up after going missing for so long, but few supervisors will 'tell you off' – you're not at school, for goodness sake. Instead, they will probably just calmly remind you of the consequences of your current way of proceeding. We're usually very pleased and relieved to see our prodigal supervisees again. If you haven't done much work, then tell your supervisor; they can help to get you back on the one true path again. The chances are that you will get a better grade by doing this than if you struggle on to the end without any help.

- 'I don't like my supervisor. I don't want to talk to them.' It happens. The remedy – assuming you have tried to talk to your supervisor and find that it's as bad as you feared – is obviously to ask for a change, though naturally you may find this awkward. The best thing is to talk to somebody else – somebody you do get on with, such as your personal tutor. In most institutions it is easier to make these kinds of changes than it used to be. It may be that while you are unable to change completely – perhaps because your allocated supervisor is the one subject specialist for your topic in the department – you can also be allocated a co-supervisor for more general discussions and support. Don't let the problem fester, anyway: do something about it, and soon. Otherwise it will turn into one of those excuses that we use to 'justify' inaction or impending failure. 'I made a mess of my dissertation because I just didn't get on with my supervisor and I was doomed.'

- 'I'm so brilliant and independent minded that I don't need a supervisor. It would be an admission of failure and inadequacy if I went to see her.' Oh yes? Hmmm. In one way or another everybody needs a supervisor for this kind of work, even if it's only as a foil to try out ideas. Sometimes it is precisely those students who are bursting with all kinds of ideas and overflowing with confidence who get into trouble soonest, or who find it most difficult to shape those ideas into a concentrated and controlled form. Sometimes it is a kind of insecurity that is being manifested: 'I am really brilliant but I'd rather not test myself on this point, thank you, just in case you mistakenly think that I am not.' Or is it just arrogance? My advice: overcome your ego and start visiting your supervisor as soon as you can. It is a very low-risk tactic: if you really are brilliant they'll enjoy basking in the glow of your intellect; if you're not they won't tell you.

Once you have made contact with your supervisor, sort out the basics of your relationship: how often will you meet, for example? Most supervisors will have their preferred ways of working, based on their experience, subject area and their knowledge of what has worked (or not) in the past. Some will offer a fairly fixed programme of regular meetings and contact hours and may set tasks for you to do in between; others will offer a more *laissez-faire* regime. I always ask my students how they prefer to work – do they like to be left alone or prefer to be nagged, for instance, and do they want regular visits or instead come along when they feel the need? Other supervisors may present you with a fixed, printed list of things they will and will not do, and in truth there must be an aspect of this in all supervisor–student relationships: you need to know what you can expect of each other.

Another important factor is whether your supervisor is also going to mark your final dissertation or report. They may do, depending in part on departmental or university policy and in part on resources – a very small department will have less choice over the allocation of supervisors and markers. In turn, this inevitably influences how much your supervisor can say and do when they read your drafts. How far should a supervisor go in helping you to correct a glaring problem in your final draft if in a few weeks' time they are also going to assess and mark it? (In practice, your dissertation is likely to be assessed by more than one marker: a common method is double marking, where two people mark independently and then come together and compare their marks and findings.)

The basis of your relationship may be established via formal statements of policy issued by your department, university or supervisor, or it may all emerge during your early meetings. However it is done, make sure that within the first few weeks of your relationship you have already established the following (don't be afraid to ask if you're not told).

- How often will you meet, and where?
- Regular or *ad hoc* meetings (booked in advance or arranged when they seem necessary)?

■ Who will initiate the meetings if they're not pre-booked – you or your supervisor?

■ Have you discussed your preferred ways of working?

■ Will your supervisor read your drafts, and if so which ones?

■ How do they see their role? (What can you expect from them?)

■ What do they expect from you? (You might have to ask them.)

■ Have you established the primary means and frequency of contact (e.g. email)?

■ When will your supervisor be away for significant periods . . .?

■ . . . and what provisions can you make for those weeks or months?

Your supervisor is a most valuable resource – one of the most precious you have at all stages of the dissertation from first concept to final delivery, and through all the ups and downs in between.

> Use your supervisor: email them, visit them, talk to them, ask for their advice.

That other resource . . .

I hope by now that you've guessed what that other essential resource might be, the one that is not part of the university environment, like supervisors and librarians, or external to it, like archives and workplaces or out in the field.

Yes. It's you.

It's important to realize that although you are a special resource – indeed the primary resource – and although you may well value yourself highly, you are also strictly limited. The two most glaring limitations are people and cash. Except in the unusual instance of collaborative working, you do not have a team of people working for you or with you – no research assistants, no administrators, no technicians, no specialists such as statisticians to process your results for you. Nor do you have a major grant from a public or private body that will allow you to travel to distant centres to interview people or buy time at a key facility.

You're all you have, so build your plans around that special resource. It doesn't operate 24/7, nor does it operate evenly under all conditions and at all times of day. If you have ever been on a time management course

– and by the time we reach a certain age most of us have probably been on a great many – you will know that people have times of day during which they work well, with great energy and application, and other times at which they slow down or become vague and sluggish. And we all slow down after main meals – the period after lunch is a notoriously bad time to attend or give lectures, for example. On top of that we all have different personalities, abilities, strengths and weaknesses, memories, attention spans …

What kind of resource are you? This is really an invitation to know yourself as far as you can, and to be honest about that, and build the reality of you as a resource into your project planning and schedule. I am not advocating here some 'corrective' programme that turns you into some deluded fantasy of an ideal student: even if that were desirable (and I think it would be a ridiculous plan), there's no time. The dissertation, your project work, your research, will occupy a large part of your waking life, and you'll find that it even creeps in when you're trying to get to sleep too. You don't have time to become Superstudent, even if you wanted to.

So in this book you will not find me advocating a 5.30 a.m. cold shower, followed by 1,500 words, followed by a breakfast of grapefruit and black coffee, followed by a 20-minute run, followed by two hours in the library, then another 2,000 words before a lunch of low-fat oatcakes and an apple, and so on. Some study guides are full of that kind of stuff, which is probably more suited to improving and morally uplifting works for young people. Of course, there will be some people who really do thrive on the dawn-cold-shower and 1,500-words-before-breakfast routine. But I am assuming that they form a small minority, and it's one that doesn't include me.

What counts is what you are. Be honest about it – by the time you are of an age to write a dissertation you are already quite established as a real person with a distinct personality – and incorporate that into your plans, your schedules, your expectations, and your dealings with your supervisor.

> Remember that if you are unrealistic when you make your plans then you are building in failure.

A little postscript: take responsibility

A dissertation is all about you and what you do. Good or bad, it's essentially yours all the way through. That's what you want too – if you get a good mark you want to be able to say 'I got that mark because of what I did.' So take responsibility for it at all times.

What do I mean by this? It's that all of the elements I've been discussing in this chapter depend on your foresight, planning, resource management and other crucial factors. Add in the dominant element of your research itself, and you may see what I'm getting at. Each of these things can be quite difficult, but taken together they are a real challenge and show why a dissertation on a degree transcript says so much about you to another academic institution or a future employer. A successful dissertation shows the world that you have matured into an independent, self-directed and critical learner as well as a researcher in your own right. It shows that you have moved far away from school-based modes of learning, and also past those intermediate orientation stages in the earlier part of your university course.

Some people make this transition very quickly and others take more time. Much depends on the intensity and quality of your engagement during the first stages of your university course. With luck, by the time you have reached your dissertation the 'I'm an empty vessel – just teach me' model of learning will be years behind you, as it is for nearly all successful dissertation students. Mercifully, few students are so passive or undeveloped by dissertation time that they are unable to take responsibility for their own progress, good or bad, fast or slow. But there are a few, so just check that you don't have any traces of this tendency. The worst of the responsibility deniers build in external excuses for failure from the start – it's the teaching, it's the system, it's the supervision, it's the library, it's the computers, it's the information they were given at the start, so no wonder they can't get a good dissertation mark. Yes, all of these things are very important, but only to support the student in taking off on their own. These passive students are like those people who blame everybody but themselves when they are caught speeding – it's the fault of the government, the council, the police, invisible goblins and so on.

Do you think the rather unpleasant fee rises taking place in some countries may increase this tendency in some students? With fees inexorably rising, they may feel more inclined to go further down the road of regarding themselves as 'customers' paying for a high-priced 'product' when they come to university, and that may undermine their willingness to take responsibility for what they do – crucial to a successful dissertation. But what you buy when you come to university is an opportunity, not some product, and what you do with that is entirely up to you. Students who simply want a 'product' can buy a worthless 'degree' off the internet (and see Chapter 9). OK, enough of that.

You, by contrast, are going to do a great dissertation, and one strong clue is that you're interested enough to read books about it.

3 Some formal elements

This is one of those parts of the book where I have a particular problem in writing for a broad range of readers, because the required elements of dissertations and project reports vary so widely from subject to subject and between universities. My own rather bizarre undergraduate experience, long ago, covered separate studies in engineering, psychology and philosophy, where I could experience the differences first hand. Yet I have to include guidance as to what these different elements are. My solution is to offer summaries of the most common components that appear in most subject areas. And apart from that my very strong advice must be that of Chapter 1: please, please read your manual, and ask staff if you are still in doubt.

The kinds of variations you will find cover not just the elements that are included but also their titles and how they should appear. Take the literature review as an example (often informally called a 'lit review'). One dissertation manual might require you to have a literature review and that you must include it as a separate chapter called 'Literature Review'; another may say you must have a literature review as a chapter but that you can call it anything you like. A third may say that you must have a component of the dissertation that is functionally a literature review but that it need not be in a particular chapter, or have that title, and may even be spread across different sections or chapters of your document. Needless to say, this kind of detail is something that you can only discover by reading your manual and taking careful note of what's required.

Similar variations apply to the degree of formality and specific requirements of what is in these different elements. Some may leave you to your own devices, whereas others may require something very precise according to your course documents or the conventions of your discipline. Let's take the lit review example again: one course may leave you to decide what you understand by a literature review (say, based on your own understanding, perhaps backed up by a reading of research methods texts); another may present you with a complicated list of rules that say it must be this, this and this, but not that, and if you are really lucky also provide you with examples of what they mean. And I hope you will also receive guidance in your research methods classes.

Changing the example, it could be that you must have a formal section called 'Results', but that you are not allowed to put anything in this section that resembles a discussion or the drawing of conclusions. In many disciplines, certain traditionally titled sections are expected in formal presentations of research and investigations, so your work must follow the pattern. In all of these examples it is very likely that marks will be gained or lost in relation to how well you follow the instructions, so once again you have been warned.

So here goes. Some of these sections may seem obvious (such as the 'Introduction' – can there really be anything I need to say about that? Well, yes) and others may seem less so ('Literature review' and 'Methodology' are perennially problematic for students, for example).

Abstracts and executive summaries

I expect you have to provide an abstract, and the exercise of writing one is a very good test of your understanding of your project, its structure and how it all holds together. In a way, the abstract is not so much part of the dissertation or report as a separate document that says something about your main document, and for that reason it is often excluded from the word count (you must check this). But its own word limit will be tightly specified – say, 150 words, or 250 or 500 in some cases, though always it must be brief because of its intended function. This enforced brevity adds to the challenge of writing a good, concise abstract.

What is its function, then? Well, apart from being something that the examiner tells you to write, an abstract is an important, short but informative document; and that importance has grown enormously as paper documents have given way to electronic ones in the academic world. Abstracts have long been used to help researchers find specific information, and there are many journals of abstracts and also abstracting services whose work covers just that. But now the abstract has become a crucial port of call during online searches for journal articles and other resources: you enter a search term into the search engine – 'maternal deprivation', say – and see what turns up in whatever search system you're using. Probably, the result will be a long list of authors and titles – far too many for you to read to discover their relevance. How do you know whether a given entry is one that interests you? You look up the abstract and there you find a summary of the paper, its objectives, its methods and its findings.

In other words, the abstract summarizes the whole of your report, dissertation, thesis, article, book or whatever it is. It includes the beginning, the middle and the end, so is not like a book blurb or similar 'teaser' text that leaves a lot unsaid and is designed to draw the reader into making a purchase. An abstract does not finish 'But what is the dark secret that Sandra has kept from her family for all these years?' or 'Now read on!' Instead, it tells all, in a very concise form, and gives the reader enough of an overview for them to decide whether to read it. And that's how you decide what to put in your abstract too.

Incidentally, an executive summary is another similar short document with the same kind of function, but it usually arises in a slightly different context. You may be asked to provide one instead of an abstract if you're studying in certain business or technology disciplines, for example. It comes from the world of company information and report writing, and you can think of it as aimed at busy 'executives' of one sort or another who are too important, or at least too self-important, to read through all of the reports they receive. Instead, they simply read the executive summaries, both for the significant details and to see whether they need to read the whole thing.

It should be clear by now that you can really only write an abstract when you have more or less finished your dissertation, at final draft stage for example, or at least when you know what's going to be in it and the general outcome. You can write one as an exercise earlier if you like, which is a good way to practise working to tight word limits, but don't spend a lot of time on it. One possible snag is that you may be asked to write an abstract for your initial proposal, as academics have to when proposing papers to conferences and so on. All you can do is write a summary of your best guess as to the overall shape of the paper and likely outcome from your current perspective.

One more thing: academic authors are now routinely asked for keywords as well as abstracts, and you may be asked for them too. Once again, these are connected to the vital business of targeted and accurate online searching. The keywords ride with the article or other document as part of the 'metadata', and are picked up by search engines to help with relevance. Think of the key concepts and terms used in your dissertation: what three or four words would you search on if you wanted to find your dissertation in a hurry on the internet?

The introduction

The introduction introduces, right? So what else is there to say? A lot, really. Your introduction is actually quite a subtle chapter. It is probably mandatory, or at least expected, and will probably have 'Introduction' as the title or as part of the title. And, yes, it comes first – or nearly first, because you may have a preface and/or acknowledgments, and you may be asked to bind your abstract before it too even though the abstract is not really part of the document.

The subtleties and variations concern what you include in the introduction and when you write it – and the two are connected. You may feel that you can write a reasonable amount of introductory scene-setting material early on, perhaps right at the beginning of your dissertation studies. That's fine. One of the themes of this book is that you should start writing early, and another is the advice not to prevaricate and fret too much about what you should or should not write – the message is effectively 'Just do it'. It is good to get words down, and it doesn't matter too much if you need to change a lot of them later.

What you should not do, however, is feel that you have to write your dissertation in the order in which the chapters appear – first the Intro, then Chapter 1, then Chapter 2, and so on. You can start writing anywhere, and in fact that's a good way to get the words flowing. Have you seen the classic 1940s film *The Lost Weekend*? It's about a writer's descent into alcoholism and his subsequent recovery and was regarded as 'a bit strong' in its day, but when the hero starts to write his story he turns to his trusty typewriter and keys 'The Bottle' and immediately underneath that 'A novel by Don Birnam' followed by 'To Helen with all my love'. And then off he goes with Chapter 1 line 1 ... Isn't that the way everybody writes everything? Well, no – not outside Hollywood. And it's certainly not the way academics work or present-day students write dissertations using word-processors.

The Lost Weekend point is that it's highly unlikely that you'll be able to write your introduction at the beginning of your dissertation studies, and you shouldn't feel obliged to. Some of it, perhaps, but all of it, no. In part it's rather like the abstract, in that you need to have the whole dissertation in final draft form before you know precisely what it is you're introducing, so from that perspective the introduction is something that you will be writing, or at least completing, at the *end* of your dissertation studies.

This book is nothing like your dissertation, but I can share with you how I wrote its introduction as an example of the way in which a first, introductory chapter is constructed late in the writing sequence. In my original proposal to the publisher I sketched an outline that included all of the introduction and chapter contents. That survived until I started writing. As I wrote, I entered headings into an introduction file that I'd created; these I would later use to build the introduction itself. I didn't write the chapters in number order, but by the time I had drafted the first two, I decided to revise the chapter plan and move some materials around. I decided to cut one of my original chapters and amalgamate two others, and some of the cut material I added back into the 'Intro' file that was building as I wrote the various chapters. Eventually, all of the chapters were drafted and I sent them out for review and comment to academic colleagues and students. By this time, the Intro file was pretty full of subheads, ideas, sketchy paragraphs in need of expansion, and of course the moved material from the original chapter plan. Finally, I was ready to write the Introduction in its present form. It may sound back to front, but once you start writing your dissertation you'll see that it makes sense.

One more thing: if the terms of your dissertation or report allow you to spread formal elements like the literature review and methodology across other parts of the dissertation, the introduction is a good place to point out where the reader (and the markers) can find them. It should be obvious, but it doesn't hurt to add some signposts to make sure.

Present, past or future?

Here's a subtle question. What tense will you use when you write your introduction? Some people fall naturally into using the future tense, on the assumption that the introduction is somehow chronologically prior to the research in the main body of the dissertation. 'I will interview ten social work staff from the medical centre.' Others use past tenses, given that they're introducing a body of research that has already taken place – 'I interviewed ten social work staff from the medical centre' – or combinations of present and past tenses. I'd be inclined to do the same: the research is something that you have already done and you are introducing it to people who will read about it afterwards; they are not people waiting expectantly for an as yet unresolved adventure to unfold. The chronological priority is completely spurious; there is only a structural priority. However, your dissertation handbook or supervisor may say that you must use future tenses in your introduction, in which case you may sigh inwardly but must do what they say.

The introduction, then, is where you set up the framework of your investigations for the benefit of your reader. You describe what you set out to do, and then talk generally about how you did it – though the specifics of how you did it and the details of your analysis follow in later chapters.

Research questions and objectives

I said that the introduction is where you describe what you set out to do. Hence it is almost always the place where you formally set out your definitions, objectives and intentions, unless your handbook demands that you create a separate section or chapter for that.

Your intentions and objectives can take several forms and follow different conventions. For example, you may base your inquiry on a *research question* – perhaps also summarized or paraphrased in your dissertation title – that you set out to answer by means of your research and its exposition in your dissertation. Or you may have proposed a *hypothesis* that you subsequently try to prove for your dissertation – or to disprove using the classic Popperian approach.[1]

It is likely that your handbook or course tutors will specify the approach you should use; there may be a 'culture' associated with your discipline that you are expected to adopt, and your staff or department may refine this further or make it explicit. Your early work on your dissertation should include the refinement of an appropriate question or hypothesis. Agree it with your supervisor. It may even be something that you have to determine before you embark on the course, as a submitted research proposal or as an element of a prior research methods course.

These formal presentations of your quest will normally be backed by one or more *objectives* that you list and then later point to as achieved (or not achieved) when you discuss your results and findings. The greater the clarity with which you present them here, the easier it will be for your readers (who include your markers) – and you – to follow the connections from initial questions, aims and objectives to results and conclusions. It is a good idea to set out objectives in list form unless you are asked to do something different. Here's a rather trite example of a research question in an imaginary discipline:

> *Was the human dwelling in the woodland clearing constructed by John Peregrine Makepeace (known as Jack)?*

or in hypothesis form:

> *That the human dwelling in the woodland clearing was constructed by John Peregrine Makepeace (known as Jack).*

A set of objectives for either of these weighty and important investigations might include the following objectives (here expressed in the first person, which may or may not be forbidden in this discipline).[2]

---

[1] This is something that is more appropriate to your research methods reflections than to this book, but I'm referring here to the 'hypothetico-deductive' method proposed by Karl Popper (1902–1994), an approach that has been very influential in the social sciences. If you want to find out more, the classic exposition is Popper's *The logic of scientific discovery* (1959 translation of the 1934 original).

[2] Pantoscience, perhaps?

- I will establish that in Filbert Forest in the 1830s there flourished a forester whose name was John (Jack) Makepeace.

- I will investigate the documentary evidence that the said Jack Makepeace gatherered together during this period materials sufficient to construct a dwelling.

And so on. Presumably, you could also investigate whether Jack then went on to kill giants from the house that he built. Notice how the form of the research question suggests that the answer(s) are likely to be presented at length via discussion, whereas the hypothesis is open to being supported or rejected, depending on the methods commonly used in these vital Pantoscientific investigations. Notice too that the objectives are expressed in a way that allows them to be achieved or not achieved.

The literature review

All academic research in any field needs to find and examine prior work in that field. Some of this will be known to you from prior studies, or standard work in the field that draws on the work of established authorities such as Jürgen Habermas or Eric Laithwaite (to give two very different examples). Or it may be new or controversial. Once you have discovered this prior work, you must reflect on how it affects what you're doing and what you're trying to achieve. In many ways, this is one of the key characteristics that makes the work 'academic'; it acknowledges that you are working in a constantly evolving collaborative enterprise, not just talking off the top of your head or working in a vacuum. This is true whether you are working in science, technology, arts or humanities, and whether your inquiry is undertaking new and groundbreaking investigations or is working entirely on pre-existing secondary sources. The approaches you may engage with when working with this prior material may include:

- summarizing established material (e.g. accepted core theories in the discipline)

- finding appropriate and topic-related new material

- sorting all material for its relevance, rejecting some as not relevant and retaining other elements

- reviewing the retained portion

- critiquing the retained items, or a main subset of them that you will work with

- identifying key theories from these and the traditional or established literature

- identifying the theoretical core that informs what you do

- critiquing that theoretical core

- possibly even creating or developing your own new theoretical vantage point

- later, perhaps amending that in the light of your findings.

The literature review (which I'll call the 'lit review' from now on) is definitely one of those areas that needs wider discussion. You'll find it discussed at length in all research methods books and it will figure on your research methods course, but how you present it in the dissertation is a prime zone for gaining or losing marks so it's worth spending a lot of time on it. If you have agreed with your supervisor that they will read at least one draft for you, make sure that the lit review, or a version of it, is included in the draft so that they can see it.

A lit review is not simply: 'I read this, and then I read this, and then I read this and a bit of that, and – oh yeah – I also looked at this . . .' That's a ridiculously crude example, and is quite obviously not any kind of review, let alone a lit review, but it is intended as a caricature of what the least diligent students offer as a literature review. When you get beyond the surface of what they're doing, they say little more than that: these are not lit reviews at all, and if anything are merely discursive bibliographies expressed in an unconvincing, meandering form.

Let's go one better. Here's the next best (but still not very good) approach, again in an extremely caricatured form: 'I read this, and it was OK, and then I read this, which was a bit crap, and then I read this, which was interesting though I didn't really understand it, and then I read a bit of that, which was also interesting, and then I looked at this, which I was told to read but didn't make sense of at all . . .'

This represents in outline form what rather more students present. These slightly wiser students know that a lit review is more than just a list of things they've had to read for the dissertation – a bibliography in fancy dress – so they try to offer a few comments on the content and perhaps on its quality. But there is no depth to the comments – they are hardly reflections and there is no reasoning behind them. Nor is there any attempt to set these critiques, such as they are, into a coherent narrative that begins to build up a picture of the state of the discipline – or more likely the recent exposition of a small section of a sub-discipline – that the student is researching. There is no way in which this shallow level of inquiry would enable the student to perform one of the tasks that a lit review must undertake:

How does my work fit into, build upon, even add to, existing academic work on this topic?

I hope you can begin to see what a lit review must do. Here is not the place to take this very large topic further. You'll find much more on the lit review in almost all research methods texts,[3] and it's such a big topic that there are now books wholly devoted to the literature review.[4] I'm sure it will feature significantly on your research methods course and will be mentioned at length in your dissertation handbook. And some universities put their guidelines on the internet for other students to read too[5] – something that is true for many aspects of research methods and writing.

One common student concern is when you should start writing the lit review. Some supervisors recommend you start it early and try to write most of it by the mid-period of your dissertation. There is some value in this approach: you certainly can write some of your lit review very early – though possibly not all of it – provided you have done a lot of reading and reflection in the early part of your dissertation course. You've done a lot of groundwork so why not write it up? This has an advantage that I shall keep coming back to: it puts words on the page, and makes you feel that you have some writing in the bank. However, if you'd rather not write the lit review early – perhaps because the theoretical context of your investigations is rather complex and needs more time for reflection, or because you'd rather wait for the outcomes of other parts of your investigations – don't feel that you're failing if you leave it till later. That's fine. Start writing another part of your dissertation instead, as discussed in Chapter 6.

Another common student question is: How long should the lit review be? I'm afraid I can only give you a very irritating answer: It should be as long as it needs to be. One obvious variable is the nature of the subject you're working on and the extent of the literature around your topic, as well as more generally in the discipline. In big fields such as English

---

[3] For example, Mark Saunders et al., *Research methods for business students*, 6th edn, Financial Times / Prentice Hall, 2010, chapter 3.

[4] See for example Diana Ridley, *The literature review: A step-by-step guide for students*, SAGE Study Skills, 2008.

[5] Search on 'literature review' and the examples will flow. I've just done that very thing, and immediately found www.unc.edu/depts/wcweb/handouts/literature_review.html, www.writing.utoronto.ca/advice/specific-types-of-writing/literature-review, and www.lboro.ac.uk/library/skills/Advice/Literature%20review.pdf, all near the top of the first page of a Google search. You are spoiled for choice.

the literature could be extensive, and you'll need to use enough space to do that justice. In other fields there could be many fewer examples of journal articles and other 'conventional' literature – and what there is could be old, of indifferent quality or even superficial or worthless. In a case like that your inquiry may need to bring in many other forms of written material as a potential foundation for your discussion. Many of the dissertations I supervise these days fall into this category: students may have to mix a fragmented array of 'official' academic literature with items from trade publications, news media, internet sources, 'grey' literature and so on. But even here, the lack or fragmented nature of the literature is something that students need to discuss too, and that can make a literature review longer than you might have first expected given the small number of academic sources.

A good way to see literature reviews in action is to read academic work, particularly in journal articles or books. Go to the leading journals in your field and look at one or more issues' worth of articles; most of them will involve some kind of literature review, probably around the first third or half of the piece. You can also get a good idea by reading journals in other fields, subject areas that are not your own. You may not understand the content but the structure of the article may be clearer as a result. Some articles are almost all review, and a good way to find these is to look at review journals, whose function is to produce concentrated evaluations of multiple pieces of work, usually in very active and fast-changing fields.

Before leaving the topic I should say – as I say again elsewhere in this book – that the length of each of the different parts of the dissertation is a matter for constant adjustment and balancing. Each aspect of the document will lay claim to space, and as you progressively write up each component you will have to decide how to divide it all up within the word limits.

Methodology

I have met people who refuse to believe that 'methodology' is a real word. How can there be an 'ology' associated with methods? Nevertheless, you know that there is, and you also know that virtually all dissertations and project reports must carry a methodology section. It is another formal part of your document, and is also subject to the same variations as the lit review. A chapter called 'Methodology' may be compulsory, or you may be allowed to scatter the elements elsewhere in your dissertation, either as a section of another chapter, or across two or more other chapters.

This part of the dissertation may be obvious to you or it may not. This obviousness, or lack of it, could be a function of your subject area. If you are setting up an experiment within, say, physics, bioscience or a technology field, it's clear that you must follow a sequence of operations in order to do this, and the (academic) reader will want to know what they are – indeed, it's essential in science and technology to tell people not just your results but how you came by them. This 'how' is so often missing from popular accounts of science and technology outcomes in the mainstream media, rendering them next to worthless. But what about, say, an investigation into Early English verse, or female costume in Restoration theatre, or the thoughts of John Balguy, the eighteenth-century British moralist? What's 'method' got to do with that?

The answer is: everything. You conducted your inquiry in a very particular way, didn't you? You chose particular ways to express and test your theories or ideas, and although these may not be clearly examples of 'method' as, say, which form of chromatography to use, they represent an approach that you should declare.

That's what you do – you make very many choices as you conduct your research. You read carefully chosen things, carry out certain investigations and not others, ask particular questions of selected people, get responses, categorize them, analyse them, emphasize some things and not others, adopt theoretical positions (perhaps backed by your lit review), choose analytic techniques, and make a wide range of other informed choices . . . The list goes on.

The point is: tell us what you did, but more than that tell us why you did what you did rather than some other thing. What are the advantages and disadvantages, strengths and weaknesses of what you did, and how do these pluses and minuses colour your results? Could (and did) anything go wrong? Why did you talk to those people and not to some other people? Would you have obtained different results if you had talked to other people? (For example, somebody might suspect that you chose those people because you knew they would tell you what you want to hear.) Why did you ask those questions and not other questions? In some fields, of course, you may also have to produce diagrams, photographs, photomicrographs or other visual material to support your presentation of what you did.

Ask your supervisor for more specific advice because the concept of 'method' varies so widely from one discipline to another; but don't be afraid to discuss the limitations of your methods – all methods do some things well and other things less well – and you should say what they are. This kind of reflection may fall naturally into the discussion of your choice of methods. Method A was more appropriate for your inquiry than method B because it is more accurate, or more robust, or quicker, or cheaper, or better attuned to the range you're examining, and so on. And it's likely that though method A has certain advantages – which is why you chose it – it will also have drawbacks, which in turn will have implications. For example, method A is more accurate but is slower, so you processed fewer test pieces, and hence the conclusions you draw are based on a smaller sample, and so on.

Be careful not to appear to be saying that you chose a particular method, or a particular form of statistical analysis of your results, because it gives you the results you want in order to prove your point: that's disreputable, and a form of verification bias. You may think you are building in 'success' by doing this, but it's illusory. More on this in the next chapter. One reason for you presenting, discussing and justifying your methods is that it shows your reader that in fact you have not chosen methods simply to give yourself the 'right' answer. It is all part of the openness of rational inquiry and lets others inspect what you did and how you did it.

There's no need to cheat and seek favourable results. A negative outcome for your inquiry is perfectly respectable, and is normally a valuable result in itself. Let's say you started out with a hypothesis – that motorcyclists under 1.4 m tall in Rochdale prefer low-fat coleslaw to full-fat varieties – and that you conduct some kind of investigation that shows quite the opposite: you find that overwhelmingly (at a high significance level) they don't prefer low-fat coleslaw. What's wrong with that as an outcome? It is informative, isn't it? If your research was sponsored by the Rochdale Coleslaw Collective then it might have implications for them and the future sales of their members, but it's perfectly sound from your point of view. If you're worried about the likely outcome being far from what you expected then you must talk to your supervisor. But think: if all research questions were validated and all hypotheses vindicated, this business of rational inquiry, whether inside science or not, would fall under great suspicion.

So, just as the lit review is not simply 'I read this and then I read that', the methodology is not simply 'I did this and then I did that'. For each 'this' you adduce, you should say why you chose that way of doing things, and how that choice impinges on the outcome. If you later decide to adapt some of your methods in the light of early work or trials that change your views, then say so and talk about their implications too. All the time, think of it as an exercise in transparency, so that other researchers, who may want to build on your work, can be sure that your approach was sound and that your findings are justified. In the sciences, for example, it may be important that other researchers can *replicate* your findings by following the same method.

And when you are writing your lit review, it is likely that you'll be discussing the methodologies employed by those other researchers whose work you're examining.

Results and outcomes

This is perhaps one of the less mysterious sections of your dissertation, and the main pitfall is that you may include more than the required content, depending on how tightly your dissertation rules specify this aspect of your inquiry. As I've already mentioned, you must be clear about precisely what is appropriate: is it the raw results and nothing else, or should you also provide some contextualizing discussion that helps to explain the outcomes but that falls short of analysing them? I can't answer that question directly – 'It depends' is about as good as I can do – though your familiarity with your own subject should mean that you have a good idea already. As always, ask if you're not sure.

How should the results be presented? Are there particular forms of tabular or graphical matter that you should use, for example? And if you are putting numerical results in tables should you also include any statistical outcomes in the cells – p values for significance, say – or does that count as analysis in your dissertation rules, and hence something for your discussion chapter(s)?

In arts and humanities dissertations your results are less likely to be in numerical form or even quantitative at all, and may not be suitable for tabular presentation; but the same general principles apply. There are things that you have found out, discovered, and here is where you should put them.

It is in these disciplines that you are most likely to be able to choose not to have a formal 'results' chapter at all, and instead may present findings across several parts of the dissertation – perhaps spread across chapters organized by period, or case studies, or some sectoral analysis. Remember that in many important ways, qualitative findings and other more nebulous outcomes still count as a form of result, so do report them with as much clarity as a scientist would present quantitative data. If the reader is unable to find what you discovered without spending hours digging through the entire centre section of your dissertation, you are doing them a disservice. Somewhere, somehow, you must present your results in a form that says 'These are my findings, my results.'

Case studies

I mentioned case studies above. Many dissertations use them to form part or the whole of their inquiry, and naturally they can be valuable when undertaking comparative or representative studies. A common way of incorporating them is to have a chapter for each case study, but you must then decide where you incorporate the outcomes of each case and other elements.

The 'results' aspects of each case will naturally fall into each separate case study chapter or section, but what about methodological aspects and analysis? Are you going to have mini-methodologies for each case, or does a conventional separate methodology do the job (or do you need something of each?). Will each case study have its own discussion section?

If you're using the case studies in a comparative context – and there will always be at least something of this when you introduce case studies – then it's likely that you will want to pull everything together in a subsequent discussion chapter.

Discussion and analysis

This chapter (or group of chapters) is inevitably a fairly demanding one. It is here that you demonstrate your understanding of your results and their significance and also display your research insights and analytical prowess. Once again, what does your handbook say about this section and what are your tutors expecting?

By the time you come to write up this chapter you will have been eating, breathing and sleeping your dissertation for many months. It is one of those chapters that you will probably draft as you go but can only write up in detailed earnest fairly late in the process. If you are under strict instructions not to include any discussion in your results section, then you could keep the discussion chapter open on your word-processor and make notes in it at the same time as you write up your results. It is probably a good idea to do this anyway if you have to keep results and discussion separate. Whenever you are tempted to do a bit of analysis, or find that you got carried away and have already included some, just cut it out and copy it into your discussion chapter instead, with suitable links and notes to yourself so that you know what you were talking about when you return later and write the discussion.

And of course you're not just making desultory comments on your results. You're analysing them, and as part of that you bring in all that thinking you did in prior chapters such as the lit review and methodology. Is there a theoretical consequence of your findings, or at least some kind of link to the established thinking in your field? Does that theoretical context feed into what you are going to say, or even can say, about what you have discovered? Could it be that as a result of your findings a widely accepted theory is flawed, or has limitations in your area, or even that you appear to have found a counter example that 'breaks' it? What are the methodological implications for the results you achieved, and what inferences can you make as a result?

The discussion part of your dissertation is naturally a vital link in the chain that connects your objectives with your conclusions, but it must also make sense in its own right. It should be possible for a reader – or at least one who is familiar with your subject area – to jump straight into your discussion without having first read any other part of the dissertation and yet still make general sense of it. Is that true of yours? Indeed, this is not a bad test for any of your chapters: could a reader understand most of it on its own?

Conclusions

Another straightforward one, right? Well, yes, but . . . At the risk of saying something ridiculously obvious, a conclusion should *conclude*, and sometimes they don't. Here are the most common things that students worry about or make a mess of when writing conclusions.

- Its length: too short or too long?
- Does it draw all of the preceding material together?
- Does it answer the question, or resolve the hypothesis, and meet the objectives?
- Is it a new discussion in disguise?

I'll try to say something meaningful about each of these, and I hope that when you read them you'll see the nature of the conclusion chapter becoming clearer in the space between these problem areas.

How long?

This is the old 'piece of string' question again, the one that I mentioned in connection with the lit review earlier. Look, a single paragraph or even a single page is not going to be enough, and something that takes a quarter of the word allowance for the whole dissertation is probably too long – and could mean that you have included a lot of material in the conclusion that you should have put into earlier chapters, or that you've duplicated a lot.

I find that more students err on the short side than on the long side. The very worst conclusions say little more than 'Great. I've finished. Read the discussion to find out what I think. Cheers. Bye.'

The best way to avoid trivial conclusions chapters is to take time over them – give them as much loving attention as you gave to everything else. Above all, don't assume you can write your conclusions at the last minute, such as an hour before you get the dissertation or report printed and bound. I think this 'last minute' carelessness is the principal cause of feeble or useless conclusions chapters.

Does it draw everything together?

This is a significant question, and a good test to apply if you want to check your own concluding remarks. Readers, and very often markers, may look for your question/hypothesis and objectives at the beginning and then jump straight to your conclusions to see what you found. If they are still interested, they will then go back and trace the route you followed between those two points as it goes through all of the intervening chapters. Can they do that with yours? Make sure the overarching argument works overall as a linear progression that includes everything along the way.

Does it answer the question, or resolve the hypothesis, and meet the objectives?

As well as the 'drawing together' point, a connected issue is whether your conclusions actually pick up the question you first asked and answer it, whether directly and confidently or tentatively and provisionally. Or has the hypothesis been resolved one way or the other, as far as is feasible given the way things worked out? And are the objectives explicitly achieved – in other words, do you address each in turn and answer it (even if the answer is 'No' or 'It's inconclusive')? If you're not able to do these things then the dissertation hasn't really succeeded and you need to work on it until it has.

As I've already said, it may be that the outcomes are largely negative, and you might even say things that effectively say 'If I were to do this again, I would ask a slightly different question.' But that's all right, and is an interesting outcome in its own right.

Is it a new discussion in disguise?

You need to exercise judgement in deciding how much of your preceding discussion to review and repeat in your concluding remarks. There is bound to be some overlap as you restate what has gone before, but there is usually no significant redundancy because in the conclusion you try to present where you've reached in a concentrated, summary form.

I find that students often err in the other direction, though. Far from their conclusion covering old ground, they start a new discussion. This may well raise valuable and interesting points – but is formally unsupportable because it doesn't draw on the preceding elements of the dissertation. It is a new 'think piece' that wanders off in a different direction. This seems to happen most when students are trying to predict future implications of the current findings (that's fine, but only if the predictions derive from your findings), suggest topics or implications for further research and study (that's good, and a frequent outcome in academic work, but likewise only if that emerges from your findings and discussion), or in some other way look out over new and appealingly open spaces.

But that's not what you're doing in a conclusion. It is not the start of a new essay but a summary of your work and findings. By all means predict possibilities or suggest new directions for study, but only on the strength of what you have already researched, discovered and analysed in the rest of your dissertation.

Appendices and other endmatter

I don't want to say much about the kinds of things that should go in here as this varies enormously, depending on the kind of dissertation or project you are undertaking. You make the decision about what to include based on the ancillary information that you think some readers may want to see, such as space-consuming sample data and so on – anything that would clutter up the discussion if you included it in the main body of the dissertation but that nevertheless some readers would find interesting, or that specialists in your area would want to look at more closely. Examples include:

- sample or complete datasets where these are bulky
- samples or complete responses to questionnaires
- interview transcripts
- sample calculations where these are too long to include in the main text
- ancillary graphs, tables and figures
- supplementary diagrams or illustrations.

There are only two other questions that you should ask yourself in relation to appendices and endmatter: first, what does your handbook say and what is conventional for you to include in this supplementary section? Second, what do your word limit rules say about appendices? Before you append page after page of supplementary information, make sure that this does not have to be included in your word count. And of course show very clearly in your design and signposting (Chapter 6) that endmatter and supplementary material are just that – distinguish it all very clearly from the main text.

4 The rigours of reasoning

In the Introduction I reminded you of something that you already know – that a dissertation is built around a reasoned discourse that starts with a proposal, usually expressed as a question or hypothesis, and proceeds to a conclusion. But these beginnings and ends must be linked together by a chain of reasoning, otherwise the dissertation degenerates into the 'bag of bits' that I warned you about. You will spend a lot – probably most – of your time on the various elements that make up this chain, so it's important that you present your findings and conduct their discussion in the right way: you don't simply inject random ideas or say the first thing that comes into your head. That's what this chapter is about: making sure that your work appears as a reasoned whole, especially in those sections that – to change the metaphor – make up the engine room of your dissertation.

Your dissertation handbook, research methods classes and course staff will have made it clear what kinds of elements are appropriate for a dissertation in your field. They may even be fixed and have specified titles that you must use. I am assuming that even if you had been out of the academic environment before you started your current course, by now you will have produced many kinds of different written material – essays, technical reports, laboratory, practical or fieldwork reports, reviews, or whatever else is appropriate in your field – in your immediately prior terms or years of university study. You may also have written a dissertation before.

So to that extent I don't need to go into detail about the precise elements to include, nor shall I waste words and insult you by telling you what you know. The standard processes and writing styles of your discipline are already familiar to you. Instead, I'm going to stand back a little, and talk generally about the application of theory and remind you about several aspects of the process that we call 'reasoning'. Part of that will involve very careful use of the terms that express this reasoning and convey it to the reader (and, as always, that means the marker too). It is so easy to use loose forms of language that say things you don't want them to say. These can get you into trouble, so I'm going to list a selection of them and offer some advice. I have quite a lot to say about this topic – and could say a lot more if this was a longer book. However, it's an important one so don't ignore this chapter. First, though, let's look at theory.

Theory

You have undertaken enough academic study to know that your subject is riddled with theories of one kind or another. They may be grand theories of everything, or tiny localized ones conjured up to explain some small phenomenon; they can be current or obsolete, modified, attacked, supported, countered, replaced, evolving, studied for historical interest only and so on.

However you encounter them and in whatever form they appear, they are supposed to have some kind of *explanatory value*, to inform, to make sense of something that otherwise appears fairly chaotic or impenetrable. Another important use of theory is that it should have *predictive value*, for example by suggesting what will happen to a country's economy in the future, or when and where a volcanic eruption or earthquake may occur. By applying theory in general – in the form of a theory in particular – to some aspect of your area of study, you should start to feel it make sense in a way that it did not before. So in different fields we have string theory, critical theory, field theory, the theory of surplus value and myriad others. At times, you may feel rather cynically that some theories obfuscate more than they clarify, or don't explain anything, and that some academics simply make up new theories or trash existing theories in order to have people talk about and cite them; but that's another story.

The point is that you will expect that your academic dissertation or report, in order to be 'properly' academic, should include a good dose of theory. How should you get the theory in there, and how do you manage this theory once you've included it?

This is one of those areas where the level of generality I have to maintain in this book makes it difficult for me to say anything that applies universally, but I will make observations where I can. So much depends on your subject area: in many areas of science, for example, there are large areas of theory that have evolved over the course of the discipline to the extent that they imbue and inform more or less all research and discussion within that discipline. In some ways, that kind of theory will be implicit in your research and your findings without you having to do anything special to bring it in. Of course, at the edges of the discipline, where researchers and theorists are pushing forwards, there will be more controversial theories or sub-theories, perhaps vying with rival views to see which will win out as new evidence is gathered to test them. When you work with this kind of theory, you will clearly need to justify what you're doing and make this explicit; your understanding of what you're doing will link into other parts of your course and studies, and will possibly require the advice and help of your supervisor too.

In non-scientific disciplines there could be more of the controversial theories and fewer of the grand and widely agreed ones, and if so your need to explicitly justify what you're doing is stronger. In the arts and humanities it is not uncommon for there to be several current theories about a particular phenomenon or set of phenomena, and different academics will support different theories and debate with each other about them in the literature and at conferences. In areas such as politics, economics and public policy, these theories may well be applied 'in the wild' too as politicians and policymakers draw on them to decide what to do about, say, economic policy in a recession. When that happens, the nature of a theory – and its 'rightness', for want of a better term, or its closeness of fit to 'reality' – becomes a big deal. It can affect all of our lives and is not simply part of a private game played among academics.

My comment about the literature and conferences above is a clue to the part of the dissertation where theory may be introduced, and this may well be the main or only point at which this happens – apart from its incorporation in your later discussion of course, and if you're not going to introduce the theory into your discussion and analysis, you've taken away perhaps the main reason for including it at all.

I'm referring to the literature review, as you know. It is not the only place to insert theoretical musings but it is the most natural one, given that you're evaluating the writings of others, including their theoretical stances and claims and, where appropriate, their methods. The critiquing and sifting of theory is also one of the key functions of the lit review, and it may well result in you adopting a theory in the literature as a matrix for your own research, or at least a variation of a theory – so, for example, you say you will follow Haverstock's Ribaldry theory (to return to our imaginary friends from Chapter 1) except that you are proposing a different hinge vector in phase 2, or propose turning it up to 11.

This indeed takes us back to the kind of reflections I rehearsed in Chapter 1 about making use of what academics produce and the assessment of its quality and value, but there is one further thing I need to say about applying theory. It is that some students first work out what they're doing – experimentally, through primary research and so on – and then come back and look for some theory afterwards.

Bolt-on theory

As you can see, I have a name for this approach to theory, and the name I use does reflect this 'afterthought' approach. I think it's more likely to occur in fields where theory is fluid or controversial, and is much less likely to be seen where the subject area is dominated by long-established theories that are part and parcel of what everybody does. In those cases you have to use the established theories to get going so they are integrated from the start and can't be an afterthought.

I think the bolt-on variety often comes about like this. A student starts work – and this can be with a good topic, sensible ideas for investigation, and a plausible methodology – and then goes off to conduct archive work, experiments, interviews, online surveys, or whatever it is they're doing. (I've added the comment about the good topic and sensible ideas because I don't want to suggest that only weak students do this: it's a risk for everybody, and you can even find evidence of it in professional academic writing.) They also do some sensible reading and put together material for their lit review. Later, quite a long way into their studies, they have pulled together their principal results and have made many notes, and feel they've achieved a lot. Which quite probably they have. Then they think to themselves that they need some theory, otherwise their dissertation will not be 'academic' enough. This is where the problems start.

In order to find their theory they trawl through their textbooks and past notes, scan plausible literature or look for connected discussions in some corner of the discipline. And then perhaps they discover one – they take it off the shelf at the theory shop, so to speak. 'Shall I wrap it for you?' 'No thanks. I'll drop it straight into my dissertation as it is.'

You can see what is wrong. A theory obtained in this way is stuck on as an afterthought. It doesn't inform what has already happened because that took place without any recourse at all to this mysterious theory. It is, as I say, bolt-on theory. It can't by its very nature add to your understanding of what you did, except by accident or if you retrospectively work it in and then redo your primary research. If you find yourself in this position – and it is not uncommon in certain subjects because the wilder frontiers of some disciplines can be substantially theory-free – then talk to your supervisor about what to do. And it is clear that you should do this early in the process too, and not leave it until you're deep into your analysis phase. It could be that they will accept that you are working in a theory-deprived region – and isn't there an opportunity here? You could form the outlines of a theory, perhaps by analogy with a comparable theory in another discipline, and have it associated with your name. If your work ever escapes into the world, it could even have your name on it and be a reason for you to be cited.

Generalizing from this idea, here are some ways in which you can misuse theory in a dissertation.

- Adding theory as an afterthought (bolt-on theory).
- Using controversial theories without justifying their inclusion.
- Not understanding the theory you apply.
- Mistaking metaphors and analogies for theories.

Careless talk costs marks

Now I'm going to talk more about varieties of loose language that can lead you astray. It may be that this loose language is a symptom of loose thinking, or it could be that you are just using habitual expressions – such as we all do – that are perfectly acceptable in everyday conversation but that harbour dangers when used in academic writing. If you are going to use these terms and expressions in the more controlled environment of the dissertation, then you must use them deliberately and consciously, and you must try to mean what you say.

These terms can creep into your early proposals and part of the dissertation, though they are prone to crop up particularly frequently in objectives and questions, discussion sections and conclusions. They can also find their way in when you're working fast to meet a deadline, or when you're tired and filling in a few more paragraphs before stopping for the night.

I think the best way to show what I mean is to list some of them and describe the pitfalls associated with each. I don't mean to make you neurotic and self-conscious about every word you use, but some terms should have a hazard warning on them.

So before I list them, let me reassure you that I'm not wishing to make you frightened to say anything at all. Of course you can use these terms; just don't use them in a casual, throwaway sense as you might if you were talking to friends over a drink or expressing ideas on your blog. Here's the key guideline for using these risky expressions.

If you use one of these terms or expressions or others like them, use it accurately and make sure you mean what you say.

'Because . . .'

Let's start with a commonplace and harmless-seeming term. It's an inno-cent, everyday word. We use it all the time, as well as cognate expressions like those using 'as' to mean because (in the sense used in, for example, 'I never play with matches as ['as' = because] I'm afraid I'll burn the house down', but not in the sentences 'I am as fit as a flea' or 'I heard a noise as ['as' = when] I stepped out of the room'). But the word 'because' will serve to exemplify the problem, whichever of these words we use in this sense (that is, as conjunctions with a special explanatory function).

The issue is a simple one: when you say something like 'People are leav-ing Spotsville because local unemployment is rising' you are expressing or at least implying a causal relationship between two things – in this case between an observed event (people leaving) and a condition or state of affairs (rising unemployment). Is that what you meant to say? I've deliberately chosen a non-silly example because it is an example of a plausible-sounding statement. We read things like this in newspapers all the time. But if you intend to make that rather strong claim, then in the academic context you face a question: are you justified in saying that?

Let's turn to more direct claims of causality to see what's going on. This is, after all, what 'because' means – 'because of' is 'by cause of'.

'Causes ...', 'is caused by . . .'

We naturally talk about things or events causing other things or events, and this notion of causality is a very familiar concept. It's a very tempting one in a dissertation too – how nice it would be to show that a phenomenon that interests us is caused by some other factor that we can investigate.

You are investigating the declining Spotsville population and you believe that rising local unemployment is the key. (You might even make this your hypothesis.) Spotsville's tractor factory shut down two years ago, last year the glue works followed suit, and the insurance company head-quarters has just moved away to Clackthorpe. Unemployment is up, so people move elsewhere in search of work. Of course, there may be something else behind all of those failures – one or more prior causes – and there may be other associated factors too – people can't stand the stench from the nearby Glerwick sewage works. How do you find out? And anyway, how do you *show* that A causes B, either on its own or in company with other 'causes'?

I'm sure you've looked at this in your research methods classes or else-where in your studies and reading, but *showing* causation is actually rather tricky. How do you separate the possible multiple factors and/or prior causes in the Spottsville case, for example? The nature of causation itself has also been the subject of debate and analysis for centuries. It's not enough just to show that things regularly happen together ('constant conjunction' as the philosopher David Hume called it) to claim that one causes another. You need more. Whenever the wind blows I notice that trees bend and their boughs wave about. Aha! The wind is caused by trees bending and moving their branches about.

This is not the place to discuss these niceties, but my point is that you must be very careful about claiming causation, or confidently stating that you are going to show that A causes B. At that level, it's down to research method and topic choice. You are choosing to work with causes so you can read your research methods texts and take advice to see how to go about this.

But the problem when you come to write the dissertation is that you can unwittingly and unintentionally make causal claims, especially when you use everyday words like 'because' and 'as', which so often imply a causal relationship. Once again, I'm not suggesting you become paranoid about these things to the stage of being afraid to make any direct or general statements, but this is another area for care and self-checking.

Correlation

It's slightly less strong to talk of correlation instead of causation. In some disciplines and areas of study, demonstrating correlation is an everyday pursuit, often backed up by statistical analysis that might include the calculation of correlation coefficients.

The nature of correlation is that it implies some kind of connection but doesn't go as far as claims of causation do. It says that there is a link between A and B but not that A causes B or that B causes A. Once you have established a correlation then you may want to look for causation too, whether between A and B or to see whether something else, C, causes both.

Be careful not to confuse correlation with coincidence, which is simply where things happen together but you have no reason to suppose they are connected. They happen together by chance. Let's imagine that you are examining the behaviour of swallows nesting under the eaves of houses, and that as part of your work you have remote cameras trained on 33 Clissold Street in Scunthorpe and 41a Bontoft Crescent in Redruth. Every summer morning you watch the comings and goings of swallows from these sites from the comfort of your remote monitoring station at the University of Nuneham Courtenay.

Then, during idle moments, you start to notice that at 7.30 a.m. each day a person (it happens to be Letitia Mimms) leaves 33 Clissold Street and enters the newsagent's shop two doors away. At precisely the same time each day, a person (it is Anwar Kletzmer) leaves 41a Bontoft Crescent and walks south. You observe these events occurring together at the same time throughout the summer, and postulate that there is a correlation. In some ways, this kind of observation and postulation is what all correlation studies do, but in this case you'd be hard pushed to find anybody to agree with your judgement of correlation. We'd simply call it a coincidence. Both people are creatures of habit: Letitia happens to buy her paper each day at that time (or perhaps it is her shop and she is going to open it up), whereas Anwar is going to catch the bus at the end of the road (or is visiting his mother, etc.). There is no plausible link between the events, unless you want to make some bland claim about them being 'caused' by the general morning routine in developed countries – a claim so bland that it has no value.

This tendency to observe and propose connections between events is a strong human propensity, and is no doubt highly important for our survival, such as when our forebears noted that when the rains came at a certain time in the year the crops flourished, but when they came later in the year the crops failed. It is also something that can mislead us, such as when the high priest Sklaer observed that the crops failed after a comet appeared in the sky – which is bad news if you're next in line on the human sacrifice rota down at the temple.

'Therefore . . .'

From what I've said about 'because' you can probably guess what I'm going to say about 'therefore'. It's the same kind of problem. You may indeed want to make deliberate, intentional claims about consequence, about something following from something else, but equally you may just be using this familiar, everyday word without meaning to say anything as strong.

And just as there is an equivalence of 'because' and 'as', we can express 'therefore' by 'so', in the sense of 'Unemployment rose in Pottsville, so the people started to leave' (but not of course in the separate adverbial sense of 'I was so tired'). 'So' is such an innocent little conjunction – a joining word like 'and' and 'but', though with a very different import (try substituting 'and' and 'but' instead of 'so' in the sentence to see the difference). The sense is one of 'following from', as I say, and this can be in either a logical sense as in deductive reasoning, where a conclusion follows inexorably from one or more premises, or in a so-called inductive sense in the familiar sense of real-world investigations.

Think too of that informal rhetorical technique based on 'so' that you see a lot in television interviews. The interviewee says something like:

> I am worried about the rising crime rate in the southern suburbs of Grimston.

and the interviewer immediately responds with:

> So you're saying that the police should increase stop-and-search patrols and introduce a curfew?

Well, no. That's not what the interviewee was saying, and is more to do with what the interviewer wants them to say or admit. There is no true 'so' there, in the 'proper' and careful sense that you will be using it in academic discourse. This is yet another topic that belongs in your research methods reflections rather than here, but do take care that when you write the familiar words 'therefore' and 'so' in this sense you are not making claims you don't mean – and can't support. You may not have meant to say that B follows from A, but your reader/marker may interpret it that way.

'Impacts on . . .', 'influences'

Yes, another one. Students often want to show how something 'impacts on' or influences a state of affairs or people's behaviour or something similar. These are also favourite words in research questions too. Once again we have familiar and everyday word use, but we soon hit difficulties. How do you *show* impact or influence? If you set out with these aims in a dissertation, what kind of evidence is going to support your claims?

In a way these are variations – less strong or more indirect versions – of the causation problem mentioned above. Things may happen together, but how do you show they're connected?

Before you collapse in despair, and think I'm saying you can't use 'because', 'therefore', 'influences' and the rest, let me say that it's nothing like as bad as that – otherwise nobody could ever show anything: the degree of rigour and standard of evidence would be impossibly high. In academic investigations a great many relationships are established to a high degree of probability, and correlations are adduced and analysed with that in mind – often using concepts like significance and other statistics, of course.

To reiterate: my point in this chapter is simply that you should be careful when using these terms, not that you should stop using them.

'Proves that . . .', 'shows that . . .'

Here are two other expressions frequently used to link phenomena or events. 'Proves that' feels stronger, but 'shows that' can often be used to mean the same thing – a kind of 'therefore' term that once again is hinting at causal or similar relationships. In cases in law, where of course 'proves' is a key term in legal process, the legal system will normally incorporate standards of proof that have evolved over a long period. In English law, for example, there are sterner standards of evidence behind proving something in the criminal law than in the civil law.

You're more likely to use 'shows that' in an unwitting manner than the more obvious 'proves that', which probably carries an inbuilt warning that reminds you to be cautious when using it. The message is the same: if you write these terms, take care.

Here's an example of what I mean (and I bundle in an 'influence' for good measure). Let's say that you quote a statement from a publisher in the UK made during wartime – something that you uncovered during your research – who said 'We couldn't get enough paper so we cut back on our output, and reduced the number and size of pages in each book by using smaller type.' Then in your lit review or later discussion you adduce this quote and say 'This shows that paper shortages influenced the output of publishers in the war years.' Well, y-e-e-e-es, and you might get away with saying it if at that point your marker is distracted by a knock at the door or a nice cup of coffee. But taken at face value and on its own it is too strong a claim – certainly if 'shows' is taken to mean 'proves', which it often is. It is just one statement from one publisher. It is illustrative, certainly, and suggestive, perhaps, but if you are being rigorous you need more evidence to show and claim influence. (Yes, I've deliberately made the example plausible, if bland, because I wanted the 'show . . . influence' claim to appear perfectly reasonable rather than ridiculous.)

Am I being pedantic, over-fussy in these examples? Perhaps, but I want to remind you that the rigour of your approach is something that distinguishes good academic writing from the sort of things you could say if writing a newspaper or magazine article about the same topic, or when declaiming in your blog. In the internet age we are surrounded at all times by vast quantities of unsubstantiated knowledge claims and strident opinions, as I said earlier, and your academic writing must distinguish itself from this noisy 24/7 background.

'Is evidence of . . .'

I don't need to say much about this now. Statements claiming that something is 'evidence of' or 'evidence for' something else are linked to the 'proves' and 'shows' family of claims. Use the terms with care, so probably not like this:

> Crop circles are evidence of intelligent alien life visiting our planet.

'Clearly . . .', 'obviously . . .', 'of course . . .'

Here are some terms that you may have been warned off before, possibly far back in your schooldays. When starting a sentence they are often known as 'sentence adverbs', serving not so much to impart content or information (though in a way they often do), but to set a conversational tone. Some people – the kind of insecure and controlling folk who imagine all 'good' writing must be governed by a comprehensive set of tiny, rigid rules – hate them unreservedly, and want them all shot on sight.

They are risky in your dissertation, though. I have intentionally used them fairly often in this book, including in this chapter, but this book is not a dissertation: it is functionally very different. You can look for them and decide why they're there if you like. Partly they help to keep it conversational and informal – a book like this mustn't be too much of a chore or a challenge to read – but often when I use one of these tags I'm saying something like: 'Look, I know you probably understand this and have come across it before, but I have to say something about it because it will be new to some of my readers, so bear with me for a moment.' This kind of implied aside to the reader is not appropriate to the text of your dissertation.

So again be careful. Some sentence adverbs – 'however', 'furthermore' and so on – can be functionally effective in a dissertation if used cautiously. 'Of course' and 'clearly' are more dangerous – and even looser adverbial expressions like 'needless to say' and 'it goes without saying' are thoroughly unsafe. There is also still a debate about 'hopefully'; while some people use it routinely and see no problem, others hate it with a passion. The objectors would say that 'hopefully' is an adverb that means full of hope; it should not be used as equivalent to 'it is to be hoped that . . .' or 'I hope that . . .'

'Unfortunately', 'sadly', and ravaging decimation

At first sight, tags like 'unfortunately' and 'sadly' are simply more examples of the 'obviously' class of adverbs, but they add an extra layer. They introduce another dimension – your evaluation, whether ethical, aesthetical, political or whatever, of what you then go on to say. I'm not suggesting that academic endeavour consists only in striving to uncover crystalline 'value-free' truths, but these are risky terms and should not be sprayed around carelessly. Look at this pair of sentences:

> *A: The preliminary polls conducted for next year's general election suggest that Torvald Smith's Nasty Oligarchic Party will win an overall majority.*

> *B: The preliminary polls conducted for next year's general election suggest that unfortunately Torvald Smith's Nasty Oligarchic Party will win an overall majority.*

You can probably see what I mean. The A sentence is a straightforward prediction expressed in neutral language, presumably based on current evidence and good psephological reasoning. But the B sentence just drops in one innocent little word that changes the character of the statement completely – it puts *you* into it. We learn that you don't like the idea of the Nasties winning the next election – well, neither do I – but that's not something that should figure in your dissertation unless there are very special reasons for it to do so. I fully accept that the B sentence would not appear out of place in much contemporary journalism, where comment is now such a dominant form, and in the wider blogosphere such a statement would appear mild given the declamatory tone of so many blogs and their love of invective.

It may seem that I am going over the top and that the addition of that little 'unfortunately' is not going to change anything significant in your dissertation. Well, all right, but if you find you want to include a term or two like this then I suggest you talk it over with your supervisor. Now have a look at another pair of examples:

> *A: In 1350 the ravages of plague decimated the population of Glumhampton, killing 60% of the adult population and up to 85% of those under 10 years old.*

> *B: In 1350 the ravages of plague decimated the population of Glumhampton, sadly killing 60% of the adult population and up to 85% of those under 10 years old.*

Applying my comments from the previous example you may say that I'm suggesting there is an unwonted element of you in there again. But isn't this case very different from appearing to express a political opinion in a neutral dissertation? You could say that here is an event from centuries ago and that nobody with even a trace of humanity would suggest this is not 'sad' – surely[1] something from seven and a half centuries ago is safe to express an opinion about, and that historians make such judgements all the time? Possibly. Discuss. Or as I said above, have a word with your supervisor if you're planning to use any of these B sentence forms, even very mild ones.

If I had used 'tragically' instead of 'sadly', would that make it different? Possibly. In spite of the overuse of 'tragically' in our everyday culture ('Tragically, I scratched the screen of my new iPhone on the corner of the kitchen table') you could argue that 'tragedy' has a particular meaning that applies in this case and that would allow 'tragically' to be used without any problem at all.

But there's more. When creating the Glumhampton pair of sentences I also smuggled in some other terms that add further colour to these ostensibly neutral or 'objective' statements. What about 'ravages'? Is that too florid for a dissertation? I don't know – it depends . . . You could probably make a case for it being an interesting and not particularly harmful term that relieves the flatness of neutral academic language. Different markers would have different views. And what about 'decimate'? There are two schools of thought on this: one says that 'decimate' has come to mean destroy or devastate, whatever it might have meant in the past; the other school says that the original meaning should stand: 'decimate' refers to a nasty punishment from long ago where one-tenth of a population were killed, usually as reparation or to keep the rest of the population polite. You choose. We all apply different thresholds. I'm usually quite *laissez-faire* about the evolution of language and the corresponding constant change of usage and meaning that comes in its wake; I don't insist that etymology should always determine current usage (which in any case would be a ridiculous policy if applied uniformly). However, for some reason I don't like the new free 'decimate' and instead still use 'devastate', a word that may have been the reason for the change of use of the similar sounding 'decimate'.

One more thing concerning the second pair: I deliberately used 'up to 85%', but what exactly does that mean? I've included it as an example of loose language around numbers and quantitative data. This 'up to' device is insidious – and a favourite device of advertisers and tabloid journalists. When you think about it the expression can mean so many different things. An anti-immigration tabloid may claim 'Up to five million immigrants are expected to enter this country next year', and not be abashed[2] when the number actually turns out to be 97,032 or 12,201

---

[1] I know – don't call me Shirley.
[2] Not that a tabloid newspaper is ever likely to be abashed by anything.

or 254, or even if there is a net emigration and it's a negative number. Why? Because all of those figures could be claimed as included in 'up to 5 million'. An advertising slogan like 'Up to 15% off your grocery bill if you shop at Herbie's World of Buckets this weekend' may lure you to buy that new galvanized bucket you've been promising yourself for so long. But when you reach the till at Herbie's you are offered just 1% discount. You are outraged and demand to see Herbie (who turns out to be Beryl, because Herbie sold the business two years ago and moved to Oklahoma City), but she calmly reminds you that 1% is covered by 'up to 15%' and that if she wanted to she could even give you nothing because 0% is 'up to 15%' too, and why don't you stop bothering honest folk who are just trying to earn a living?

I'm not sure how Herbie's bucket discount would stand up in a trade descriptions dispute, but the point is that you should avoid 'up to' language in any quantitative contexts that you use in your dissertation. More generally, be careful when presenting numbers and quantitative data not to use vague or shifting language to embed it. And another message from the Glumhampton example is to see how many potential issues can arise from just one short sentence.

Business plans

In contemporary discussions and investigations we frequently encounter an expression that was once rarely used but is now a part of everyday informal language. In dissertation work in business studies, politics, social studies, media subjects and more you may need to use the term 'business plan' in your analysis to describe something that an individual or a company or sector needs to produce, but the term is now so embedded in our everyday language that it's tempting to use it too loosely to mean 'anything that makes money' rather than to refer to a strategy that could sustain a business. However, if your project or dissertation is based on the creation of a business plan, then it's unlikely you will fall into this trap because you will have a much clearer focus. It may even be a term you take care to define at the start.

'Relevant', 'important'

These terms are examples of another problem, one that (if you want it to) links into wider discussions of ethics, absolutes versus relatives, and so on. I'm going to claim that terms like these, so common in everyday discussion – not to say everyday disagreements – are disguised relational terms. A fellow student might say that they would like your university course to be 'more relevant' (something heard a lot in the 1960s). Or you may ask a key question in your dissertation of the form 'Is X important?' – perhaps even in your research question or title. Quite apart from the evaluative (good, bad, right, wrong, strong, weak, etc.) and comparative (more than, less than, etc.) elements of these statements, which you may well be able to argue for, there is another dimension. Here's an example of 'important' used in a research question:

How important was the Net Book Agreement to the survival of independent booksellers in the UK?

What kind of answer would a dissertation need to give to satisfy this question? In summary terms, it would be something like 'very important', or 'quite important' or 'unimportant', so that's the kind of conclusion your dissertation would support and argue for. Although you'd have to provide evidence to support the evaluation you make, it's easy to understand what's being asked here because of the phrase 'to the survival of independent booksellers'. In other words, we have the other part of the implied relation. Where it gets tricky is when this is missing. Have a look at this simple statement:

It is important that independent booksellers survive.

You or I may think this is correct, although it is clearly a judgement, an evaluation. But beyond the bald statement we can ask: important to what or to whom? Is it important to independent booksellers and to those who support and value them? Yes, presumably. But what of the vast number of other possibilities: to the high street, or the publishing industry, or to 'culture' or to 'civilization' – and so on? If you're one of those people who believe that markets are the only fit measure of humankind then it might even be seen as a contradiction: if independent booksellers fail it is because the market – supposedly aggregating all human decisions and choices – has not supported them; hence if through the market people have rejected them it is not open to people to say it is important they survive because they have freely decided they shall not. And so on. This can be quite a subtle issue, depending on the context. Just be sure you have assessed that context and can relate the use of 'important' or 'relevant' to it.

In everyday discussion we say things like 'It is important to remember that . . .' as a kind of shorthand for 'Please remember that . . .' or 'I think you should remember that . . .' but in the straitened confines of a dissertation you should be careful. Unless you adopt some kind of 'God's eye view' of importance that treats it as a kind of absolute (a *sub specie aeternitatis* view in the jargon), you'll need to make clear what the other side of the relational term is. Important, relevant to what, to whom?

Significant

You probably know that this term is not only a common word in every-day language but has a set of technical uses too. If you're using it in this formal sense – say, you're trying to show whether or not something is statistically significant – then you'll be aware of the technical pitfalls. If you're using it informally, such as in:

> *There was a significant change in the behaviour of the Henrician Court towards the king.*

> *The engine was operating at significantly higher temperatures than its original design parameters.*

then you need to be careful that you understand the implications of what you're saying whenever you say that a shift, or a difference, or a level, etc., is significant, and you should be able to justify that (often rather strong) claim if need be. In this informal sense, 'significant' is like 'important'.

Revolution, revolutionary

Here is another example of language use that is much affected by the language of the internet, journalism and advertising. The traditional business of identifying and analysing revolutions belongs to history or politics – the French Revolution, Russian Revolution, American Revolution, Glorious Revolution and so on. But now the term is caught up in a kind of continuous background hysteria: in this world of rapid change every new product, way of working or means of communicating is described as a revolution or revolutionary – the digital revolution, the internet revolution, social media as revolutionary, and all of those other things we hear every day. Any kind of change is immediately described as revolutionary.

In part the use of 'revolutionary' links to framing (see below), but many of the claims for revolution are specious, venal or just plain false. They are made by all kinds of people, but prime culprits include those in IT and Nerdland who want to be seen as gurus; or those promoting and selling advanced technologies who want them branded as tomorrow's way (and hence to have increased sales); or journalists for whom 'revolutionary' is an easy impact-gaining device; and bloggers and general declaimers who want to be seen as up to speed in the contemporary world.

I advise you to maintain some academic sobriety here and use 'revolution' and 'revolutionary' wisely. You should assess whether something is or is not a revolution using the reflective criteria used by the traditional evaluators of revolutions, such as the historians and political studies academics I mentioned above. At the very least, you need time after the events or innovations to assess their effects and to see the proverbial 'big picture'. It is only from that perspective that you can really assess the existence, extent and effects of any supposed revolution.

Community, movement

Here are two other commonplace terms that it is easy to misuse, and again their casual adoption could undermine your argument or the credibility of your discussion. Think of the familiar expressions:

- the local community
- community leaders
- the open access movement
- the motoring community
- the anti-war movement
- the online community.

You can supply many more examples, I have no doubt. These kinds of terms are, like many of the others I've been looking at, all over the news media and online. The problem? Well, particularly from your dissertation perspective, where you have to weigh words carefully and address your precise meaning, there is a pressing question: what makes something a 'community', or a 'movement'?

So many of the contemporary uses of these terms are really dead metaphors, likening groupings such as those in my list to physical settlements where people are living in some kind of close connection with many shared resources, values and interests. Would you say there is something identifiable as a 'local community' where you live, and if so what characterizes it? Where and/or what are its boundaries? Are there people who you would describe and accept as your community leaders? I don't recognize myself as being under the thrall of anybody who I would accept as 'my' community leader, and in particular I have not authorized any such person to speak on my behalf; but notice how often ethnic or minority groups are presented in news media as people who can be represented by and spoken for by 'community leaders'.

Once again, this is a plea for you to be careful before describing something as a community, or a movement, or before using some other similarly bewitching group term. To take a couple more from my list, what is the 'online community'? Even a moment's thought should convince you of the fragility of such a term used to lump together the millions of disparate individuals who connect to the internet all over the world, especially as a group that could be ascribed shared interests. And what is the 'motoring community' (or more subtly 'the motorist', as the token of this alleged group)? There are millions of drivers in a country like the UK, but they are not a community with shared interests; they are just everybody who drives. Motoring lobbyists and pressure groups might talk of the motoring 'community' (the poor motorist) to make political points, but this is an approach that is not acceptable in your dissertation.

People's motives

One more set of risky things to say concerns *why* people do what they do, whatever the subject area or context you're operating in. In part this is to do with the same considerations that apply under the heads of causation and consequences, but here you have another layer – or, rather, two other layers. I mean why people do what they do, collectively in groups, and what people say about what they do and why they do these things. Naturally (another one of those words), the first layer is going to figure largely in psychology, social psychology, sociology, political studies, economics and the like – and these fields may have a strong interest in the second too. But the scope for the second layer is much larger, and could creep into a wide range of different fields. Some of this may well result in attitude surveys, interviews, market research and similar. Then you have to talk about the links (or absence of them) between why people do things, and what they say about what they do – and this is something to sort out in research methods again.

You know why this is. People are not necessarily truthful, or self-aware, or careful, or possessed of suitable information when they answer questions about their actions and their decision-making, on occasions where you try and uncover reasons as well as causes, so you must be careful in the use of language that appears to be imputing motives to people. There is always theory behind this too – for example, the theory that people will make rational choices when they have enough information (itself a controversial topic) about alternatives. Notice that there was a component of motivation in our Spotsville example: you could have asked people who'd left recently why they had done so.

So, be sure that you accept the implications when you are searching for reasons, motivations, choices, either as part of your research question/ hypothesis or during the discussion. You can't just measure these things with a suitably calibrated stick.

Begging the question

Insisting on the correct use of this expression is probably now a lost cause, but do you know what it should mean? Perhaps I should now ask 'Do you know what it originally meant?' To listen to most people using the expression now, across the media and the net, you would think that it has to do with raising a further question.

> *Today the Prime Minister lost a vote of no confidence in the House, which begs the question as to whether he should now call a general election or sit tight and ride out the storm.*

That is not the 'correct' use of the expression 'begs the question', and it's certainly not one I would use – though I have to accept that as part of the normal evolution of English the expression is moving towards the position where this is becoming the accepted use. And there are fewer and fewer people who know or will say that it isn't.

The term 'question begging' is actually used to refer to a particular fallacy, a logical failure that breaks any chain of reasoning that employs it. It is essentially what I have been reminding you about when I said earlier that your definitions should not have hidden within them a prior assumption of the truth of what you're trying to demonstrate, and also links to the problem of verification bias below. To do that is to *beg the question* at issue: in argument terms, the truth of one or more of the premises presupposes the truth of the conclusion. Ah well. But whatever the usage has become, you must avoid the fallacy itself.

Verification bias

Beware of anything in any part of your research, from first idea to final discussion, that looks as though the choices you made were directed towards achieving a particular result. And by 'particular' result I mean the result that you wanted, or that is most favourable to your hypothesis, or that you would love to be able to prove, or even that you really, really believe in.

The place where you're most likely to drift into this problem is in your methodology, but aspects can creep in elsewhere in the dissertation, such as when you define terms at the beginning – are there assumptions lurking behind your definitions that presuppose or imply that the outcomes or theory you're examining are already true? This inbuilt skewing towards a favourable result – verification bias – is also a special risk when you select case studies, interviewees, specific methods of inquiry, particular statistical techniques to analyse your data, and so on. In these and similar instances, you should always be able to justify your choices and answer questions like 'Why did you choose to interview those people?' or 'Why did you choose those people for the focus group?' You will probably answer this kind of question pre-emptively in your methodology in the usual way, by saying for example that they are an elite sample, or a quota sample, or a convenience sample, etc., and discussing the pros and cons of your choice.

Frames, stereotypes and platitudes

There is a whole category of loose and casual speaking that could get you into trouble if you use it in your dissertation. This is another one of those things that can be subtle and easy to overlook when you check back and assess what you've written, but it is something that does creep into student dissertations. The easiest way to show you what I mean is through an example. Have a look at the following text extract:

> The target group was divided into three non-overlapping age bands: 'Baby Boomers', 'Thatcher's Children' and 'Digital Natives'. It is widely known that people are affected by technologies and attitudes that prevailed in key periods in their younger lives. For the Baby Boomers that means the 1960s; for Thatcher's Children it is of course the 1980s; and the Digital Natives are naturally influenced by their contact with IT and computer technology, which they have always known, unlike the older cohorts. Thus Digital Natives are fully familiar with the use of standard software for all main office and analytic functions.
>
> As a result of these groupings, the team designed three different training programmes, carefully shaped to the characteristics of each group. For the Baby Boomers the programme is based round flower power and sixties music, which will make the learning easier through familiar and much loved associations. This group obviously has great difficulty in understanding and using computers so the course follows a slow pace and runs for two afternoons per week over seven weeks. Thatcher's Children follow a faster learning programme of only three afternoon sessions as computers were beginning to appear on the desktop in their key decade, hence they will find new computer skills much easier to learn. The course materials use images of power-dressed characters such as bankers and business leaders and they emphasise acquisitiveness and self-interest to provide a familiar and attractive motif for the learners in this group.
>
> Finally, for Digital Natives the team has produced a short and accelerated course using cartoon images of Madonna, the Kaiser Chiefs and Dizzee Rascal, which should provide something for all tastes among this group. Their course lasts only one full day. A long course would be regarded as boring and patronising by these younger people and is believed to be unnecessary because of their high familiarity and skill levels.
>
> From Nathan Spiller-Worth, Eleanora Briggs and Nehemiah Tilsley,
> 'An investigation into computer training for civil servants', *European Journal of Computer and IT Based Learning*, Vol. 15, No. 2, 2011

What did you think of that? It was thoughtful of the authors (Spiller-Worth et al.) to shape the course to the three different groups, wasn't it? It makes perfect sense, doesn't it? But you'll have noticed other things, and a glance back at the heading I used to introduce this section should make you rather wary of what the authors are saying.

Stereotyping as a formal idea was developed in disciplines like social psychology some decades ago, especially in the work of people like Henri Tajfel. From your point of view, there are multiple dangers in the casual assignment of people into categories, and the equally casual expression of platitudinous statements about people in these groups or about other 'facts' about the world. Students do fall into this trap – often in quite a small way, but occasionally in a rather large way.

It could well be that as humans we can't do without stereotypes. We may need that ordering mechanism, with all its flaws, in order to make rapid sense of the world and cope with its constant changes. It would be impossible to evaluate everything that happens on a kind of existential-ist, situationally specific way, and instead constantly have to make rapid judgements based on 'pre-filed' categories. If we see a mad dog we run away; we don't stand there making separate evaluations that it's an animal, a quadruped, stocky and well muscled, apparently producing a frothy substance between its teeth, and so on (and besides, these obser-vations are themselves categorizations . . .). Also, without stereotypes there would be no stand-up comedy or sitcoms (I could add 'Discuss' again). But stereotyping actions – the lumping of people into catego-ries of 'them' and 'us', of 'in-group' and 'out-group', 'decent people' and threatening 'others' – have of course been responsible for some of the most dreadful episodes in human history and our own time. It is some of these that first inspired Tajfel to work in this field. From your disserta-tion's standpoint the threats are less dramatic but nevertheless real.

Let's go back to the extract (Spiller-Worth et al.). You should have noticed at least two things about it. One is the creation of three arbi-trary groups organized by age (though we don't learn precisely what the age bands are). You may feel that the authors were justified in doing this for practical training reasons, in the same way that a text designed for teaching English as a foreign language (EFL) to adult business people is very different from an EFL text designed for 8 to 11 year olds. Perhaps, but the catchy names they give to the groups suggest that each age band is being loaded with a large number of characteristics. Are all young people naturals and all older people dolts when it comes to digital equipment? That brings me to the other thing you will have noticed: the authors' assumptions about each group's abilities, outlook, preferences, interests and so on. 'Digital Natives' are fond of Dizzee Rascal and good with computers, whereas their ancient cousins the Baby Boomers are computationally incompetent and swoon at the sound of flower power music. Meanwhile, the people in between are grasping money-grubbers who fall midway between the other two in IT prowess. This sort of categorizing, with its attendant allocation of characteristics that shape perceptions and expectations, is often examined in media and communications studies using the concepts of *frames*, or framing.

Let me come clean and say what many of you probably suspected: I made up the whole extract. It is based on an exercise I produced for a research methods class. I must also say that neither the authors nor the journal are intended to be remotely like anybody or anything really out there in the world. I only added the 'source' as a kind of credibility code to make the extract look more plausible. (Remember what I said in Chapter 3 about not taking such material uncritically? Here's an example of why you should not: look behind the label and assess the material itself.)

'Ah yes', you may say. 'You laid it on a bit and made it extreme, whereas I would never write anything like that.' But my point is that it's sometimes difficult to avoid drawing on this kind of thing; it's such a habit and, like so much else I've talked about in this chapter, so heavily embedded in the media and internet noise that surrounds us that it is almost second nature. For example, the 'baby boomer' is now treated as a member of a distinct group in society with associated characteristics that anyone can confidently assign to him or her; it's a staple of lazy journalism, a feature of contemporary politics (as a more recent variety of identity politics), and still more it's *de rigueur* in advertising. One of the more depressing aspects of growing older is the way in which you find yourself moving from one arbitrary 'demographic' (a word that used to be an adjective) to another. The holiday business is riddled with this: eventually, you are supposed only to be interested in dreary and undemanding holidays with people of your own age in dull hotels that are presumably only a few minutes by mobility scooter from the nearest funeral home. You wait and see.

When did baby boomers first appear anyway? In 1945? From May? And when did they finish? Was it 1955, or 1958, or 1962? Is it a generation, whatever that means? What generation are you in, and did you have any choice in that? Are you old enough to be part of Generation X, for example, and what does that 'say' about you? You can see the dangers.

Generations and decades seem to have a particular hold on the human imagination, and you'll be hard put to avoid using them if you're talking about events in time or about people and their doings. What's a generation, for example? Is it 25 years? That used to be the rule of thumb, but think about it – at any given time in any population there are people at all ages from birth to death, so the allocation of groups of these people into generations is arbitrary and may also be one of those subtle unwitting ways of ending up with foregone conclusions when they are studied. Yes, there are life events in most societies, such as starting and leaving school, or retiring, that cut across groups and suggest life points or stages, but that doesn't automatically create neat generations. Not only that, but generations can have any length now, depending on the field of inquiry you're looking at. Some fields, like IT and popular culture, have very short generations: I was reading the other day about a group of rock guitarists who were supposedly inspired by the previous generation, and then further down the page I discovered that for these people (who started in about 1962) this 'previous generation' meant players who started in about 1958.

And what is it about decades? It is one thing to divide up sequences of years by decade when you present data such as GDP, oil output, number of school leavers attending university and so on. That is a familiar way of organizing and summarizing data to make it manageable – though it is not entirely without its problems either. For example, sometimes it's possible to shift category boundaries and produce a different effect, or create a different curve on a graph, etc. I'm talking more about the fascination for groups of ten years and the widespread notion that each ten-year period must somehow have a distinct character and be completely different from the one before it. And it's not just any ten-year period either: 1974 to 1983 is a decade, but there's no great identification with that (I haven't heard anybody say 'I'm a child of the seventy-four-to-eighty-threes'). No, it has to be 'the thirties', 'the sixties' and so on. What magical force is it that determines that everything shifts as we go through midnight at the end of the last day in December in a year ending in 9? Perhaps it is a relic of numerology that we can't shake off.

Think about 'the sixties', for example – a decade praised or vilified by so many people as the cause of all they like or hate in the world. What do you assume, or know, about 'the sixties', and what would you say in your dissertation about people who lived in that time, or were born in that time? Was 'everybody' a hippy or possessed of 'hippy ideas', for example? It's now very difficult to get beyond this kind of framing, or the multiple stereotypes if you prefer; instead the common representation is of a caricature of a caricature of a caricature of an arbitrary period of years, unless you take the trouble to look beyond that.

If you do that, you may avoid the kind of problems that Spiller-Worth et al. fell into. You may also avoid the kind of thing I read in a student dissertation some years ago which described baby boomers as the 'generation shaped by *Catcher in the Rye*'. Really? How did that work, then? You can see how tempting it is to say such things, but beware.

The perils of platitudinizing

If you want an instant guide to the kinds of things that come under this head, most of them could be summarized as statements amenable to being prefaced by 'Everybody knows that . . .' They are the casual generalizations of our time, continually dropped into everyday speech and rarely troubled by detailed evidence, that should not find their way into your dissertation. Blogs, comments and the internet are modern bastions of these kinds of trite, declamatory utterances.

Have a look at the Spiller-Worth extract again and you'll see examples of explicit or implicit uses of the 'everybody knows that' meme. Sixties children love flower power, Thatcher's children (generation X?) love money, and so on. Where's the evidence that these generalizations are even vaguely or partly true? Well, *everybody knows* that they are. Notice too that there is a slightly more plausible-sounding presentation of them in Spiller-Worth: 'It is widely known that people are affected by technologies and attitudes that prevailed in key periods in their younger lives', they say. In a 'real' academic piece there could well be some 'justificatory' citations cued after 'widely known', but even they wouldn't do much to defend the weakness of the statement. While we're at it, let's do that to see what it looks like:

> It is widely known (Cremble, 2008a; Foible and Garwick, 2010) that people are affected by technologies and attitudes that prevailed in key periods in their younger lives.

This adds the credibility code (using author–date or 'Harvard' forms in this case) that I mentioned before, but you would need to look up those two sources to see whether they do anything to support that glib 'widely known' statement. If you find that Cremble, 2008a, had indeed reviewed a large range of studies that supported the 'people are affected by technologies' claim with some rigour and precision, then that would help. But without that kind of backing 'It is widely known that' is only 'Everybody knows that' in pseudo-objective disguise (see Chapter 6 for more on impersonal passive constructions).

Assumptions of time and place, of viewpoint, etc.

Whatever your use of tenses and persons of verbs (again, see Chapter 6), your dissertation and its context are rooted in a particular place and time, and also in a particular culture come to that. But let's start with place and time as they're easy to see. Imagine you're discussing some results in a survey of comparative data and say something like this:

> Over the last ten years there has been a steady increase in the Knarling index in this country when compared to the Irish Republic or France, where it remains static.

That sounds innocent enough, albeit boring and probably unintelligible.[3] It wouldn't cause a problem in a transient and nationally located publication either, by which I mean a newspaper or periodical. In these kinds of publication, 'over the last ten years' and 'in this country' have an instantly identifiable meaning because these publications have a very short life in the here and now. But imagine you were writing this sentence in a textbook designed to be used in the UK, Australasia, North America and other parts of the world. Imagine that the book takes a year to write and that the edition will last for three years. This would mean that the sense of 'over the last ten years' shifts with each passing year until the next edition, and 'in this country' will mean different things to people in Accrington, Allegheny and Adelaide.

All right, you're not writing a textbook; you're producing a dissertation at a time and place that your markers know and share. But there are still good reasons to avoid the 'local references' and write in the actual times and places instead. One is that it's a good academic discipline to do that; another is that your dissertation may be a reference for a future student or academic, who may want to quote your Knarling index sentence in their work. If they did they'd have to do something like this:

> Over the last ten years [2001–10] there has been a steady increase in the Knarling index in this country [the UK] when compared to the Irish Republic or France, where it remains static.

---

[3] At least I hope it's unintelligible – I made up the Knarling index.

Now to extend the 'local reference' or perspective problem to the 'cultural' context. Here's another example:

> *The architect has a difficult task when setting out the interior of today's smaller homes for those of limited means. First, he has to design a kitchen space that will please the mistress of the house, yet he has to find enough space for the breadwinner to unwind when he returns from work. And there must be enough storage space for Jill's vacuum cleaner and Jack's toolbox so that in the evening both can settle in front of their giant plasma TV to watch their favourite soaps and reality shows.*

And so on, with apologies for laying it on a bit. Yes, it's all a bit obvious, but is designed to show that unwitting assumptions of the reader's vantage point are not just restricted to time and place. This is another factor that links to the earlier discussion of stereotyping and framing. The example is patronizing and full of stereotypes, including the roles occupied by 'Jack' and 'Jill' as they get ready to watch undemanding lowbrow programmes on their gigantic bling TV. The architect is a 'he' too, naturally. The message: be careful that you don't assume that your reader shares your vantage point, which may be more likely to happen when you're making qualitative assessments – for example, you shouldn't automatically suppose that your reader shares your disgust that Torvald Smith's Nasty Oligarchic Party will win an overall majority, even though you could if you were writing this up in an anti-Torvald newspaper. Newspapers are different in this respect too, of course, and not just in the time and place case: all newspapers some of the time and some newspapers most of the time actively reach out and massage the prejudices and assumed points of view of their readers. But that's not for you and your dissertation.

Explanation

This is actually a big topic – yet again too big to examine here in detail. But it is important so I must mention it and add it to my list of key topics for you to use with great care.

What does it mean to explain something? Why do we accept some statements and descriptions as explanations and not others? Or, to put it another way, why do we accord some candidates for explanation higher standing than others? Here's an example. You are 21 years old. You find presents are left for you around your Christmas tree on 24 or 25 December, or whatever is your custom (and if you don't celebrate Christmas then substitute another example). That's nice. But how do you explain it? How did the presents get there? Here are two potential explanations.

1. Your friends, relations, partner, etc., bought these presents for you, wrapped them up, and placed them there as a surprise for you to open as part of a shared annual celebration and holiday.

2. They were placed there by a fat elderly man who entered your house unseen during his annual present-delivery service, which he undertakes by reindeer-drawn sledge to all Christmas-observing parts of the world in only one day.

Which explanation is more convincing? I imagine you opted for the first explanation. (If you are five years old rather than 21, the second explanation has more appeal and is probably the one you prefer.) But why? In terms of our understanding of the world, which for most rational people is an understanding substantially informed by science, the second explanation is simply not feasible. It flies, like the reindeer, across the whole of our understanding of the world and how it works – an understanding that we're not prepared to change or give up in order to admit one bizarre example, one that is great for children and nice to believe while it lasts, but that is essentially nonsense.

This example already shows how explanation is linked to our larger understandings and other contextual elements; and in turn any explanations that you use or claim to have uncovered will do so too, and will draw on the theoretical underpinnings of your area of inquiry. You could, of course, have talked of the examples 1 and 2 as 'theories' rather than 'explanations', which is a common way of using these terms interchangeably; but that is a loose usage. We could accept the Father Christmas version as a theory, but not that it counts as an explanation – not by the time you reach the age of 21 anyway. Unless you're holding out, in which case *of course* Father Christmas is true and I hope he brings you everything you want. We expect something more from our explanations, something that makes them convincing in some way – and notice how that leads us into deeper waters, because 'being convinced' would seem to be a psychological state and now we're not just talking about theories of the way the external world is.

All very interesting, but not a discussion we have space to explore in more detail here. But you certainly won't be justifying your explanations and theories in your dissertation by saying 'I have an intuition about this.' Even though you might have a 'hunch' that something is true you can't make that a ground for presenting it as such; at best you can use it to set up a research method that investigates the phenomenon or theory to provide acceptable evidence.

So when you come to write in your dissertation a sentence that includes something like 'This explains why . . .', just make sure that it really does explain in a meaningful sense.

Argument

And now for another grand topic that I can only discuss in a brief way here, just enough to remind you of its importance, though it features at other points in this book. Here is as good a place as any to talk about it, but it affects the discussion in most of the other chapters. By 'argument' here I mean the main reasoned sequence of your dissertation – the thread that holds your entire dissertation together, or the connective tissue (to switch metaphors) that stops it being just a bag of bits or a collection of separate discussions, however clever they may be. And I'm sure I don't need to say this, but let's get it out of the way: by argument I don't mean shouting at people and stabbing your finger towards them and going red in the face – or whatever else you do when you have such an emotionally laden disagreement with somebody (throw things, cut up their clothes, go on daytime TV and scream, etc.).

You may be very familiar with the term 'argument' in an academic, even a technical, sense, or you may not. A lot depends on the discipline you're following, your subject, your topic and your general academic experience. In certain types of formal discourse – the study of logic, for example – an argument may have to be constructed precisely and can only work in certain predetermined ways. You'll know what they are because they've figured largely in your prior studies. In other disciplines an argument can be expressed or presented in very many different ways, some of them implied or informal rather than explicit, but all argument has certain characteristics in common.

Whatever it is that your discipline requires of you in setting out an argument, you should try and sketch it as soon as you start your dissertation work. It's the old journey-planning metaphor – how do I get from here to there? One good reason for working on it from the start is that your argument links naturally and intimately with your methodology, which you can't begin to construct without being aware of how the various stages of your planned work will fit together to connect your starting point – question or hypothesis, objectives and so on – to your results, discussion and subsequent conclusion.

Perhaps the best way to think about your main argument is to reflect on how you'd respond to challenges to your conclusion – in other words, to get back to the journey metaphor, how would you answer somebody who asked you 'How did you get here, then?' The journey you describe reveals your argument. Hence, if you can't describe how you reached your conclusion by the time you've produced your first complete draft then you need to give the connectedness of your dissertation some urgent attention.

Your argument will use a lot of 'so', 'hence' and 'therefore' language, and you may find yourself using such related expressions as 'it follows that' to join the various stages together. I've already gone on at length about those terms and won't repeat the caveats; but I ought to look briefly at logic.

It's logical innit

I'm using 'logic' here to refer to something more precise than its use in such expressions as 'Logically, we should go that way' or 'It was logical for me to try and get a new job', where it means something like 'it seems sensible to do that' or 'it's common sense' or 'it's a good idea'. That doesn't mean an excursus into formal logic or anything equally scary, but whether or not you believe that logic is the language of thought, it is a tool that can be used well or badly to check the correctness of your underlying reasoning. Even in the most informal contexts it is still possible to make mistakes in the chain of reasoning that can be characterized and cured using some simple logic. In other words, be careful when you say something like 'If follows logically from this that . . .' In some disciplines or with some markers, that might be safe, but in other disciplines and with other markers it might not be. For example, a marker might assume 'it is logical' means 'it follows deductively'.

In case this all sounds a bit sinister and robotic – perhaps your dissertation or project has a strongly intuitive character, and you feel that 'logic' has no place in it – I think I'd have to disagree and then reassure you. Fallacious reasoning can't support any kind of academic argument. Or, to look at it another way using a different kind of formal example, the fact that we accept the addition of numbers is not a threat to, say, a purely qualitative analysis based on five interviews. You'd freely say in such a case that you conducted five interviews, which is not remotely threatening; you wouldn't add them up and deliberately say there were eight interviews (that is, pretend that $1 + 1 + 1 + 1 + 1 = 8$) as a defiant gesture to keep the discussion free of the corruptions of formal thinking.

So I'm just going to allude briefly to the difference between deductive and inductive reasoning and then look at one simple (logical) argument. If you know all about logic you can of course skip this bit; if you don't, and logic sounds hateful, then this will be like giving you a snake to hold and saying 'There. It isn't so bad is it? Doesn't the snake feel nice?' Well, to get to grips with the snake let's first have a look at Sherlock Holmes, who was always claiming to deduce things. But he hardly ever did. Look at this example from the story 'The Adventure of the Blue Carbuncle':

> I [Dr Watson] took the tattered object in my hands and turned it over rather ruefully. It was a very ordinary black hat of the usual round shape, hard, and much the worse for wear. The lining had been of red silk, but was a good deal discoloured. There was no maker's name; but, as Holmes had remarked, the initials HB were scrawled on one side. It was pierced in the brim for a hat securer, but the elastic was missing. For the rest, it was cracked, exceedingly dusty, and spotted in several places, although there seemed to have been some attempt to hide the discoloured patches by smearing them with ink.

And what does Holmes 'deduce' from this hat examination? That the man who had lost it is highly intellectual (because he has a big head – a piece of nonsense from the long discredited 'science' of phrenology), that he was well-to-do in the last three years (because of the cost and style of the hat) but has now fallen on hard times (the make-do and mend evidence, etc.); that he probably drinks, that his wife has ceased to love him, but that he still has some self-respect; that he is sedentary and goes out but little, is unfit and middle aged; that his grizzled hair was cut in the last few days and is dressed with lime cream; and that he probably doesn't have gas in the house.

All this is great fun, but it is not deduction. It is more to do with guesswork based on supposed probabilities associated with the physical evidence. Deduction, on the other hand, is much more like the classic 2 + 2 = 4 case in arithmetic; it tells you what follows inexorably from what, but doesn't tell you anything new about the world. So just as you should be careful when you claim that something follows logically from something else, so you should use 'deduce' and 'deduction' with great care.

Here's an example of a classic simple argument known as *modus ponens*:

If it is raining then the pavements are wet [premise 1]

It is raining [premise 2]

Therefore the pavements are wet [conclusion]

The point about this is that *modus ponens* is a *valid* argument form, which means that if the premises are true then when they are plugged into this argument the conclusion must be true. My point in introducing this simple little argument is go on to pervert it and show you an alternative form that is not valid, the use of which would result in the fallacy known as 'affirming the consequent':

If it is raining then the pavements are wet [premise 1]

The pavements are wet [premise 2]

Therefore it is raining [conclusion]

This is not valid so you could not use it to support a chain of reasoning, as part of an argument in our grand sense of holding the whole dissertation together. If you were to engage in reasoning that was underpinned with this sequence you'd be incorporating a fallacy. Perhaps it's unlikely that you'd do this, but once again be careful with these logical terms.

One recurring problem is that investigation and reasoning about things in the world don't seem to work in a straightforwardly deductive way. Deduction doesn't tell you anything new about the world, as you can see from the conclusion of *modus ponens* above. Philosophers talk of the problem of *induction* in this regard, puzzling over what one can reliably say about the world based on observable regularities and whether this approach can provide a good enough basis for science and scientific reasoning. This is often expressed by the familiar example of the sun coming up: if the sun has come up every day throughout human history, then it is highly likely to come up tomorrow. And we go about our lives assuming that it will. But we can't be 100% sure (and we also believe that one day in the distant future it won't), hence is this probabilistic knowledge good enough?

One more caveat about arguments. Be careful not to get drawn into appearing to present polarized arguments, such as 'If A is not black then A must be white' and 'If Jenkins doesn't support the measure then Jenkins must be against it.' When I put things as baldly as that it may appear that you are unlikely to say anything so unconvincing, but such positions can hide within more plausible sounding statements. Here's an example:

Hembleton (2008, 2009) fails to show that the phlogiston pod relocates in the dormant position after the surge vector fails, hence my contention that the pod is protoplasmic must provide the correct explanation for pod relocation.

Apart from this being nonsense, you could only use this kind of reasoning to support your contention if you had already performed some prior analysis to show that your theory is the only possibility if Hembleton's doesn't do it. Otherwise, on its own the fact that Hembleton's theory fails doesn't show anything more than that. There might be any number of other contesting theories.

5 Using and managing information technology

At frequent intervals during your dissertation work you'll have to engage with some kind of technology – and by that I mean IT. If you are working in science, bioscience or technology subjects you may well be using specialist gear applicable to your study area, but my emphasis in this chapter is on the more familiar applications – applications in the computer sense of individual programs that run on your operating system – that you use to create your dissertation or report. That can cause problems enough, as we all know. Remember, I have to keep this fairly general, so things like chromatographs, engine analysers and even humble things like Bunsen burners are way beyond the scope of this dissertation. I'm concentrating on your creation of the all-important document (or documents) – the object that you deliver at the end of your dissertation work, and the thing that other people read and mark. That's common to everybody doing this kind of work.

This means that for the most part I'm looking at:

- working with applications such as word-processors
- computer usage and file management
- security and good practice.

Also important, even though they are not used directly in creating your dissertation document itself, are things like databases, stats packages, aids to thinking[1] and project management, and other programs that you may use to store or manage information. Incidentally, I do occasionally mention some operating systems, software packages and applications by name in this chapter – it's impossible not to when dealing with this topic – but my mentioning or describing an application should not be taken always to mean that I'm recommending or endorsing it.

---

[1] Such as the excellent and versatile FreeMind, an open source mind-mapping application that is completely free, so why not try it? You can find out more and download it by visiting http://freemind.sourceforge.net/wiki/index.php/Main_Page

'But we already know all about using computer software'

Yes, you probably do. You've been using word-processors, spreadsheets, websites, social networking, things like Microsoft Publisher and a host of other applications and sites for years. You may well have produced magazines, newsletters, your own websites, maybe your own applications if you can program too, and so on. As in other chapters, I'm aware that in covering material that a minority of you may not know – for example, those of you who have come to your degree course after many years away from formal education in the workplace or raising families – I am talking about things many of you already do know.

But there are still better ways to do things, and it's always good to look at settled habits to see whether what we've been doing for years is actually the best way to go about things. For example, is there now something better than that ten-year-old word-processing software you've been using for so long? (Yes, very probably.) And should you therefore change – because you've really got used to the old version and like it very much? (Well, I don't know – only you can decide; can you try out a new version to see whether it lets you do a lot more? And there are security implications, as I point out later in the chapter.) Have we developed some inefficient habits and got stuck with them? We can still fine-tune applications, choose better packages, discover the bottlenecks in our own ways of working and decide to work more productively. And in case that 'productively' aspect sounds a bit grim and oppressive, surely it makes sense to reduce the time and energy you expend on writing your dissertation if you can?

Not only that, but as you are well aware, students operate in an environment in which the pressures are not just from the volume of work. Your own laptop will be vulnerable to damage if you carry it around all day, and may go wrong or wear out even if you don't; and sadly it is also vulnerable to theft. You are also working in a flux of both settled and changing relationships and friends, whose effects on your IT life may or may not always be helpful. I once supervised a student who lost her whole dissertation with only three weeks to go before it was due in. I asked what had happened, and she told me how she'd lent her laptop to a friend whose own computer had broken so that he could finish his own dissertation. Then one day the friend couldn't make the computer behave, so being a computer 'expert' (as he insisted he was), he did what he always did with recalcitrant computers and reformatted the hard disk, in the process wiping out my student's entire stock of files including her dissertation. Some friend he was! And, no, she didn't have a backup, and you know all about that.

Which brings me on to the best reason of all to be super-efficient with IT. If you are, you will never be in the position that my student was in. You will never lose your dissertation because of a computer problem and you will be able to hand it in on time. I have to say this. Yes, computers break down and get stolen – annoying but true. But 'My computer is buggered [or stolen] and I've lost my files' has also become the universal 'the dog ate my homework' excuse for the twenty-first century. It won't do. You simply cannot have just one version, one copy, of your dissertation. You must back it up. Then, even if your computer is eaten by a vampire or just spontaneously combusts, you can still hand in your work on time. Many colleges and universities (my own included) now expressly disallow IT equipment failures, breakdowns or thefts to count as reasons for not handing something in on time. Why? Because we all know that IT equipment does this – it can be very disloyal – so we are expected to take steps to protect ourselves. Backups are a principal defence.

In other words, the 'computer excuse' is not allowed at all. So my reasons for spending a little time on IT in this book, even though you are an experienced user, could be grouped as follows.

- Security: avoiding malware and the work of bad guys.
- Security: preserving your precious documents and files.
- Efficiency.
- Personalization.

These are not the section headings in this chapter because I have other things that I want to emphasize, but I hope that together they will persuade you that it may be worthwhile to read this chapter. Even if you're an expert (a real one, not like the hard-disk formatter, I mean). Even if you're busy. Go on, go on, go on. Just skim it to see if it contains anything interesting – you never know.

Backups

Do you perform regular backups? Always? This is like one of those reliability or 'truth' questions they slip into psychology questionnaires, such as 'Have you ever done anything wrong?' (well, it wouldn't be that obvious), which if you answer 'No' suggests you are a liar and that your answers should therefore be discarded.

If you do remember to back up regularly, then well done. If you don't, then you urgently need to change your methods and start backing up now. The 'broken computer excuse' is not allowed, remember. Actually, we probably all fail to back things up quite a lot of the time, but the more important something is, the more likely we are to back it up. For this book – which I would have hated to have had to write all over again, as it was so difficult to find the time to do it the first time round – I had copies of all the files on my university office computer, my home office computer, my main laptop, my netbook, at least two USB sticks and also a mobile hard drive. These were manual backups that I managed myself. Besides these I also had the general system-wide backups that I have set up to work automatically on my PCs. Paranoid? Maybe, but at least I could hand the finished book to my publisher without using the 'computer excuse' – er, even if not exactly at the original date (sorry, publisher).

My backup tale immediately throws up some of the main choices facing you when you back up computer-based materials, and we find ourselves engaging with wider issues. Which files do we back up? What backup media do we use? How many copies, and all the same or generational? And what about timing (how often), location (where do you keep the backups), and version (aaagh! – which file is which, and which is the one you want to work on, or hand in)?

Which files?

Backup software can help you choose the files to save in regular backups. I am assuming that you are using some kind of software that has 'backup' in its name or description, and probably 'restore' too. Operating systems tend to have these built in, and many antivirus/anti-malware and office software suites do too. If not, you can do it all manually using a file manager – just select the files you want to duplicate and copy them manually to your chosen medium.

If you are using backup software it usually gives you the choice of copying and replacing everything each time you do it, or instead doing an 'incremental' backup, which is a more time-efficient process that only copies the files that have changed since you last backed up.

You probably don't want to copy application (program) and system files, as that would create a huge number of files to back up and take ages. Besides, you can usually restore applications and operating systems from the disks they came on, though in the case of operating systems and major office suites they are so heavily patched and updated these days that any restoring you performed from disk would need a lot of extra downloading to bring it up to current specifications.

It's your own creations that are your primary concern, so it does help to have all of your own files stored in the same directory of the hard disk. If you are somebody who just saves your files anywhere, based on wherever you happen to be working at the time, you'll find organizing your backups that much harder. Some of the pre-given directory names sound a bit naff, like Microsoft Windows' famous Myfiles which has echoes of 'My very first big balloon book' – but it is much easier to organize your files knowing that they are all in one cupboard, as it were, than if you have to look for them all over the house. With everything organized in this way, applications can all be pointed to the basic directory structure.

The organization of filing systems should be familiar to you, but because some people do still indiscriminately scatter all of their files around on a single directory, I'll just remind you that it's normal to use a hierarchical system of subdirectories, sub-subdirectories and so on. Computer operating systems like Microsoft Windows, Apple Mac's OS X, and the varieties of the open source GNU Linux organize their file storage and directory structures in different ways, but the main approach is to use hierarchies.

You may have set up your systems to save your working files automatically at preset time intervals, and you can also configure an application (such as a word-processor) to generate separate backup file creation and autosaves.

Storage media

Most computers still store and access their software and files using some kind of hard disk, an electronic device but one with a mechanical heart – the rapidly spinning platter inside, on which the information is stored by largely magnetic means. The rotating component is a favourite part for premature failure and is also prone to excessive shock, so hard disk failures are not uncommon.

Hard disks represent a successful and highly evolved technology, resulting in high-capacity disks, relatively small form factors, much higher reliability and endurance (life) than older types of disk, and – an important factor – a relatively low price per unit of storage. This is why they are only slowly being replaced by purely electronic, 'solid state' forms of storage. The occasional disk crash is therefore likely to remain a part of the computer experience for some time to come.

If a traditional hard disk fails it is normally a complete write-off and totally unrepairable. Sometimes they make funny noises and become temperamental and hence give you some warning, but very often not. They just break and stop. Replacement is the only answer and after that you have to start again, loading your operating system, applications, etc., on to the new disk. But any files you had stored on the old one – precious dissertation files, perhaps – will be lost unless you had copies elsewhere. There are some specialized data-recovery firms who can take disks apart in special dust-free environments and recover at least some of the contents, but they charge astronomical amounts of money that only major companies can afford. They are not an option for students.

Beware of software that automatically saves your backups to another part of your hard disk. Many proprietary systems of the kind that you find on your computer when you buy it are configured this way. You should immediately reconfigure it to use a different backup medium if yours is like this. Look carefully, as all may not be what it seems: you may have a hard disk showing on your system as C: and another site called D: chosen for the backup, apparently another disk. But these default save areas are almost never on a separate disk. Instead, D: will be a virtual disk, a partition of the same disk that C: is on, so if your hard disk fails *you lose both*. Secure backups must therefore be saved to something separate. The choices are now mainly:

- portable hard drives (connected to your PC by USB or similar)
- USB 'sticks' (also called thumb drives, data drives, etc.)
- space on networked drives, perhaps online (part of the 'cloud')
- CDs and DVDs (sometimes called 'optical' storage).

I'm assuming that you won't be using magnetic tape, traditionally an important backup medium in the business and academic worlds but not an option for you; and you are probably not using magneto-optical storage such as ZIP drives, though these are still around. If you do use ZIP drives take care of the bulky disks because they are expensive.

If I were writing this ten years ago I would have floppy disks at the top of the list as the 'cheap and cheerful' solution. Floppies have been around for most of the personal computing era, reducing in physical size but increasing in capacity as the years passed, but present-day PCs and laptops don't have floppy drives fitted so these once-familiar items of portable storage are passing into history. If you have the drives and the disks they're still usable, of course, though treat them with care rather than fling the disks into the bottom of your bag.

Portable hard drives use the same fast-spinning devices as the ones in your computer but mounted in a separate case with some electronics and a connecting cable. USB cables already carry power so you normally don't need a separate power supply as you did with the older styles of external disk.

USB sticks, as I'll call them for short, are easy and cheap to buy. Storage capacity has gone up in recent years. They are extremely portable, of course, and are fairly reliable. Because they are fairly cheap you could buy two or more and use them for generational backups (see below). Their main problem is just that they are small – it is so easy to lose them or leave them stuck in a PC. I find I have to attach them to lanyards to make them bigger and easier to spot. Still, if you do lose one it's cheap to replace and need not be a disaster if everything on it was copied elsewhere.

Network drives covers things like any central shared workspace that your university may give you as a student. You need to be able to access the network to upload or download your files, so that may be a factor in how useful this option is. Alternatively, many major software companies such as Google and Microsoft now provide free save space along with email services, and these are normally available 24 hours a day so access is less likely to be an issue. But it's one you should consider: you need a backup urgently because if your computer breaks down just before you need to print out the finished report, but you find the university server is offline for maintenance . . .

CDs and DVDs have become much less exotic than they were a decade ago and are now commonplace means by which people exchange digitized materials such as documents and images. They too are cheap, and as you know you can get both 'write once' and rewritable kinds. As with most ubiquitous and cheap things, they can induce carelessness. If they have important material on them, keep them in a sleeve or jewel case, identify the contents with a suitable pen, and don't chuck these in the bottom of your bag either. They do break, and they can become unreadable if damaged.

Reading and writing

Here I mean the process by which information is stored on a medium and later retrieved; these are usually identified by processes called 'Save' and 'Open' in most computer systems and software. I mention them because it is not just media failures like broken disks that cause problems: here is another area where things can go wrong. Writes (saves) can fail or become corrupted – one reason to keep generations of saves and also multiple copies, as I mention below – and reads can hit problems too. Back in the bad old days of slow computers and flop-pier floppies it was possible to write a disk on one PC but not be able to read it on another one because the two drives were differently aligned. These kinds of problem have several implications.

- When you write (save) to a medium like a CD this usually overwrites and replaces the previous version of the file, so what happens if the save is corrupted?

- When you are connecting or disconnecting drives, say from USB links, make sure there is no reading or writing still going on, or you will get corruption.

- Whenever you write to a medium (save a file as backup), check afterwards that you can read (open) the file and that it is not corrupted.

Some media are set up to use delayed reads and writes, and it may be that although a drive looks idle it still has unfinished business. If you then disconnect it carelessly before this is done, then the write will be incom-plete and file corruption is likely. Although USB was designed for 'hot swapping' to some extent – you don't need to switch everything off to connect or disconnect items, as you did with old systems – you should still do a software disconnect first to keep your files safe. On Windows, for example, this involves clicking on the 'Safely Remove Hardware' icon on the taskbar before you remove the drive or stick etc.

Location, location

Finally, before looking at another implication of backing up – the mass of different files it creates – there is the issue of location to resolve. The most dangerous form of backup is, as we've seen, storing the backup files on the same disk. CDs, USB sticks and the like have the virtue of being separate, so they are unaffected by computer disk failures. But how 'separate' should separate be?

The more dramatic types of problem – I'm thinking now of things like flood, fire and theft, and abduction by aliens – could affect both your PC or laptop and the 'separate' backup storage. If your room is devastated by a deluge of water from the bathroom upstairs, this could wreck both your laptop and the portable drive you have beside it on your desk. If that sounds unlikely, here's another less colourful scenario. You leave your laptop on a bus and nobody hands it in, so it is gone for good. You had backups on a USB stick and also separately on a labelled CD – hooray – but you kept both of these in your laptop bag, so they've gone too. Oh dear.

All of this should remind you that to be really safe you should keep more than one backup and keep copies in different places. This might sound like paranoia again, but the laptop on the bus scenario is not highly unlikely; it's the kind of thing that happens. So, for example, for a cheap solution leave a CD backup copy at a friend's house or with your parents, say – anywhere that is in a separate location from your main PC, whether that is a desktop or laptop PC. But if you do this you should consider the safety and security of any material you leave with another person – remember the 'friend' who reformatted the hard disk? There are at least two dangers to consider (sorry to seem paranoid again): one is that somebody could copy your files, perhaps to use them in their own coursework if they're a fellow student and hence commit an academic conduct offence; another is that a prankster or malicious person could modify your files or add malware.

Versions, keeping track and generational backups

Every time you amend a file you create a new version of it. If you add in all those backups you're making too, it doesn't take long for your hard disk to be full of different files, many with similar sounding names. Do you always know which is the latest version? Or, to put it another way, which is the version that you want to hand in? This has become a significant problem. One way of identifying files in professional publishing environments, such as for journal articles, is to use a Digital Object Identifier (DOI) to distinguish different versions of the 'same' article – such as the one on the author's website, another one on her university's repository, and a third in the journal itself.

You won't be using a DOI yourself,[2] but it is very important to keep track of all those files over the period of the dissertation – such as your notes, separate files for things like bibliographies or table files, files in supporting programs such as 'mind map' and note-taking programs, various part or full drafts of the dissertation, and the final submission version itself. The principal weapons in your armoury are, first, the date stamp and other automatically recorded information belonging to the files themselves, and more directly and obviously the filenames you choose to label them with. I'm assuming that you also keep things in organized and well-named directories and subdirectories.

Let's take the automated stuff first. Every time you save a file, it is written to your disk along with information about its name, attributes (such

---

[2] Have a look at www.doi.org/ if you want to find out more.

as 'read only), and the date and time. As you know, when you save the file it will overwrite the previous save of the file unless you have configured your operating system to behave differently. Most users don't edit the attribute and date stamp information directly, but these are accessible if you know where to look (for example, in the 'Properties' submenu in Microsoft Windows). It's unlikely you will want to change this kind of detail, and indeed sometimes such changes would cause suspicion (think about why, and turn to Chapter 9 if you're unclear about what I'm alluding to). Filenames you can change at any time, of course – and you can rename both parts of it including the suffix, so 'diss.doc' could be renamed to 'dissertation.doc', 'dissertation.docx' and so on (changing the suffix may have other implications, though). Depending on how you have configured your file management software – usually an application that comes with the operating system – the attribute and date information should be visible in your file listings, or at least when you hover your mouse over a file.

Filenames themselves are an important way to maintain sanity when trying to keep check of files and their versions. Always choose informative names. Unless you are using a non-standard or very old operating system on your computer, you are no longer restricted to the old '8.3' system of filenaming. You can now let your hair down and use names that actually say something about the file. However, it still pays to take care: a filename such as 'latest dissertation save.doc' is worse than useless. You should be able to see why.

Instead, always take care when giving names to important files. Think about what information would be useful in the filename if you come across that file again in three months' time and can't remember what it's about; the filename may save you having to open up the file or search all the content in the directory to find out. Whether or not you put your own name or student number as part of the filename probably depends on whether it will be sent out into the wild, so a file for submission for marking certainly should have that information (and your university may specify a particular filename). Apart from using part of the name to refer to the content, there are two simple ways of making filenames useful and an aid to version control: either put the date and time information in the filename too, or use a version numbering system. Let's take the date system first. Here's a filename showing how this might look (and here I've added some imaginary university details too, such as the student's number and a course code):

clara peggotty 17965487 dissertation D5555 second full draft 14-00 hours 3 July 2012.docx

I've used a hyphen for the time so that there's only one point (dot) in the filename, between the main name and the suffix. Most operating systems allow dots in the filename itself now, but I think leaving just one is clearer. Also, I'm not using initial caps in these filenames but of course you can if you want – though using all capitals looks a bit old fashioned. Then of course when you come back to it and write more three days later, the name becomes something like:

> clara peggotty 17965487 dissertation D5555 second full draft 17-30 hours 6 July 2012.docx

This naming convention actually duplicates the automatic date and time stamp information, but it makes it far more obvious. You can see exactly which file is which as soon as you open the directory and start listing the filenames. The other simple system you could adopt uses version numbers, which you can number either in a single sequence or according to a software style numbering system. So on this system Clara's dissertation is something like:

> clara peggotty 17965487 dissertation D5555 second full draft ver 12.docx

which just assumes that the last version was 11 and the next will be 13, or you could be more subtle and use software version style numbering, which has a main version and then uses the numbers after the decimal point to show the level of modification the version represents. So version 0.95 might be a pre-release version, version 1.0 the very first published version, version 1.01 the same but with a very minor change, and version 1.10 is the same with a more substantial change, and so on with 1.50, 1.51 . . . A completely new version would then be version 2.0, later slightly tweaked to be 2.10 and off we go again. Clara could use:

> clara peggotty 17965487 dissertation D5555 second full draft ver 1-03.docx

again using the hyphen instead of the dot, or she could use the main number to indicate the draft version too, so the second draft would be:

> clara peggotty 17965487 dissertation D5555 full draft ver 2-0.docx

and the next full draft, with a couple of minor corrections here and there:

> clara peggotty 17965487 dissertation D5555 full draft ver 3-1.docx

You could even combine version and date numbering, give more content information and the like. It's up to you. Anything is better than 'latest' type names, which will soon fill up your disks with indistinguishable files all claiming via their names to be the latest versions. Just remember when you save versions with these informative filenames and overt identifications that you must use 'Save as' and modify the name when you do the final archive save to disk rather than 'Save', which simply overwrites the previous write with the same name.

Forking files

Let's imagine that you are working on the latest version of your dissertation. You've been working on the file during the week using your space allocation on the university server, and backing up the copy on to your USB stick. You take that home each night and use it to copy your work on to your laptop, where you sometimes do additional work during the late evening. On Friday you worked as usual on the university version then went out in the evening. Over the weekend you fire up the laptop and put in a good few hours of work on that. But then on Monday you realize that the work you did at uni on Friday was not backed up to the USB stick, so the work you did over the weekend was on the last home version saved on Thursday night. Oh no! You now have two sets of diverging amendments – a fork, so called because it resembles a fork in the road. Neither of them is an update of the other; instead, each is a separate update of a previous version.

Actually, this scenario is not that serious at this stage, largely because you have realized what is happening before the divergence got too great. You have two different versions, yes, but you can combine the two files either manually, paragraph by paragraph, or much more easily by the compare or combine option that most word-processors have. For example, MS Word has a Combine option under Compare on the Review menu.

Using informative filenames (see above) is not an absolute guarantee against forking files because you could give the same upgrade name to each different file (especially if you're using version numbers), but it should help to avoid most of them.

Check before burying granny

One more thing. Before you delete an old version of any file make sure that you can run the latest version. It would be galling to delete lots of old files only to find that the latest one is corrupt and won't run and that you've deleted your backups too. If there is a large number of successive versions of a file on your disk it's usually wise to delete only some of the old ones but keep more recent ones.

Some people use a generational system of backups too, where you have say three generations of versions – the latest file (the daughter) , a previous version (the mother), and the earliest of the three (the grandmother). Then, when you save the latest version you overwrite the oldest version (the grandmother) to produce the new daughter file; the previous mother becomes grandmother, and the previous daughter becomes mother. Or you may have configured your word-processor to save backups, in which case whenever you do a new save the previous save is retained as a backup – a kind of two-generational system with no granny. This backup function is not the same as the 'autosave' function that much software allows you to do – and that is enabled by default in many application suites. This automatically saves a version of the file at fixed intervals that you can set, but usually not in your main files directory. These autosaved versions are the ones that the software tries to recover if you have a computer or application crash.

Malware

The rather clunky word 'malware' has been coined to cover all of those problem such as viruses, trojans and worms that wicked people create for nefarious purposes that can be anything from parading their vanity to causing irritation to creating major damage and theft. People tended to call everything a 'virus' in the past, but the new name has a wider scope, reflecting the very broad range of threats out there. It used to be a particular problem for the PC family of computers because these are so widely used, and hence the bad folk would reach a wider group of people by writing PC-specific malware. But the problems are now spreading to Macs and can be expected to grow on Linux-based systems such as those running Ubuntu – not to mention other devices such as iPads and smart phones. I'm assuming you all know about the need to observe appropriate 'hygiene' when confronted with unknown files and the lures of click-through links in unsolicited emails, as well as the importance of having at least one application on your computer that is dedicated to protecting you from such threats and eliminating any that it finds. Computer scientists have conducted experiments by connecting new unprotected computers to the internet to see how soon it takes for them to get infected – and it is a matter of minutes.

I suggest that as well as one main antivirus suite – there are many, so read the reviews, including well-known free versions such as AVG – you have at least one other ancillary one. The secondary ones can be scanners designed to detect malware on demand rather than automatically, because permanently running antivirus suites tend not to coexist well with each other; they burrow deep into systems and tend to regard each other with suspicion. I find it useful to run separate scanners designed to pick up tracking cookies and other 'spyware' as these run on demand and there are very good free ones. But don't just do a casual internet search and download anything that comes up high in the search engine's hit list claiming to be your malware saviour. Unfortunately, the bad guys have also designed fraudulent anti-malware suites that pretend to find problems on your computer then lock you in to some expensive scam. Some of these even install malware too.

The problem of malware has increased enormously since the advent of always-on high-speed internet access, but that doesn't mean the old ways of transferring files are not still susceptible. One likely vector for transferring infected files and hidden nasties is the ubiquitous USB stick. The ease with which it can be inserted into computers and other devices means that it's a wonderful device for moving malware about. To keep safe (or safer), you can think about it in STD terms: regard unknown computers and USB-enabled devices as potential sources of infection and be careful about lending them to other people. Use your antivirus software to scan them separately, or when you are doing system-wide scans leave the USB stick connected so that it is scanned too.

Remember that malware can do all sorts of horrible things. It can corrupt and destroy your files, including backups if you are careless or not vigilant; it can turn your computer into an infected zombie that spends much of its time in a 'botnet' that is busy sending out junk to infect other computers (unknown to you, though it will slow your computer down); it can install programs on your computer to do unpleasant things like log your keystrokes and web activity as a prelude to discovering your passwords, and so on. Be vigilant, because malware has the potential to wreck your computer, your bank account and more, and of course your dissertation. Here's a quick security check.

- Use and run antivirus software and keep it up to date.
- Consider running second or third scanners too.
- Never reply to emails from unknown sources.
- Use the highest level of spam protection that you can for emails
  - occasionally check for genuine files in your spam folder before emptying.
- Don't click on links in emails, even from banks, etc. (who should know better).

- Never click on links on websites or pop-ups that advertise 'checks' on your computer
  - these are almost always scams.

- Regard disks and USB sticks (thumb drives) as potentially infected by the other machines they've been used on and check them regularly.

- Use strong passwords and never give them to anybody, either personally or online
  - which means not writing the password on a sticky note and putting it on your computer!
  - and not having passwords like '123', 'password' or your date of birth.

- Don't use the same password for all sites or purposes, and change them from time to time.

- Don't allow others to work on your machine, still less repair it, unless you are confident of their ability
  - university computer support facilities are usually good places to go for advice.

- Always have backups of all your personal and important files, and ideally keep these separate from your computer.

Keep up to date

In the first item of the above list I mentioned keeping your antivirus and security software up to date. The simplest thing to do is to configure it to download updates automatically, and if you've done this you will already know that these updates are extremely frequent, even several times in one day.

There is another side to this, though, which is that operating systems and application software are all subject to constant updates. Partly this is for product improvement purposes and to correct bugs, but mainly it is because of the risk of malware. Significant product improvement is something that commercial software producers like to reserve for paid-for upgrades – after all, the challenge of the software business is to sell you the same thing over and over again. (You have a word-processor and it does everything you want, so why buy another one? Well, because this new one is version 6.0 that does wonderful things like make toast and produce synthetic birdsong, and besides has a lovely new lilac menu system.) Alas, the people on the dark side are constantly looking for ways to exploit flaws in software so that they can spread malware, so software producers have to update their products at frequent intervals to patch the defects. Again, the safest thing to do is to activate automatic updates because sooner or later you'll forget.

As part of this constant – well, frantic – update environment there comes a time when all software goes out of date, in the sense that it is no longer supported by the manufacturer. Although you may feel that you are on some kind of upgrade treadmill, once the support stops then so do the updates; any flaws that the bad guys find from that point onwards remain unpatched. Unfortunately, this means that your favourite and familiar old software does progressively become more of a liability and a risk. So do keep your operating system, your word-processor and other 'productivity' software, and your browsers, image viewers and other recreational or multimedia software up to date. And do ask yourself from time to time whether you need to buy a new version or a different product, especially if the updates have stopped or the file format you save in is becoming obsolete too. Of course, there are now some very well established top-quality open source products such as Firefox, Thunderbird and OpenOffice.org,[3] so if you use these it will cost you nothing to upgrade.

Configuring software

Commercial software is designed to please as many people as possible and be as widely useful as possible in order to sell in large numbers. Bespoke software that is designed for particular small groups is produced in highly targeted versions but has the drawback of costing a small fortune. The software that you use to write your dissertation is likely to be a word-processor, possibly part of an office suite, and as such will have features for very many different types of user – students and academics, authors, PAs and secretaries, mailing operations and the like. Most software of this kind is therefore configurable to enable users to shape it more closely to their own purposes. The strange thing is, though, that so many purchasers and users just use the software straight out of the box without changing anything.

Here's a tiny example. In Microsoft Word, which is typical of these broad-brush pieces of software, if I key a '1' followed by an 's' followed by a 't', I get 1st rather than 1st. Why? Because by default the software is configured to turn ordinals like this into superscript form (a 'superior' in typographical jargon). That's what it does out of the box. But do I want that? As it happens, no I don't. I dislike it, and it is not useful in files that are intended to go for publication where the typesetter or editor may not want that to happen. And if I key the character ASCII character ' (usually used only as a prime rather than an apostrophe or quote these days)

---

[3] For Firefox and Thunderbird visit www.mozilla.org/; for OpenOffice.org go to www.openoffice.org/

in association with words or letters I will get the familiar typographical quote instead. Do I want that? Well, it usually happens that I do, but the point is that these are small examples of things that can be reconfigured.

I am suggesting that you, as a user of the word-processor or other software, should go and find the configuration and options settings and change them to your own preferences. There are usually quite a lot, and they include the configurations of menus and button bars as well as backup and file-saving arrangements. Don't just use software straight out of the box. The location of configuration menus can vary, but a common place is on the Tools menu. The name is usually something like 'Configuration' or 'Options', which can be interchangeable terms or mean something slightly different, depending on the software. Microsoft moved theirs in later versions of their office suites, so for example in Office 2007 you click on the big button at the top left and then look for the item on the bottom frame of the box that opens up (with a name such as 'Word Options'). Making these kinds of changes puts you in greater control. When you drive a strange car for the first time you immediately adjust the driving seat and mirrors, so why use somebody else's choice of features for your software?

6 Stop dithering – just write

It's a familiar cliché of authorship and writing that the blank page exerts a certain tyranny. Even nowadays – when entering text is such an easy thing to do and the result is so easy to change – it makes a real difference to get started and to write something.

This chapter covers three aspects of that writing challenge. It stands aside from the technicalities of your content, and to a certain extent from your argument and progression (though I can't leave those out entirely) and looks at you as a creator of text: first, in how to get going and get over that fear of putting it down, and then what do about style and structure.

Just do it

It may seem strange to be talking about how easy it is to enter text, but that's because word-processing is so familiar for the great majority of people reading this book. It wasn't always like that. You know this, but it's worth looking back for a moment to remind ourselves of the opportunities and drawbacks associated with this ubiquitous way of entering text. I'm not suggesting we go back to ogamic or cuneiform writing, or even to the days of scribes, but just a few tens of years. I believe the change in the way in which we write has not just altered the speed and ease of text entry, but also *what* we write. It's very difficult to demonstrate this, but intuitively it seems right.

An exercise in experimental or investigational design: How would you try to show that present-day authors, who nearly all use word-processors, write differently – in both style and content terms – from their equivalents in previous decades who used earlier forms of technology (pens and typewriters)? Think about how you would plan your investigation, and the things you'd need to take into account.

Think about it. In 1920 or 1930, say, most authors would write longhand and then somebody, the publisher or more probably their typesetter, would work directly from their handwritten copy – a genuine *manuscript* – to produce the finished version. Then the typewriter gradually assumed a greater importance, first manual and then electric, and it began to reach writers beyond the province of the journalist and professional author. Typewriting was still a largely specialized skill, though, with typing being the preserve of the trained typist and everybody else just amateurs using 'hunt and peck' two-fingered typing. In academic styles of writing this carried on until quite recently. It was very common to see departmental secretaries thanked for their typing in the prefaces and acknowledgements of academic books. It is only in the last twenty years or so that these tributes to the typist have all but disappeared.

Then the word-processor came along. First this was in corporate and institutional settings – they were large stand-alone machines with large noisy printers attached. But then personal computing arrived and through the 1980s this brought word-processors to people's desktops. People started to key their own material, an increasingly widespread practice that saw typists disappear and the rise of the general expectation that we type all of our own work, unless we are very so-called important people. This is where we are now, and what seems so familiar.

In handwriting days, and even in typewriting days, the cost of change and correction (in time, and in resources generally) was so much higher. Changing things was time-consuming and painful, even when whitening fluids and correcting ribbons on typewriters appeared. The consequence, I would claim, is that people were so much more careful about setting down their text. If you got it wrong, you may have been able to correct the line but for anything major you'd have to pull out the page and start again. This could only add to the tensions created by blank space – that clichéd tyranny I mentioned at the beginning. What about that first sentence – so important for journalists? Perhaps you'd make separate notes first and then key the final version.

So what's this little historical diversion got to do with you and your dissertation? It's a reminder of the freedom that word-processing gives you, a freedom that means you really can just start writing without worrying about the time-cost of making mistakes or changing your mind. It's so easy to change and move material when you word-process, so stop agonizing about it. And you can start anywhere too. Forget the 'Lost Weekend' model (see Chapter 3). It can be in the middle if that's where you are able to set down some fairly finished text – anywhere, really (see below) – so get those fingers working. Of course, when you are first starting you can't write your conclusions or set down outcomes, because normally you don't know what they are, but there are plenty of things that you can start to write.

When I say 'get those fingers working' I assume you're not using speech recognition software or an amanuensis. But even if you must use a note taker or other methods because you can't use a keyboard, the present-day alternatives create equivalent opportunities. Write something now – and I mean draft 'proper' text rather than just generate more material in note form, because of course I expect you to be making notes for much of the time.

To paraphrase the old election joke,[1] write early, write often. This will save you from one of the biggest bugbears of dissertation students – doing weeks or months of research and preparation but without writing anything other than notes, so that the business of writing the main text becomes an ever larger problem as the deadline looms. In extreme cases, students just become paralyzed with fear at the size of the task they have left themselves to do in the small amount of time remaining.

Don't feel that writing 'proper' text early on will tie you down. Later in the process you will want to go back and change much of what you write in these early stages, but that's fine. Word-processing lets you do that without too much pain. This familiar tool has done a great deal to reduce the tyranny of the blank page that I mentioned at the start, so do please get on with it.

There are a couple of caveats. One is about time of day and the other is about starting and stopping. First, it should be obvious that you have more alert and less alert times of day, and these will depend on your body clock, not to mention other aspects of your physical condition – drunkenness is not a good basis for writing academic prose, for example. A whole litany of time-management literature and courses has grown up around these basic ideas. The principle is that you observe yourself and reflect on your habits, then decide when you are at your most alert and when not, and plan your time accordingly. Do add this consideration to your deadline and schedule management and your writing plans. How much can you write in a day, for example; and when are you at your sharpest or most alert during the day or night? How often should you take a break from writing, and from staring at that screen?

---

[1] In case you haven't heard it it's a joke about corrupt electoral systems – 'Vote early, vote often'.

When you answer this question, don't just consider the quantity you can turn out. The *quality* is very important too, and this applies particularly at the end of a long day or in the early hours of the morning. Have you ever written something very late at night and then been disappointed when you read it back the next day? I certainly have, and have often had to discard things I produced late at night or at least to rewrite them. Ideas that seem great at 3 a.m. can look rather less good at 10 a.m. When I was young I was a regular night owl for working and writing, but I am now much more careful about the quality of material from the extremes of the day. Many years later I still have the late-night habit, but I no longer entirely trust what I generate. (For the same reason, it's a good idea to leave emails and letters that you write late at night and only send them the next morning, when you've had a chance to assess them in the light of day.) The quality consideration is key, and is one very good reason why you should not leave all the writing until the last minute. All you can do at that late stage is generate quantity, and that's why so much last-minute writing is anything from poor to awful – there's not enough time to reflect or revise.

And that brings me to the other point, which is to do with each writing session itself. Whisky makers know that the beginning and end of a particular distillation sequence don't produce good spirits – they discard these 'foreshots' and 'aftershots' and put them back into the system for reprocessing. They only use output from the main central run of the still. That's not a bad way to think about a writing session either: be particularly suspicious of your foreshots, the material you produce early in the session when you are getting going, and your aftershots, the stuff you are writing when you're about to stop. Even if you're not tired at that point, your concentration may be starting to flag. I'm not saying you should discard those beginnings and ends, but they may be good candidates for extra reflection and revision.

Which bit do you write first?

There is no right answer to this, and a lot depends on what kind of research you're doing. But in general, anything that you know early you can write about early. Having some chunks of text already written, albeit in draft, is a real confidence booster.

Some supervisors advocate writing the literature review early – and certainly you can make good progress with a lit review because your reading and desk research are likely to go back to the very start of your dissertation work and may precede it. Therefore you have at least some material that you can start setting down early. Other supervisors would disagree, or partly disagree: a lit review written early in your programme might be insufficiently analysed and turn out to be more like an extended bibliography, so it may be better to write it later because you then have a better idea of how it informs your findings and your thinking in general. Perhaps a compromise is the best thing. Get down the framework of your review early, but don't just leave it at that. Make sure you come back to finish and revise it later in your schedule. This assumes it is better to have some text in the bank in month 1 of a project stretching over an academic year, even if it has to be revised later, than have virtually no text in the bank even in month 5 or, worse, month 8.

Methodologies are good candidates for early writing-up too, because much of how and what you're going to research needs to be established before you can undertake any primary research. It's likely that even in the first month or six weeks of your project you have sketched out your methods and their strengths and potential weaknesses. So get that all written down, and do it in a polished way too – take trouble and expend some care rather than simply sketch some notes; that way you have some good-quality text already written to use in the finished methodology rather than rough text that is little better than notes you then have to write up from scratch.

When should the other content come in your writing programme? The logical sequence of the dissertation is unlikely to be the precise determiner of the order in which you write the content. Yes, you'll need to write your conclusions somewhere near the end of the whole project – something's wrong if you try to write them at the start – but think of the introduction, which is a chapter or section you're almost certain to have. It comes at the beginning in the document but not in the process: you can only write it in full when you have all of the material ready, so it's not something to do on day 1, 'Lost Weekend' style (Chapter 3).

For much of the rest of the material that falls in the body of your dissertation you can follow the pattern I suggested for the methodology. There will be many things that you must wait to write up, but equally there are many 'islands' of largely settled content that you can write up early. Once again, write these islands carefully so that you don't have to write them all out again later. There will be gaps between the islands – in some chapters large gaps – but not only does this give you some text in the bank, it also gives you a good early idea of the probable structure of the dissertation.

The importance of revision and checking

I come back to this in the 'final frontier' chapter (Chapter 10), but it's very important so I'll mention it here too. The fact that it's easy to start writing, to bang in text at low cost, makes the need for careful checking and revision much higher. That's the principal drawback of our present system. In the old days (yes, them again), you would probably take much more care before you committed a line to paper; now you can bash in any old thing because it's easy to change it later. But there must be a 'later' for this approach to be worthwhile and safe.

Partial checks and then final proofreads are thus very important, partly because of the ease of text entry but also because of another benefi- cial factor of word-processors – ease of amendment. You can change things endlessly, which is great and fits your need to update and modify, but eventually you need to draw this process to a close. This has impli- cations for version management (see Chapter 5) as well as for quality control. And when you have finished all your local rewriting, tinkering, tweaking and so on, that's when you do your final inclusive proofread. More about this in Chapter 10, as I say.

Style and detail

Right. Now you are writing. Because you're writing a dissertation you've reached a certain stage in your academic life and you are an old hand at being a student: you are aware of 'academic' approaches to writing and how this governs your content and what you say – in particular, you know how to avoid the pitfalls of casual and inappropriate language that betrays sloppy reasoning (Chapter 4). But what about the language itself? Is there a special kind of language that academics use that you should follow to the letter? And how are you on the basics of style, gram- mar and punctuation? All right, you're perfect and brilliant at all that, but I hope you won't mind me mentioning such things as punctuation and spelling for the benefit of those people who aren't.

Teachers and supervisors in higher education differ in their views about the importance of accuracy in matters of style, punctuation, spelling and grammar. Some have a *laissez-faire* view – 'It's what they say that mat- ters, not how they say it' – whereas others take a very different view – 'If they can't write accurately and carefully at this stage of their academic careers, then they should lose marks for it.' You can expect to find every shade of opinion among academics. (And, believe it or not, some aca- demics are very bad at this themselves. In decades of academic editing I have seen some truly dreadful stuff . . . But don't tell them I said so.)

The approach your college or department adopts should be clearly expressed somewhere – in the course documentation, at the very least. If the course guide says that there is a strict approach to grammar, punctuation and the like, then you know where you stand and you won't be surprised if you lose marks for ignoring these aspects. If you can't find any information on this when you RTFM, or perhaps in your university's wider academic policy statements, then ask your supervisor what the policy is. But remember that even if your supervisor says something like 'Well, it doesn't bother me personally', they may not be marking your dissertation; and even where they do mark your dissertation it's likely that there will be at least one other marker too, who may have a very different view. Hence:

> Assume that you will lose marks if your dissertation is badly written and is careless with spelling, grammar and punctuation.

That's the only safe thing to do. *Always* assume that it matters, and then you build another defence against losing marks. This book is about not wasting all that time and energy you put into your research when it comes to writing it up. Here is one of the most straightforward ways of not losing marks, so take it seriously. If you don't, you create one or both of the following impressions:

1. 'I don't know about these things'
2. 'I don't care about these things'.

Unfortunately, neither of these looks good or convincing by this stage in your academic career. It is not inspiring that you are unable to spell and write your own language by the time you reach your 20s, unless you are dyslexic or have similar good reasons (which of course your markers should know about). Also, even if you feel that spelling and the mechanisms of language are beneath you – just petty stuff for anal and small-minded people – that's not how it will be received. They create the impression that you don't care generally, and that is an impression that will spill over into the way the marker thinks about the other aspects of your dissertation. Modern academics are trained not to allow themselves to be distracted by ancillary factors, but if you don't care about the details and the presentation it's almost impossible to avoid the impression that you didn't care about the rest of your dissertation either: you just threw it together in a hurry. Think about it. Perhaps some aspects of your dissertation are causing the marker to think about how the quality of what you're saying and their decision may go either way; but however professional and experienced a marker they are, if they think you don't care they may not give you the benefit of the doubt. 'This student looks as though they just threw this together at the last minute. Hmm. I think it's probable that they don't understand the main aspects of Thurdling's theory after all.' And the effect of this will be cumulative if your language use is poor for page after page.

Some pundits say that current students can't write, and blame all sorts of factors for this – such as wicked schools, the internet, texting, and that all-purpose phrase 'declining standards'. I think it's more complicated than this. One thing is that language use changes all the time. The ubiquity and adaptability of English make it a language that is particularly susceptible to this; but the line between acceptable and unacceptable usage is a difficult one to pitch. People disagree about it, and the age and the cultural background of language users are factors, as is whether English is their first language. Undoubtedly, texting and the internet have an effect too, as has the changing emphasis in schooling over recent decades: it's highly unlikely that 11-year-olds now will have the kind of education I had, which is in many ways a good thing, but has consequences. That kind of education was much more inflexible and narrowly channelled towards academic outputs and language; for example, when I was 11 I was learning clause analysis and had to study Latin, so for me thinking about the way language worked became second nature. It wouldn't have been possible for me to write 'Attlee could not of maintained a Labour government for another full parliament' or something similar (see the 'Mark of Cain' for horrors like 'could of').

There is another factor, or set of factors: higher education has become much more diverse and accessible than it once was – it is available to more people, with more varied backgrounds, across a broader range of subjects. This change has been very marked in the UK. In spite of the whining in some quarters from old-style graduates who resent the passing of their own exclusivity, to me this seems an excellent development for both individuals and the larger society. How can a well-educated society not be better than a poorly educated one? Whether or not it will be sustained politically is another matter – things are not looking good – and the complainers also worry about whether there are enough plumbers to unblock their loos and install their new kitchens. But when you have finished your dissertation and have graduated you can always retrain as a plumber if you want to.

The Mark of Cain

I'm sure that you don't do this, but perhaps a friend of yours does and you may be able to save them from themselves when they submit their dissertation. It appears more often than it should in academic coursework, and is a really awful mistake. It is very likely to catch a marker's attention, suggesting as it does an unreflective, unthinking use of one's own language.

The error is simply this: the preposition 'of' can *never* function as an auxiliary verb, so for example 'would of' is *always* wrong for 'would have'.

Here are some examples of the error in all its awfulness, with the offending parts italicized:

I obtained a higher value for x_p than I *would of* expected.

The experiment *might of* turned out very differently with proper controls.

The senior accountant *could of* told me about the disparity but chose not to.

As you know, these sentences must use *would have*, *might have* and *could have* respectively. They are easy to search for in your final checking phase, though you may want to restrict your search to whole words otherwise a search for, say, 'would of' will stop on sentences like the following one:

He would often visit Mary and her family at the cottage.

Why am I mentioning this? Because an outcome of this breadth of background is that larger numbers of people are coming into higher education who have less training or a more fragmented background in academic writing, and many students reach the stage of writing a dissertation without having made much progress in this respect. It depends of course on the subject area as well as a student's background. You may or may not fit this profile, but it could be worth reading this chapter even if you do not. I have known students who scoffed at basic reminders such as the ones in this chapter – 'Oh, come on. Don't insult our intelligence. We know all that stuff' – but then submitted dreadfully written dissertations with appalling spelling and grammar of the 'could of' variety like the Attlee example above.

If you have special problems

I am sure that if you have dyslexia, dyspraxia or a similar condition then by this stage you have had that investigated and you will be registered. But some people still slip through the system: if you are somebody who has always struggled with grammar, spelling and punctuation, and also can't really see how it all works, then it might be worth inquiring further with the appropriate support centre at your university or college. If you are diagnosed with a condition of this kind then this will be recorded by your college and taken into consideration for coursework and examinations.

Markers take such conditions very seriously and adapt accordingly. So if you are dyslexic, dyspraxic or similar, always include your blue card when you submit your dissertation or other coursework.

What does all this mean for your writing?

Let me say immediately that none of this means that you should be discriminated against if you are not a naturally gifted or elegant writer. I'm not suggesting that the aesthetic dimension of your personal style, something that is largely outside of your basic competence as an academic writer, should affect your marks. Some people do this aesthetic thing well and some not so well, although if you want to do it better there are things that you can identify, reflect upon and change. But that's not what I'm looking at here. Instead, I'm concentrating on what's appropriate at a basic level, and I organize this under four headings: the right register, structure, grammar and style, and spelling and punctuation.

The academic register

Students sometimes imagine that to be properly 'academic', your writing must have a complicated structure, be full of difficult words and jargon or other impenetrable technical stuff, and littered with as many references and notes as possible. Unfortunately, a proportion of academics seem to think this too, and if they start off with that outlook, modern academic training is likely to drill it in to the point where it's a habit that is almost impossible to change.

This kind of thinking might lead you to the absurd assumption that something can't be properly academic if you can understand it, or that an article with 190 footnotes is more 'academic' than an equivalent one with only 40 footnotes, and so on. This is nonsense: the best academic writing is clear and easy to follow, even when it is dealing with fiendishly difficult concepts.

This is not to say that you can always avoid complexity, or technical 'stuff', or notes and references, or even jargon – and what is jargon to outsiders may be essential terminology to insiders. Each of these elements has its place if it can be justified on functional grounds – that is, if it is actually doing some work that couldn't be done without it.

Take jargon. What counts as jargon, which we assume is something undesirable and to be avoided if possible, is the important thing. While you should avoid obscurantist terms, every discipline has its own special vocabulary of key terms and definitions that have a fixed meaning for people working in that discipline. There will be times when you must use those terms in order to be understood and to engage with the discipline and its theoretical bases.

You will probably also introduce your own defined vocabulary of key terms and operational definitions, etc., early in your dissertation or project. These are the terms outside the 'official' vocabulary of your discipline that you still want to use systematically throughout your dissertation. They may even be ordinary everyday words, in which case it is particularly important that you pin down these terms to stop them 'drifting' in meaning between one part of the dissertation and another. As an example, let's say you're doing some primary research into a group of people and you want to see whether high-status individuals achieve more success than some other lower-status individuals. You should be able to see immediately that you must define what you mean by 'high-status individuals' (and of course the other groups you're using too) and also what counts as 'success', right from the start.

As for notes and references, I talk about these in the next chapter – they are important features of academic writing, especially references – but here let's just be clear that on their own they don't turn something into academic writing. Once again, they are items that have a particular function within the piece. They are there because they do something that academic discourse needs to incorporate.

There is an appropriate type of writing for the academic world, though. It is reasoned and structured and backs its statements with evidence, data, theory or some similar underpinning that makes the piece part of a wider and continuous discourse. It is different from journalism, even sober stories about important themes, and very different from the declamatory tones of most blogpseak, or the language of 'commentards',[2] or our

---

[2] In case this word is new to you, it is an unkind term applied to those people who regularly append comments to online news articles, blogs and so on. It is unkind because the ending '-ard' comes from the pejorative US term 'retard', which towards the end of the first decade of this century was already being adapted and applied to people who expect everything to be free on the internet ('freetards') and has since been extended to other groups.

everyday ways of talking and writing for each other. It is also quite different from the language of this book, which is looser and more familiar because it has a very different function from that of a dissertation.

That leaves prolixity, pomposity and circumlocution as the other characteristics of bad academic writing – that is, the deliberate use of complicated and high-sounding prose, obscurantism, and never using one word when ten will do. This is emphatically not the way to produce good academic writing. It is used by the pretentious, the status seeker, those who don't want to be understood (or are afraid that they might be), people who believe that elaborate language confers 'authority', and by all who insist this is the 'proper' way to write academic prose. But a common use of this overblown writing is to cover up the banal, the trivial, the trite, in the hope that the language will conceal the lack of substance in the writing.

To see this kind of pompous and empty writing in action, take a look at this article[3] by Jeremy Evets, an author very well known to me,[4] who took one simple, banal statement – that the candidate who gets the most votes tends to win elections – and turned it into elaborate and excessive multi-page diatribe with a great many unnecessary notes and references. It's a spoof of this kind of academic writing. But it's not just a piece of meaningless nonsense – it does actually say something. It is internally consistent and correct, all of the definitions, notes, etc., work perfectly, and you can unpick everything in the piece to find out what it means. But the overall effect is of an impenetrable mass. To show what I mean, here is a passage from the article where the author is saying something very simple – that getting votes is not enough to win elections because other parties may win more votes than you:

> Let us turn first to an important point: the mere accrual of opinion tokens is not in itself enough to achieve declarative governmental authority acquisition because there may be other representational or quasi-representational units represented in the framework. To see how this might work, consider a case in which there are two representational units . . . RU1 and RU2 who are contesting an opinion token accrual event in a particular zonalised accrual contest region. . . [5]

---

[3] Jeremy L. B. Evets, 'A Synoptic Outcome Survey of the Quantitative Accrual of Opinion Tokens in Western Democratic Polities', *The Political Quarterly*, vol. 79, no. 4, 2008, pp. 605–12; you can access this online by searching or via the site direct at http://onlinelibrary.wiley.com/ where you will be able to download the article free as it's open access.

[4] As to why, you might like to reflect on the surname – write it backwards and place it as a forename instead of a surname.

[5] Evets, 'A Synoptic Outcome Survey', ibid., p. 605.

Writing like this most definitely does not make you a 'proper' academic. You are simply being deliberately unintelligible. And that is a very unwise thing to do in a dissertation, especially when you want a marker to reward you for what you are actually saying. But as there are ways of writing academic prose that convey your ideas clearly to your marker, let's look at those in terms of structure, and then style and the details.

Structure

It's pretty obvious that all documents have some kind of structure. There's the basic stuff that we're all familiar with, and at the lower levels this include sentences and paragraphs. Sentence structure in particular is often associated with an author's personal style – for example, the historian A. J. P. Taylor was noted for his use of short, staccato sentences, which made what he said easy to follow. It would be unwise to copy this approach, though, as variety in sentence length is valuable and will normally emerge naturally when you write. Nor is it true that because short sentences are easy to follow, long sentences are unintelligible: well-constructed long sentences are as easy to follow as short ones. Bad or novice academic editors sometimes err in the direction of believing that they must simplify everything that looks complicated, rather as a parent might mash up food for their infants. Besides, some things just are complicated and hard to understand, and there are limits to how simple can be the language used to present them.

Paragraphs make up the next level of obvious structure; here the length of paragraphs creates impressions in us about the accessibility of the text. Very long paragraphs create a dense mass of text that looks 'serious', which might be your intention, but it may also appear impenetrable, which definitely should not be your aim if you are trying to write a good dissertation. At the other extreme, if your paragraphs are so short that they only contain one or two sentences each, then your writing will lose coherence and fall into a mass of small fragments. Tabloid newspapers use short paragraphs like this to provide bite-sized bits of text for their readers, assuming that they don't want to read anything very complicated that takes more than a few seconds. But tabloids have a very different function from your dissertation. I hope.

What's the way to proceed? I think it's more a question of writing naturally and seeing how it looks after you've completed each page or two. If you're one of those people who writes in 'stream of consciousness' style and just keep keying text without much thought for how the sentences and paragraphs are working out, this is more important for you to do. It might mean going back and adding paragraph breaks and moving things around – but do this according to sense, keeping groups of ideas, themes, emphases, etc., together rather than putting breaks in at random intervals just to even up the paragraph lengths. The divisions you put between sentences and paragraphs should be meaningful, related to the shift of ideas and information as the text develops, and are not about word counts. If you find this kind of thing easy and natural then fine, but many people don't. If you're one of the people who find this difficult, try the above suggestion of reviewing and dividing as a first step.

Design is not the same as structure

I need to remind you here about the difference between a document's structure – how its various parts are organized – and its design or layout – the decisions about how it should look in terms of fonts, heading size and so on. The two are connected: as all publishers and typographical designers know, a good design will make even the densest and most forbidding text easier to access. But they are different. I am talking about structure here. Of course, you will want to choose typefaces and type sizes (fonts and sizes) that are both readable and aesthetically pleasing, and you may have established your own preferences and always use the same range of fonts for your coursework. You can get books on typographical design or word-processor use to help you if you don't have a good feel for this kind of thing. Or you can use the ready-made styles and layouts that come with your word-processor. Be careful not to use anything too florid or extravagant, however, and avoid layouts and designs that look more like greetings cards or award certificates than plain text. On the other hand, your university or department may tell you to use particular fonts and sizes, paper sizes, line spacing and so on, in which case you have little or no choice. As always, if it's an RTFM thing, then make sure you do that. In general, for the design:

- use a reasonably large typeface (font): 12 point is commonly specified for stock fonts such as Times New Roman
- although there are several sans-serif fonts designed for ease of reading on screen, most legible text fonts for print on paper have serifs – Times New Roman is a common (if boring) example
- use generous margins all round, even if they are not specified; this is related to page depth and line length
- the longer the line, the harder it is to read, which gets worse with smaller typefaces; this is why designers organize text into two or more columns on large pages such as newspapers – the short lines are easier to read

- use clearly distinguishable fonts for headings, so that the reader can see at a glance the difference between your headings for chapters, sections and subsections; make them different from the text font too

- avoid script and fancy fonts – these are often hideous and are unlikely to enhance your work.

But, as I've said, your chosen (or required) design is not the same as your structure, so let's get back to that.

Spelling and grammar hints

Here is a brief list that covers a selection of common spelling problems, together with recommendations where appropriate. Occasionally, it drifts into looking at grammar or usage too. But it's just an arbitrary collection of items based on what commonly turns up in dissertations, and shortage of space stops it being longer (it could take up tens of pages or even a whole book).

Incidentally, in this list you'll see that I'm using two different ways of distinguishing the mention of words as opposed to their use, by means of either italic or quotation marks. Hence I can mention the word *green* or the word 'green'. If you are mentioning terms, as you might be in fields like languages, literature, philosophy, linguistics and the like, you should pick one system and use it consistently in your own work (unless you are working under an edict to follow one form or the other).

Always use a good dictionary. Whenever you have doubts about a word, look it up. And while you're there let the rest of the dictionary seduce you and read neighbouring entries. Also, if you want to find out more about some of the topics here you can look them up in usage guides as well as dictionaries.

Distinguish US and UK spelling

This is a fairly fundamental distinction and you'll be familiar with it. Whichever you use, be consistent. Hence US *color* or UK *colour*, *behaviour* or *behavior*, and so on. You can help yourself to be more consistent by setting your word-processor default language to whichever form you're using.

Remember that US and UK English differ in a great many ways, and not just in spelling. But even the spelling aspects can involve subtle distinctions, such as practise/practice and license/licence. These come down to different treatments of the verbal and noun forms. Here's a rather odd sentence that summarizes it for you.

▶

UK form: 'It is normal practice for me to practise daily and I am effectively licensed by my neighbours to do so, in the form of this document, which I treat as a licence to make a noise.'

US form: 'It is normal practice for me to practice daily and I am effectively licenced by my neighbors to do so, in the form of this document, which I treat as a license to make a noise.'

In the UK there is a driving licence, in the USA a driver's license. In the UK, it should not say over a pub doorway something like 'Hermione Pring and David Willibrod are licenced to sell . . .', though it often does; it should be 'licensed to sell . . .'. Also, 'licensing authority' is correct in British English because 'licensing', like 'licensed', is a verbal form.

Words ending in –ise or –ize

First, remember that this option doesn't apply to all words with these endings, because some words like 'advertise' are always '-ise' forms.

It's not simply a US–UK distinction. It's true that *utilise* would not be used in the USA, but *utilize* is definitely used in the UK. In fact, –ize variants are recommended in some publishers' house styles, such as OUP's.

If you want to alter the system you have used, don't change it with a simple global search. If you casually replace all –ise with –ize, for example, you'll end up with 'rize' and 'praize' for 'rise' and 'praise', etc.

Possessives generally

As you know, the apostrophe position varies with the singular and plural. For more on this, see 'Points of punctuation', and also topics like *its* versus *it's* below – *its* is the possessive form, which often causes problems.

Possessive pronouns (yours, theirs, etc.) do not have apostrophes (so it is just plain wrong to write your's, their's, etc.), but this can be confusing when they're mixed with ordinary possessives, so:

Whose ball is this? Is it yours, Stephanie's or the others'?

The others' may look awkward here but it means 'the others' [their] property'.

Elisions, contractions and variations

Is it all right to use 'don't' instead of 'do not', 'I'm' instead of 'I am', 'there's' instead of 'there is' and so on?

It may not be, and it's probably safer to avoid them or keep them to a minimum. I've used such forms freely in this book because they feature widely in conversational English and help the language to flow – that's how they come into being in the first place. But this book is not a dissertation and is not written in an academic register. If you're not sure, then check with your supervisor. Some academics don't mind, whereas others are more strict. And some are fanatical and would regard a single instance of 'don't' as a sign of the terminal decline of civilization.

The family of contractions includes many of the problem words of our time. What follows are some alternative forms that seem to cause a lot of trouble. For example, people seem to use 'your' for 'you're' routinely, judging by online language. Perhaps it's the most common because of the general level of casual abuse in online discussion, as in depressingly incorrect examples like 'Your an idiot'.

They're their there

The correct uses of these similar-seeming words are embodied in this sentence:

> They're [= they are] going to collect their [possessive] bags when they get there [place].

Similar considerations apply to 'you're' and 'your':

> You're [= you are] going to be taller than your [possessive] father soon.

It's and its

An old philosophy professor and tutor of mine used to announce to students that the failure to distinguish the correct usage of *its* and *it's* was 'the hallmark of the semi-literate'. We academics are much kinder to our students these days, ahem, but it's [not *its*] a serious mistake in formal prose. If it's [not *its*] repeated many times its [not *it's*] effect is to undermine confidence in the quality of your work. It's true.

Might of?

For the truly dreadful 'might of' instead of 'might have', etc., see 'The Mark of Cain' above. However, quite apart from these erroneous forms, the correct uses of 'may' and 'might' and 'could', with or without 'have' and other auxiliaries, introduce subtle variations that you can read about in usage guides like *Fowler's*. A minority of markers make a fuss about the use of 'may' versus 'might'.

That, which, who

The alternative uses of these relative pronouns can excite angst in people, but their usage seems to be getting even looser than it was in the past – and that's saying something. In the words of *Fowler's Modern English Usage*, 'The relations between *that, who*, and *which*, have come to us from our forefathers as an odd jumble.'

I suggest you try to use them in a systematic way, using 'that' for defining clauses and 'which' for non-defining clauses, and 'who' rather than 'that' when appropriate. I've followed this approach in this book. What am I talking about? Look at these sentences, which are variations on a very familiar old sentence.

- This is the house that Jack built.
  - That is, *the* particular house, as defined by Jack's building it.

- Here is a house, which Jack built.
  - That is, a house, which happens to have the characteristic that Jack built it.

- Jack is the person who built the house.

Notice the comma before 'which' in the second sentence, whereas it is not appropriate to put a comma before 'that' in the first sentence ('This is the house, that Jack built').

As for 'who', I don't know what this poor word has done to be so widely shunned, but many people would now write the third sentence as 'Jack is the person that built the house'. I like to use 'who' here – which is after all its mainstream use. (In case you're wondering, 'whom' is the object form of the pronoun, as in 'Who gave it to whom?') Actually, 'who' and its related forms are perfectly fine to use for more than just human beings, as in the example 'Frogport is a town whose population expanded rapidly in the post-war period'.

While on 'whose', make sure you distinguish this from 'who's' (= who is, who was, etc.). The correct uses of each can seem similar at times, as in the following two sentences, but if you're confused just think about what each means and you should be able to pick the right one.

Whose scarf is this?
Who's responsible for this?

Correct and pseudo-correct plurals

Some people have problems with the plurals of words like 'referendum' and 'forum'. And what about 'data', a very common word in dissertations: is it a singular or a plural, so should you say 'these data' or 'this data'? 'This data' used to be almost universal, then 'these data' became more common as some asserted that it was 'correct' because 'data' is a plural.

Yes, etymologically it is, but it isn't the plural of 'datum' in English usage – the senses of 'datum' and 'data' have diverged. And nobody says 'these agenda', which would be an equivalent to 'these data'. The sensible thing is to choose a form and use it consistently, bearing in mind any preferences or requirements of your department or course.

'Referenda' would seem to be the plural of 'referendum', and there are other words like this. But though that looks like a Latin third declension neuter plural (*-um* singular and *-a* plural), the original Latin term is not a simple noun and doesn't have a plural form, which arises only in the word's descendant in English. Hence on this reasoning it should take an English plural, 'referendums', which is what many guides recommend. 'Forum' is rather different, as 'fora' is a genuine plural in the original Latin. However, I still prefer 'forums' in general usage on the grounds that 'forum' has long been established as an English word and outside of technical uses 'fora' sounds unnecessarily pompous.

But some words still have distinct and non-optional singular and plural forms that people frequently get wrong. Two to watch out for are:

- *criterion* (singular) and *criteria* (plural) – so 'this criteria' is simply wrong (it should be 'this criterion' or 'these criteria')
- *phenomenon* (singular) and *phenomena* (plural), so 'this phenomena' is similarly incorrect

A spelling and usage miscellany

Here are a few more pointers. Many of them concern similar forms that people frequently confuse. A good dictionary is always your best bet.

Are you bored of it already?

Use of the form 'bored of' (also 'fed up of') has burgeoned recently but is also disliked by many. I suggest it is not yet completely acceptable in formal or academic English. Use 'I'm bored *with X*' (which suggests the boredom emanates from within yourself somehow) or 'I'm bored *by X*' (which suggests the boredom emanates from whatever X is).

Different from, different to, different than?

This is another example that provokes surprisingly strong reactions in some people. 'Different than' is now common in UK English, but some see it as a US form that's crept in, and there are yet others who think it is an abomination and insist that only 'different from' is correct, because 'from' is the only preposition strong enough to do justice to the sense of 'different'.

Publicly

The adverbial form of 'public' is 'publicly' – 'publically' is simply incorrect.

Continuously/continually?

These usually mean different things – 'continuously' means without inter-ruption, non-stop, whereas 'continually' means repeatedly, persistently, on a regular basis, etc. So your neighbour is continually playing loud music – perhaps for several hours at a time and on most days – but not con-tinuously doing it, which would mean 24 hours a day, seven days a week, without a break.

Inquiry/enquiry

Sometimes people use these to mean different things (say, 'inquiry' for a formal investigation and 'enquiry' as an informal one), but these kinds of subtle system are often not evident to readers, who just think it's an inconsistency. They're usually now treated as alternatives, so choose one and stick to it. Which do I use in this book?

Affect/effect

Here are a pair of words that can cause trouble, and even good writers and spellers get them mixed up when they're tired or lose concentration. Here are the main uses:

This change will affect everybody in the department.
The change did not have the desired effect.

But it's not simply a question of 'affect' as verb and 'effect' as noun, as these other uses show:

Cyril was trying to effect a change in the dominant culture.
Psychotherapists frequently talk about affect.

Form/from

Using the wrong one of these is not a confusion you will ever intention-ally make, but your fingers may let you down at times and jumble them up. Always make sure you have the right instances of 'form' and 'from' when you're proofreading and doing final checks. There are several other jumbly-finger traps too, such as 'causal'/'casual'.

Acknowledgement, judgement, moveable

These are words that can appear with or without that 'e' (so 'judgment' and 'movable' are OK too). In many contexts these are simply alterna-tives, so – as always when faced with a genuine choice – just pick one form and use it consistently (you would tend to use the same variant for both 'acknowledgement' and 'judgement' too). However, in certain fields, such as law, an author may try and maintain a systematic difference; for example, 'judgement' and 'judgment' could mean different things – everyday informal judgement and a legal decision by a judge, respectively. Check to see whether you're required to do this.

You don't wanna use this

The mainly US conversational form 'wanna' for 'want to' is never acceptable in academic or any other formal English. However, my impression is that it features widely in the English taught in many Asian countries, particularly where US English is the dominant form. In general, if English is not your native language take extra care not to use 'wanna' in your coursework and the dissertation.

Mitigate against?

No – look up the meaning of 'mitigate' and you'll see that's a nonsense. It's *militate against*, not 'mitigate against'.

'Loose' usage

So many people mis-spell 'lose' (in the sense of mislay) as 'loose'. It's a tiresome error, and one of those that stands out and makes you look careless, so double-check. Misuse won't normally show up in spellcheckers or style checkers because each term has legitimate uses, including as a verb. For example, you could *lose an arrow* (drop it in the grass and not be able to find it) but also *loose an arrow* (in the air, and have it fall to earth you know not where, in which case first you loosed it and now you've lost it).

Is it all right to use 'alright'?

I suggest you use 'all right' in formal English. All right?

The principal principle

Which is which? Search for each of them at your final check and make sure you've used the forms correctly. The head of a college is a *principal* (main, chief, head, foremost), but if you resign because you feel strongly about something you did so on a matter of *principle*. And Occam's Razor is also known as the Principle of Parsimony. That means you really could talk about a principal principle without it being nonsense.

Precipitous/precipitate

If you act hastily, was your action *precipitous* or *precipitate*? And which of these two words refers to the steep cliff? You should not act precipitately, and a cliff falls away precipitously.

Chapters, sections and headings

Like books and journal articles, most dissertations and reports are organized into separate blocks, normally called chapters or sections. The terminology isn't exact, but in publishing and typography a section is part of a chapter, and the term 'part' itself is used to mean a group of chapters. Sections can in turn be divided into subsections and so on, though it's usually unwise to carry on this subdivision too far – to sub-subsections, sub-sub-subsections and so on – partly because the whole thing starts to fragment but also because the difference between these various levels is difficult to convey to the reader. This book is divided into chapters, sections and subsections, and each of these elements is introduced by a heading. When I typed it, I used bold for my main subheadings and italic for the sub-subheadings – such as 'Chapter, sections and headings', the one introducing this block of text. Then when the publisher designed the book these were translated into the headings you can see now. The point is that you can tell at a glance where the chapters begin and end, and whether a block of text is part of a section or a subsection. If you are free to choose your own structure, then you should look at introducing these features too.

There are few things worse in a dissertation than an undifferentiated and unbroken mass of text that has few or no breaks from one page to the next. It's not just that it looks forbidding and not user-friendly; there's also no clear way into it – or, rather, there is only one way into it. You have to dive in at the beginning and follow it all the way through to the end. This is fine for a novel, but no good for a document with a very different function such as a dissertation or an academic report. One of the key aspects of organizing this kind of text is that you need to find ways to help the reader jump in to find specific points in the discussion or argument. This requires a structure with added signposts – headings and subheadings at various levels, lists, tables and so on – and ways of organizing your information, ideas and arguments. Linked with this there should be a navigation system that helps your reader to find the right place quickly, so at the very least you should have a prominent contents listing at the start.

I said 'if you are free to choose your own structure' because you may not be. Just as with the design, your college, department or some other authority may require that some or most of the structure of your dissertation must follow a specified pattern. This is more likely in contexts where the work nearly always follows a set pattern than in disciplines where dissertations will vary greatly from one to another. Naturally, if your rules say that you have to follow a particular structure – you must have particular named chapters with certain titles, for example, or number all of your headings in a nested and numbered sequence – then that is what you must do.

I'll say it again: your structure and your design are distinct from one another. Structure is something that refers to the elements and their organization – something that might be tagged by XML in an electronic document – whereas the design is how the elements will look in this particular instance. For example, you may choose to include main sub-heads and sub-subheads in your dissertation (a structural decision) and choose to represent them by 12 pt Calibri and 12 pt Times New Roman italic respectively (a design decision).

Other text elements

Publishers have a word – 'display' – for text elements that are used to set out material that is intended to be in contrast to the main text. This includes bullet and numbered lists, equations and similar expressions, formulae, definitions, passages of quoted text, verse, dialogue and so on. Some of these kinds of elements are likely to feature in your dissertation, depending on the subject area. They can be very valuable and are a way of summarizing information in a clear way so that the reader can find it quickly. As with masses of short paragraphs, however, it is possible to overdo it. Take lists, for example. A bullet list is a handy way of presenting brief pieces of information or ideas, but if you use too many of them, or they are too long or complex, they soon lose their value and your document starts to break into fragments. There are authors who produce text like this, possibly because they think in that way, but they need a lot of editing to restore a narrative from that mass of small pieces. A list is a contrastive element, so it should be used sparingly – bulleted when the order doesn't matter and numbered when it does.

Sometimes it's not easy to tell whether an item divided into rows and columns should be treated as a list or as a table.

Grammar and style

This is not the place to go on about grammar or style at great length. That would take a whole book. Indeed there are books that do just that such as the long-standing *Fowler's Modern English Usage*, which has been running in various editions since 1926, and if you are interested in this kind of thing then you might like to read one of those books. Instead, I'm going to look at one or two aspects of grammar and then look at some of the stylistic choices authors make – and how these can help or hinder what you want to say.

First, what is 'grammar' anyway? Strictly, it's to do with the rules that govern the way language is put together, its 'well formedness'. So, for example, in formal written English we say 'Yesterday I went to London' rather than 'Yesterday I am goes to Londons'. In the second version the verb forms are wrong and I've also added an 's' to London, making it a kind of plural that would suggest it's a spelling mistake (which is how your word-processor's spellchecker would probably see it).

However, a lot of the apparent rules that people call 'grammar' are not like this; instead they are usage fads that date back to the prescriptions of earlier times, such as 'Never start a sentence with "and"', or 'Never use a preposition to end a sentence with' (which is also a self-referring joke, if a feeble one), or 'Never start a sentence with "Firstly" and instead use "First", though you can use "Secondly" to introduce the second item', and so on. If you were to ask people the reasons for these 'rules', they might say something like 'Everybody knows this is good English', or 'I was always taught that this is what we should do', and so on.

How strongly these and similar apply now is debatable: for some people – I'd guess a dwindling number – they are absolutely mandatory, for others less so; and there will be yet other people who are not aware of them at all. I can't tell you how far you should apply them, but in most cases they are probably trivial from your point of view. If one of your markers has an attachment to one of them, say, it won't be very significant – for example, it may mean a ring around 'Firstly' at the start of a sentence if that's what you use, meaning you should have used 'First' in their view, but then you may already have learnt about that marker's preferences and foibles earlier in the course. No: what is far more significant are failures of the first kind of grammar – the 'well formedness' kind – and spelling or punctuation errors. These are examples of what I was talking about at the beginning of this chapter: they create a bad impression that can rub off on how the rest of your dissertation is received.

'The present writer'

By now you have evolved your own way of writing, an aesthetic and technical fingerprint that is characteristic of your own use of text. This covers things like expressions and constructions you habitually use, words that you employ frequently, and your approach to punctuation. Within reason, this personal style should not affect the character of your dissertation and hence the marks you get for it. As long as they can understand what you're saying and it's expressed in a reasonably competent way, they'll look beyond your personal style to what lies beneath.

So how much of 'you' should there be in what you say? Harking back to the example I used in Chapter 1, should you use the first person, for example, and say things like:

I interviewed 35 quota-selected non-league footballers.

Or should it be:

The present writer interviewed 35 quota-selected non-league footballers.

Or must it be something that appears to leave you out altogether, such as:

Thirty-five quota-selected non-league footballers were interviewed.

In cases like this I strongly prefer the first person on the grounds that if it was you who did the interviewing, and it's germane to the discussion that it was you (and it certainly was in this example, and you'd feature that in the methodology), then for goodness' sake say so. The expression 'the present writer' is a hideous mealy-mouthed euphemism that says nothing other than 'I', as is clear from the first two of the example sentences about the footballer interviews. I'm not suggesting that you should introduce an unwanted personal dimension into an 'objective' environment, so what is going on and why did expressions like this grow up in the first place?

Passives, and impersonal constructions

This is more than just a campaign by me to rid the world of the idiocy of the expression 'the present writer' – though by all means sign up to that and march on the capital with your demands. It is to remind you that academic writing involves a mix of expectations and conventions that combine with a relatively sober style of English. It is this combination of forces that shapes the way you write your text. Each discipline will interpret this in a slightly different way, and as well as these variations there will also be the lesser expectations of individual markers. As to this last aspect, it's almost impossible to cater for that unless you know who is marking your dissertation and whether they have any stylistic preferences or obsessions. Forget that as you can't fine-tune your writing for something as small and unknowable, and instead concentrate on the other mainstream aspects.

For example, hundreds of years ago in my engineering days we were expected to write reports in the 'third-person past passive'. In case you don't know what I mean by this, verbs have different forms depending on number (such as I or you), tense (such as past or present), voice (such as active or passive) and mood (such as indicative and subjunctive, the latter being used little in English though you may have met it when learning other languages). The difference between the active (think agent, action) and the passive (think patient, passion – yes, interesting isn't it) is the difference between doing and being done by, so 'I lit the fire' is a first-person past (perfect) active statement, whereas 'The fire was lit by me' recasts the same statement into the passive. The third person is the 'he, she, it' (singular) or 'they' (plural) form. That means when I was asked to do a report on an engine test (Ruston horizontal engine – remember to keep your thumbs over the starting handle in case it kicks back) I would put sentences like the following in my 'Apparatus' or 'Equipment' or equivalent section:

A Dobbie McInnes indicator was connected to the cylinder test port.

It's not exciting but it's accurate, and notice that there's no mention of who did the connecting and how they did it. Also, a collection of sentences like this would probably be backed up by one or more diagrams. Whether illustrated or not, this deliberately neutral approach, routine in the sciences and technology, describes as far as possible an objective (discuss!) state of affairs in the world, and people are kept out of it not just to avoid distraction and irrelevance but because they should not figure in the events described in the report. One key aspect of scientific and related inquiry is replicability and repeatability – anybody else should be able to come and duplicate what you did and get equivalent results. The people don't matter. So we would not expect to find this replacing my bland statement above:

Sophia entered the room and glanced briefly at the Ruston engine, newly cleaned and glistening brightly in the corner of the thermodynamics lab. I had expected her to glide towards it in that bewitching way of hers, as I had seen her do so many times before. Instead, she swayed towards me, slowly and calmly, her eyes fixed on mine. I felt her breath on my face as she reached out. Her violet eyes flashed, my longing heart raced. Sophie's trembling hand brushed my cheek but did not rest there, pushing past me to the polished wooden box on the shelf behind my ear. She paused, then withdrew the precious container. 'Dobbie', she said in her soft Arbroath accent. 'McInnes', I mumbled in reply, barely able to speak. In an instant she had left me and was standing by the engine, her arm caressing the massive flywheel. Pausing only to slip the recording paper over the drum she coupled the valve to the engine port . . .

Quite. But it is that objective tendency, the desire to get the human out of the apparatus and the process, that leads us first to passives and then to impersonal constructions. What do I mean by impersonal constructions?

Things like this:

A Dobbie McInnes indicator was connected to the cylinder test port.

Thirty-five quota-selected non-league footballers were interviewed.

It has been discovered that people who live in glass houses should not throw stones.

It is widely believed that people who walk underneath ladders invite ill fortune.

It is the first part of the last two statements that uses the most common approach to impersonal (and passive) construction. You can probably think of any number of others. There are so many variants, and they're widely seen (impersonal construction!) in media reports too. Notice that these are not the same as active statements of a kind beloved by the media that preserve anonymity or promote a spurious objectivity, such as 'Scientists have shown that eating nettles prolongs the average human life by 180 years,' in which the vague and unexplained subject term 'Scientists' is supposed to ensure instant authority; or 'Sources close to the Prime Minister have claimed that . . .', where we are supposed to assume that the 'sources' refer to somebody like the PM's partner or second in command, but may just mean 'we made it up'.

There are two sets of problems with this approach. One is to do with the passives themselves: it is that a succession of passives – sentence after sentence, paragraph after paragraph – creates a very dull kind of prose. This is an aesthetic consideration, but it can affect readability and the reader's interest, and as your key readers are the markers that should interest you. The other problem concerns the impersonal constructions: we can always ask something like 'By whom?' whenever we encounter one. Yes, there's a kind of person-independent neutrality about them, and certainly no sign of a Sophie with her massive flywheel, but when we come across 'It has been discovered that . . .' we can ask 'By whom?', and that question is not trivial. It is more a case of a suppressed or hidden subject term than an absent one. These constructions are bewitching and easy to lapse into, so it's a good idea to search your final drafts to see if there is anything in there that is pretending to an undeserved objectivity. If there really are real subjects behind the impersonal constructions you can sometimes add sources to give some weight to such statements:

It has been discovered (Prottle, 1994, 1997) that people who live in glass houses should not throw stones.

It is widely believed (Maginot, 2008; Flaubert, 2009a; Skratz and Gosch, 2010) that people who walk underneath ladders invite ill fortune.

But even here there are problems. In the first case, the discovery claim appears to be yours (somebody might write to you later and say that it was not Prottle who discovered it but Glisby and Tow in 1987) and in the second it is your claim that the three sources are enough to constitute evidence of wide belief. (And how wide is 'wide' anyway?) An instant solution is to turn the sentences into active forms such as:

> Prottle (1994, 1997) studied people who live in glass houses and concluded that they should not throw stones.

I hope you can see what I mean. I am not saying that academic writing, particularly in science and technology, should abandon neutrality and the striving for objectivity – far from it. Nor am I claiming that you should not use passives or objective constructions. Instead, it is rather like the warnings I gave in Chapter 4 to use language carefully. Check all those impersonals and make sure that you're not lapsing into pseudo-objectivity, and where the discipline and the narrative permit use other forms to avoid page after page of unnecessary passives that will send your reader (marker) to sleep.

Spelling and punctuation

Are you a good speller? How is your punctuation? Many people can probably answer the first; possibly not so many the second, as punctuation is less obvious than incorrectly spelled words. The point is that, tedious or not, these factors influence the reader's impression of your text and indeed the document as a whole. And if you're not a good speller, what have you done about that? Of course, spellcheckers help – and perhaps grammar checkers are of some value – but have to be used with care. For example, it's only too easy to fill up your personal dictionary with incorrect spellings if you're tired, not paying attention or convinced that your incorrect spellings are the right ones. At the very least this allows incorrectly spelled words in your text, and at worst includes them in your dictionary too so that they won't even be flagged up. And here's a question for you: when in your writing and checking sequence do you run your spellchecker? Near the beginning, when you've just finished writing the draft, or near the end, when you're doing your final check before submitting the dissertation?

I don't want to say too much here about either of these two cornerstones of accuracy as they are things you can check elsewhere. And I suggest you get into the habit of looking up words in a traditional paper dictionary (for a single-volume dictionary I use *Chambers Dictionary*). Why? Because you'll get distracted by the etymology and by other words nearby, and you'll start to read it more widely instead of just jumping in for a quick fix on the target word. Dictionaries are a really good read, and you improve your vocabulary and spelling into the bargain.

You can take other steps to improve too. If you're not good at spelling, write down any word that causes you problems (for example, ones that you've had marked in previous coursework) and when you have a nice list start learning them – so many a week, or even so many a day if there are lots. If you are writing academic prose, where accuracy is still valued, bad spelling stands out in sharp relief, so please don't simply accept being a bad speller and do nothing about it. I've summarized some common or crucial spelling problems in 'Spelling and grammar hints' on pp. 113–19.

Points of punctuation

Here are some guidelines to help you with common punctuation issues and problems. It is no substitute for dedicated books on the topic, but if you take notice of these points you should avoid common errors and give your writing a bit more polish. If you are interested, read the punctuation sections of usage guides and dictionaries, and also classic books on punctuation itself – though I suggest you avoid those that take a moral panic approach and regard changes in punctuation usage as a harbinger of the end of civilization.

Full stops (periods) and abbreviations

The typographical name for this thing '.' is a point. To describe it as a full stop (or period, in the USA) is really to imply a particular use – namely its most familiar one as a sentence stop. The other extremely familiar use of this innocuous dot is to mark abbreviations, but here usage has changed very much over the decades and along with most other punctuation is much lighter than it was.

A widely adopted modern convention is to use points for abbreviations but no points for contractions (where the beginning and end of the term remain but some or all of the middle is removed), so here are some examples of each. In the abbreviations, at least one of the components has had the end knocked off, whereas in the contractions, the middle has been hollowed out:

- e.g. (*exempli gratia*, for example) and i.e. (*id est*, that is), not ie, i.e or other variants
- et al. for *et alia* (often used in bibliographies) because only the 'alia' bit is abbreviated

- etc. to mean 'and so on' (*et cetera*)
- Examples of contractions: Mr (mister), St (Street or Saint), edn (for edition), eds (a contraction for 'editors', but in some systems used with ed., an abbreviation for 'editor', which can be confusing).

One more thing. The ellipsis is usually represented by three points, like this . . . except where a sentence finishes immediately prior to it, where it is preceded by the sentence stop like this. . . .

The comma chameleon

The comma splice (or 'overloaded comma')

Perhaps the commonest punctuation error of our times is what Fowler called the comma splice, where a comma is given a load – splicing two essentially independent elements together – that it is not designed to bear. I usually describe it more straightforwardly as the overloaded comma to students. Time will tell whether it will become accepted usage as part of a simplified punctuation based on commas, dashes and points; but in formal registers, including academic writing, it is bad enough still to be regarded as straightforwardly incorrect and hence a punctuation error. Even people who otherwise write well are prone to the comma splice. Compare these three sentences to see it in action in two of them: which two?

1. I went home the other day, mainly because my father had asked me to go.
2. I went home the other day, my father had asked me to go.
3. I went home the other day, I collected the car on Tuesday and drove there.

In sentence 1 the comma separates the main clause (the 'went home' one) from the subordinate clause. There is no punctuation error there, though as a matter of style some people would omit the comma in these lighter-punctuating times. So sentence 1 does not make the comma splice error: it's fine.

Sentences 2 and 3 are different. In those, both parts of the sentence are main-clause-like and each could stand on its own as a meaningful sentence. (Compare this to sentence 1, in which 'Mainly because my father had asked me go' could not normally stand alone as a sentence.)

In examples 2 and 3 the division between the two parts is more like a break between two sentences, and the comma is not a strong enough stop for that purpose. *Using a comma in that place is the comma splice error.* So what's the additional difference between 2 and 3, if they both use the overloaded comma? It's that there's more of a connection between the senses of the two parts in 2 than there is in 3, so sentence 2 is a better candidate for the semi-colon rather than a full stop. You could almost read the semi-colon in 2 as meaning something like 'because'. Here are the examples again, this time without the errors:

1. I went home the other day, mainly because my father had asked me to go.
2. I went home the other day; my father had asked me to go.
3. I went home the other day. I collected the car on Tuesday and drove there.

Commas between subject phrases and verb phrases

Look at the following sentence. What do you think about the use of the comma, and would you have put one there?

The long barrelled revolver that he hid in his jacket, fell to the floor with a clatter.

Its awkwardness to modern eyes is more obvious if I substitute a much shorter and banal sentence with the same structure. This one has a much simpler noun phrase as its subject:

The cat, sat on the mat.

It looks odd, doesn't it? It suggests an old-fashioned rhetorical approach to punctuation that places the stops to convey the breathing points and emotional weight of the spoken sentence. Nowadays, with our 'logical' punctuation usually marking sentence structure, the comma just seems in the way and we trip over it as we read. But in the 'revolver' example the noun phrase forming the subject is more complex so the awkwardness is less easy to spot. I'm sure people don't consciously adopt 19th-century and earlier modes of punctuation, but I see this often. My guess is that people sometimes think 'That's quite complicated so I'd better put a comma in somewhere to show the word groupings.' But it's not necessary, as the perfectly intelligible comma-less version shows:

The long barrelled revolver that he hid in his jacket fell to the floor with a clatter.

Commas in lists

There are two main conventions for using commas in lists. One is probably the one you were taught, which is that you don't need a comma between the penultimate item and the 'and', like this:

dogs, cats, horses and aardvarks

There is another convention, enshrined in some dictionaries and publishing styles, which does use a comma there. This is sometimes called the 'Oxford' or 'list' comma:

dogs, cats, horses, and aardvarks

The argument for this is that every item should be followed by a comma for consistency, which I've never found convincing given that commas in lists are effectively place-keepers for 'and', hence the list comma effectively creates an 'and and'. Still, if you have a choice (you probably do), use one convention and stick to it. This only applies to commas in lists: it doesn't mean 'Never [or 'Always'] use a comma before "and"'. In clausal punctuation and other uses of 'and' you are free to do whatever the context needs, independent of this convention.

Colons and semi-colons

People sometimes mix these up, but if you use them sparingly they're unlikely to cause problems. Colons are usually used to introduce, to imply 'for example' and so on. Incidentally, never use them with a hyphen as in old-fashioned typewriter practice like this:-

The semi-colon is a more subtle stop, which leads some people to overuse them in the seriously mistaken assumption that it makes them look sophisticated. There are two main categories of everyday use. One is exemplified in sentence 2 from the comma splice example, as corrected:

I went home the other day; my father had asked me to go.

There it functions as a link between two related main clauses, as an alternative to the stronger full stop. The other main use is to separate the elements of lists where the elements are themselves punctuated with commas. That means the following list is incorrectly punctuated, as commas would be perfectly fine here:

dogs; cats; horses; and aardvarks; . . .

Here's an example of commas, semi-colons and a colon used in a conventional way. Notice that the semi-colons mark the list because there is additional internal punctuation by comma in some of the list items:

Mulligatawny and Schreiber (1994b) recognized four distinct categories of wedding gift: bedding, towels and other fabric goods; cutlery and kitchenware, not including electrical items; electrical goods, including those designed for kitchen use; and pointless clutter bought at the last minute, such as hedgehog-shaped lights and novelty toilet seats.

Notice that the colon introduces the list, and you'll also see how the structure and sense would be more difficult to follow if those semi-colons in the list were replaced by commas.

Possessives and apostrophes

The main use of the apostrophe is to mark a place where something has been omitted, such as 'That's' to shorten 'That is' and 'Let's' to shorten 'Let us'. This is also how the apostrophe came to be used for possessives over the centuries – as in 'John his book' eventually becoming 'John's book' to give us our present-day forms. And as you know, the apostrophe position varies between singulars and plurals, so 'the cow's legs' (the legs of just one cow) and 'the cows' legs' (the legs of two or more cows).

When it comes to 'its' the contraction convention takes precedence over the (derived) possessive one, which causes problems to many people.

Pitfalls

Sometimes people come unstuck with plural forms like 'men' and 'children', and are not sure what to do with terms like 'people'. As the first two examples are already plurals, the correct forms are 'the men's ideas', 'the children's books'. In the third example the right form is, for example, 'the people's charter' (the charter of the people, collectively) – 'the peoples' charter' would mean something different as 'peoples' refers to sets of humans, as in 'the peoples of Europe'.

Here's one more group of apostrophe uses that sometimes leads people astray. Which are the correct forms in each pair?

- I only managed three hours sleep last night.
- I only managed three hours' sleep last night.

- I leave for the Moon in three days time.
- I leave for the Moon in three days' time.

Which did you say? It's the second version in each pair that is correct. To test cases like these if you find yourself unsure, try the equivalent with only one of the items (hours, days, etc.), such as:

- I only managed one hour's sleep last night.

That should convince you it's a possessive-like structure. If this were only a simple singular–plural difference then the correct form with one hour would be 'I only managed one hour sleep last night'.

But don't confuse this with the superficially similar:

The town is three hours away from here by train.

In this, an apostrophe (hour's) would be incorrect; 'hours' is a straightforward plural.

Apostrophes in plurals!

Some would say that I should put this error, sometimes pompously known as the 'grocer's apostrophe' because it has so often appeared on produce price labels, in the dreaded Mark of Cain category alongside 'would of' and the rest. I mean here things like 'She gave me a box of apple's [aaagh!] and a banana'.

I am afraid incorrect apostrophes in plurals do look bad when they are repeated through a dissertation, so look out for them during your proof-reading and other checking phases. They may well influence a marker to think that you 'don't know or don't care'. If it's a plural and not a possessive, it doesn't have an apostrophe.

Hyphens and dashy things

You should be familiar with the principal use of hyphens to link prefixes and form compound adjectives. Their use is in gentle decline and some see them disappearing one day. In many publishers' style guides they're proscribed in '-ly' compounds, meaning they want 'heavily used road' rather than 'heavily-used road', for example, and indeed that's the style I have followed in this book as I prefer to use a minimum of hyphens. You can add polish to your dissertation by using hyphens consistently throughout, so for example don't use 'pre-war' in one part of it and 'prewar' in another.

Another 'professional' touch is to use the longer 'en dash' (en rule) for purposes like parenthetical dashes (with spaces), or in, say, 'red–green colour blindness' (where somebody can't distinguish red from green), as opposed to the hyphen in 'She wore a blue-green cape' – that is, a cape of a compound bluey green colour.

Quotation marks

Here is another case where consistency helps to add polish to what you do. Do use the same type of quotation mark ('quote') throughout – single or double – if you have a choice. Whichever one you pick, it's normal to use the other form for 'quotes within quotes', as in this example: 'John would always become emotional whenever he saw the word "Samantha" in the newspaper.' (Or vice versa if you're using double quotes.) Most modern word-processors automatically generate typographical quotation marks unless you tell them not to. More complicated schemes (single quotes for some things, doubles for others) can be unsuccessful because it's often not clear to the reader what the scheme is.

The other aspect to watch is the relationship between quotes and other punctuation, exemplified by these two sentences:

'I would like you to stop what you're doing immediately,' said Inspector Narble, 'and give the knife to me.'

'I would like you to stop what you're doing immediately', said Inspector Narble, 'and give the knife to me.'

In each case the closing quotation mark comes after the final full stop because the whole sentence is inside the quoted passage. In the first, however, the comma after 'immediately' comes before the adjacent quotation mark – a traditional order that some people always use habitually, as they've been taught to do it that way – and in the second it comes after it – reflecting a so-called logical sequence because the comma belongs to the outer sentence and is not part of what the inspector actually says. As before, use one system and stick to it. I use the second 'logical' approach myself.

I asked about your punctuating ability and commented that people are not always aware about their own style – but you will have one. Punctuation is just as much a feature of your own writing style as your choice of words and sentence length. I have also summarized many of these punctuation issues in the 'Points of punctuation' list on p. 127. Once again there are books of the *Fowler's* variety (including *Fowler's* itself) that advise on punctuation, and there are also one or two polemical books. Present-day punctuation styles tend to be lighter than those of a few decades ago, and if you read a 19th-century novel you may be struck by the larger number of stops (here meaning commas, full stops, semi-colons, etc., collectively) than you would expect to find nowadays. Another change has been the steady move away from rhetorical punctuation, in which the placing of stops was related to the spoken utterance and its intended effect. The following examples would now seem rather stilted to most people:

I always find that, I suffer from wind after eating asparagus burgers.

The bus I am waiting for, is very late.

Though the one about the bus is an example of a style that some people adopt. In today's more 'logical' or structural approach to punctuation it does not make sense to put a comma between a subject term and its verb like this. Some people seem only to use commas and dashes to punctuate; others use a greater variety of stops but not always correctly. But as with spelling and grammar, the fairly formal register of academic writing needs careful punctuation or you will once again create that 'I don't know or I don't care' effect. This doesn't mean heavy and laboured punctuation, or inserting huge numbers of semi-colons in the mistaken belief that this will automatically make your writing look more sophisticated.

Perhaps the most common spelling problem today is what is sometimes called 'the comma splice', though I call it the 'overloaded comma' when talking about punctuation to students. This could be one of those shifts in usage that will one day no longer be seen as an error but as part of normal practice, but I don't think we've reached that point yet and certainly not in formal contexts such as academic writing. Here's an example:

I am still waiting for the bus, it should have been here twenty minutes ago.

Perhaps it looks innocent. Is this how you would punctuate the sentence? The point is that the comma isn't 'strong' enough to hold the two parts of the sentence together (or to hold them apart, if you want to look at it that way). The simplest way would be to turn it into two sentences:

I am still waiting for the bus. It should have been here twenty minutes ago.

But in this case because the senses of the two parts of the original sentence are closely connected, with the pronoun 'it' linking back to the bus in the first part too, you could certainly use the more subtle semi-colon:

I am still waiting for the bus; it should have been here twenty minutes ago.

Isn't that better? The thing about the comma splice is that once you've recognized it as a problem you'll start to see it everywhere, across all media.

Oh yes. The answer to the spellchecker question I asked earlier. I suggest you use it at the beginning of the process. It enables you to get the major problems out of the way, but because spellcheckers are not flawless tools and we can also use them carelessly, running them early means that you can find the errors and problems they create when you do your final check before submission (see Chapter 10).

7 Working with notes and references

For most of you, the use of notes and references will be second nature by now. They will have been part of the fabric of the coursework you have submitted since you started at university or college, and probably before that. If you're confident that you're *au fait* with all aspects of their application in your subject area and department you may want to skip this chapter, or just scan it in case there's a useful hint or two. You may decide you want to read it anyway for a brief review of annotation and referencing practice.

If you have less experience of writing in an academic register then perhaps notes and references are a bit more mysterious – you've been able to use them in your assignments up to now but may be less confident about why you're doing what you're doing. Or you've simply followed some departmental or course rules in a handbook (as usual, when you apply the information in this chapter make sure you RTFM too). If this applies to you – you 'sort of' know what you're doing but don't feel totally confident about the details – then I hope this chapter is of some value. I talk first about notes, and then about reference systems and bibliographies.

Notes on notes

What is a note? Well, before I come back to that let's observe a distinction that is commonly used in publishing parlance between *footnotes* and *endnotes*. It's obvious, really: footnotes are those that appear at the foot of the page, and endnotes appear either at the end of a chapter (or a similar unit of organization), in which case they're called chapter endnotes, or at the end of the whole book or publication, when they're often called volume endnotes. In either case, endnotes usually appear under a subheading such as 'Notes' or, especially if they're bibliographical notes, 'References'.

Footnotes are easy to find and very convenient, though if there are a lot of them they can draw your eye and distract you, interrupting your flow as you read from one page to the next. Endnotes became more heavily used through the 1960s and 1970s as publishers started managing their costs more tightly, because with the production systems of the time it was normally cheaper to typeset endnotes than footnotes. They divide opinion: some authors and readers like endnotes, because you aren't distracted on every page and only look at them when you get to the end of the chapter or when you otherwise want to check them. To the detractors, it's that very feature that makes them a nuisance – you have to keep a bookmark or your finger in the notes pages, and keep flipping backwards and forwards whenever you want to read them.

Whichever style you choose (though I appreciate you may have no choice), follow it throughout and use it consistently. And if you've not used the distinction before, you can use your new-found sophistication to talk of footnotes and endnotes rather than call everything a 'footnote', which is what a lot of people do. Hence I describe my general topic here as *notes*.

As to how you number your notes, you'll be familiar with the fact that most people now use a continuous sequence of arabic numbers (^{1}, ^{2}, ^{3} . . .), restarting from 1 at the beginning of each new chapter. That's by no means the only system, and you'll notice that your word-processor allows you some alternatives, such as ^{i}, ^{ii}, ^{iii} or ^{a}, ^{b}, ^{c}, and you can construct others such as [1], [2], [3] but I suggest you don't use them unless your dissertation rules tell you that you must. Sometimes these alternatives can find specialist uses, such as ^{a}, ^{b}, ^{c} being used for notes within tables or [1], [2], etc., being used for referencing in the so-called Vancouver system that is used rather more in science and technology than arts and humanities.

There are more variations. Some schemes renumber the notes from 1 after they reach 99 because note cues like ^{137} make an ugly gap in the text, though that's more a nicety of typography in published work rather than a worry for a dissertation. Besides, are you going to run to more than a hundred notes a chapter? You are? Well, read on below when I ask whether you need all those notes. Another common system was for the notes to renumber from one each page, and more basic still would be systems based on symbols like *, † and ‡.[1]

---

[1] Where * is an *asterisk*, not an Asterix, who is a Gaul from *la bande dessinée* of the same name and a friend of Obelix, whose name may have something to do with the fact that the dagger symbol † is often called an obelus or *obelisk*.

Something that's really helped with the control of numbering sequences, which used to be the bane of an author's or editor's life in the days of typewritten manuscripts, is the word-processor's native note function. Now when you want to add an extra note between 12 and 13 in your 142 note chapter you simply click on the mouse and the added note goes in and becomes the new note 13, with all the others automatically renumbered. That certainly wasn't how things were when people created books on typewriters, when you had to renumber them by hand. It's still possible to make a mistake, though. For example, you can accidentally mix two different note systems by adding a note 1 at the start of your chapter, say as an endnote, then when you find you need another one some pages later you absent-mindedly add it as a footnote. That would give you two note 1s, which might mystify you as you read through the text until you checked more closely. Naturally, you should use the same system throughout as I said a few paragraphs ago. If you find something wrong with the numbering scheme then check you're not mixing them.

When using notes in tables and figures, it's normal to use a different system, so for example if your main note sequence is running [1], [2], [3], etc., then your notes within a table would perhaps use [a], [b], [c] (starting from [a] with each table or figure) or a symbol system. Why? This is really an approach that is driven by publishing requirements. When you create a table or figure for publication you don't know exactly where on the final book or journal page it will appear, so if you were to number its internal notes within the main text sequence that would only work if the table falls in that precise place on the page, which it may well not. Hence a separate note sequence for a table or figure allows it to fit in anywhere.

Types of note

I've already identified the distinction between footnotes and endnotes, and talked about different numbering schemes, but there are functional differences between kinds of notes as well. A principal one is between bibliographical notes and what are usually called substantive notes. A bibliographical note carries the reference scheme being used in the document, so it would be like this one.[2] A substantive note is the kind that carries some kind of aside or added titbit of information that the author doesn't want to put in the text, where it would slow things up, but

---

[2] W. F. Peachtree, *My Love for the Footnote and Noteworthy Life as a Master Annotator,* Rotherham: Wheatear and Dimley, 1913.

really doesn't want to leave out either, like this one.[3] You'll notice that the substantive example also includes some bibliographical information – they often do – but that doesn't make it a bibliographical note in the strict sense. You will often find an author using both kinds of notes in the same single sequence.

Less common are systems employing two or more types of note at the same time, and one useful application of that is when somebody wants to produce an edition of a distinguished or historically important author's work and needs to comment on the interpretation of the text but also add editorial information and asides. If you want to see a dual system in action, look at the standard Latham and Matthews edition of *The Diary of Samuel Pepys*,[4] where you'll find the textual annotation cued using lower case letters ([a], [b], etc.) and the editors' own comments and added information marked using arabic numbers. Notice that both systems are footnotes and that the notes restart from [1] or [a], as the case may be, on each new page.

Two other things you can see from this example or others like it: first, in professional publishing there is a commonly used convention that unless a particular word is being cued – and sometimes not even then – the note cue follows the punctuation,[5] rather than precedes it[6]. Therefore you can add a little polish to your use of notes by observing this nicety and doing it consistently. The other point concerns a numbering scheme like the one in the Pepys diary example that restarts on each page: if you want to cross-refer to the contents of this kind of note elsewhere in the text then you need to give both the note number and the page number, whereas if you cross-refer to a note in a publication where the note numbers are continuous and only restart at the beginning of each chapter then you need to give the note number and chapter number.

----

[3]   The inventor of the chapter endnote was one Fletcher Clopton Mullet, who in a presentation to the Royal Footnote Society at Harrogate in 1927 used a novel magic lantern animation to show the transformation from foot of page to end of chapter. So radical was the device that three gentlemen in the audience fainted and Mullet was later suspended from the Society for four years. Following his premature death following a pond accident in Maidenhead he was buried upright in the garden of his family home in Stranraer. See Megan Tweed's acclaimed biography *The Life of a Noted Radical*, Builth Wells: Hulbertson Jenkins, 1955.

[4]   R. C. Latham and W. Matthews, eds, *The Diary of Samuel Pepys*, Bell and Hyman, 1970–1983. Unlike the sources in the previous two notes, this one's genuine!

[5]   Like this cue does, following the comma in text.

[6]   Like this cue does, preceding the full stop. You won't normally see this approach used in published work, but authors often create their typescripts in this way.

Is that note really necessary?

A few hundred words ago I asked 'What is a note?' and threatened a definition, but then I put it on hold. Let's put that right with a very general definition that draws on some of the things I've already said:

> A note (in the sense of footnotes or endnotes) is a text item that carries information that the author wants to provide for the reader but deems unsuitable for inclusion in the main text.

So far, so good. It's a general enough definition to apply to both bibliographic and substantive notes, though the material covered by the catch-all term 'information' is of a different kind in each case. But do you really need all those notes? If you are using a note-based referencing scheme – either because you have chosen to or because it's mandatory for your dissertation – then the question of whether to add a note or not actually translates into the question of whether a reference is necessary at that point, and that's something I'll come back to in the next section when I talk about references and bibliographies.

What of substantive notes, though? It's possible for such notes to be informative and fascinating but also, alas, irritating and intrusive. First, let's knock a falsehood on the head, one connected to the discussion in Chapter 6 on the delusion that academic writing must be complicated, abstruse and highly technical and, ideally, completely unintelligible. In the context of notes, this delusion would be expressed something like: 'Because we're doing academic writing we have to put in loads and loads of notes to show we're serious.' No, not at all (and as a reminder of pointless notes see the Jeremy Evets article that I cited in that chapter).

So how do you tell whether a note is needed? There is a common argument against notes, and it goes something like this:

> If the material is worth including then it belongs in the main text, and conversely if it's not suitable to appear in the main text then it's not worth including at all.

In other words, there is no need for notes; and this can be a useful test of others' notes and one's own notes to see if they are worth including. To some people, notes are simply extraneous clutter that gets in the way of the discussion and argument; to others they are a source of fascinating asides, rather like the side-quests on an adventure game where exotic creatures lurk and there is much treasure to be had. To give two contrasting examples of different approaches, I can first cite *The Political Quarterly*, a journal with which I have been associated for many years. There, the presumption is that articles for the journal can be as difficult and challenging as you like but they must be written in plain, jargon-free English and have as few notes as possible: the ideal number is zero, and if authors can't manage that they are allowed up to 12 bibliographical notes. This is quite a demanding requirement, especially for academic authors, but the articles are much better and clearer for it.

To see another and very different approach, one that celebrates notes as a network of intriguing byways off the main highway, have a look at Hans Peter Duerr's *Dreamtime*,[7] an ethnographic study first published in 1978 that uses volume endnotes containing both substantive and bibliographic information, not to mention an extensive bibliography. The main text of the book runs from page 1 to page 133, so is not very long – about the length of a novella. But the endnotes, which are actually in a smaller type so would take up even more space if they were not, run from page 134 to page 370 – that's 236 pages – with the bibliography in the same small type running from page 371 to page 457. It would be absurd to cut this book down to the 133 pages of the core text on the grounds of some kind of aesthetically regulated tidiness.

Before going on to look at references there is one more factor that I want to raise in relation to notes, one that you may feel bearing down on you as you progress through your dissertation and that you may also have encountered in previous coursework. It's to do with the very strong presumption in the academic world that people should cite sources in a complete and accurate way but also provide clear explanations of any detail along the way. Sometimes this can lead to very large numbers of notes, and I'm going to call this tendency *defensive annotation*, as it's really about the author looking over his or her shoulder to keep an eye on potential attacks and criticisms. Once again, it's heavily to do with referencing and rather less about substantive notes so I'll come back to it in the next section, but you may feel it keenly too. For substantive notes, you may be able to use the little argument I mentioned above to help decide whether you need them. But for a defensive approach to bibliographical notes, where we are in effect moving into something that could be called defensive referencing, it's a lot more difficult. There is much more pressure, and it's particularly difficult for you as a student to feel that you can decide this freely: you'll probably go very much in the other direction and say 'If in doubt, add it'. You may even have been told to do this. As I say, I'll come back to this in the next section.

---

[7] Hans Peter Duerr, *Dreamtime: Concerning the Boundary between Wilderness and Civilization*, trans. Felicitas Goodman, Oxford: Basil Blackwell, 1985 (originally published in German in 1978).

References, bibliographies and citation

Now for references themselves. Anybody picking up an academic book or article can see that the systematic citing of sources and the matched listing of references is fundamental to this kind of writing. It's highly unlikely that anybody reading my book now – even those of you who have done relatively little formal academic writing – has not used a reference system in written assignments or other materials in higher education. So why am I reviewing referencing here? Essentially, to look behind the scenes, which may help those who are uneasy about referencing systems and could provide a more solid framework for those of you who have so far seen it as an aspect of mundane rule-following on a par with handing your work in on time. It can be reduced to a system of rules and codified, and you could get through the whole course, dissertation and beyond by following the 'little ref. book', but I think it's better to know what's going on. Then, when something tricky comes up that's not expressly listed in the rules you will know what to do.

I'll mirror the notes section by starting with a question. What is a reference? ('Duh!', you may say, but let's go through the motions.) A first stab at a definition is that a reference in our sense is a device by which you refer to another piece of text – whether by another author or indeed by you – at a particular point in your text. At this point I'm talking about the reference at the start of the process in the sense of the act of referring or of act of acknowledging, and once that's established I can then go on to remind us of how we mark that act and create a trail that anybody else can follow and check if they want. I've also used 'text' in this rough definition when I could have used something more general like 'content', but when I talk about text I mean it to cover anything from elsewhere that you repeat verbatim or draw on in your own text. And here is an immediate distinction between verbatim quoting and a more general use:

> The reference can be general (saying in effect 'hereabouts I drew on the work of another, namely this person . . .') or it can be specific and directly related to a particular piece of text that you have just reproduced directly (saying in effect 'these words are not mine and came from this person . . .').

Both of these are of course commonplaces in academic writing, and a failure to practise them properly can be anything from a little oversight to a major breach of academic protocol that could land you in trouble (and see Chapter 9 for more on that). That danger of a failure to acknowledge is one reason why academic authors opt for long lists of references and notes, and helps to create that nervousness that leads to defensive annotation and referencing. And the preceding rough definition and distinction are a reminder that the first stage of any referencing process is to acknowledge that you are drawing on the work of another, or actually taking their words and putting them into your own academic work – normally, to use a familiar expression, 'for the purposes of criticism or review'. This is a standard element of academic discourse, and entirely proper. It is part of working in a collegiate environment of shared incremental progress.

Let's go to the starting point, then. To put it crudely, phase 1 of all proper referencing is to declare this use of another's work immediately, whenever you do it. And 'another's work' includes your *own* work in another place at another time – universities are becoming much more vigilant about this now. That means if you copy a block of text from another piece of your coursework or research that you did, whether in your present university or another institution, you must treat it exactly the same as if it were written by somebody else entirely. Yes, it's not the same as taking another person's text and pretending that it's yours, or letting it be thought of as yours. There's not an issue of copyright violation here, but the perceived problem is one of reusing the same material and in effect having it marked twice. That's one reason why it's being lumped together with the more obvious vice of plagiarism. The other reason for not 'plagiarizing yourself', as it's come to be known, comes from the sphere of the professional academic: it's to express disapproval of people who take the results of one piece of research and recycle it across different journals to gain unwarranted advantages through citations and promotion prospects.

So once you've completed phase 1 and acknowledged that the text is from elsewhere, we move to phase 2 of the referencing process, which is to say where that other material came from. That's when the whole mechanics of the reference system comes into play. There is also an implied phase 3, which is to do with present access, because the source you used – a website, say – may no longer be available. This is something that's more of an issue with 'digital' sources than it used to be with slower-moving traditional sources, though sometimes you have to point out edition shifts in books. Where there isn't a deliberate presentation of the third phase as distinct, the implication is that the reader can find the material in the same place that you did.

Here's the three-phase breakdown that I've been sketching. I've expressed it in terms of what you're effectively saying about external content that you're using in some way:

1. 'This content is (or draws on) material from elsewhere'
2. 'Here is where I got it'
3. 'And here is where you can get it now (when I last checked)' [not always used].

So we openly identify the external nature of that piece of content by some device or another, and then give the kind of information that will satisfy phase 2. This second element is what most people mean by referencing – the 'chapter and verse' details that will identify that source. And those details are probably what take up most of the space in the referencing rulebooks or guides of the kind you may be required to follow.

How do we show text is from another source? This should be routine by now. Method 1 – suitable for short extracts – is to put it between quotation marks 'like this, if you imagine it's text from another source'. Whether you use "double" or 'single' quotation marks depends on the punctuation style you're employing.

The other method, suitable for longer pieces of text, is to break off the text and set it out separately, which in printed matter can be done by using a shorter measure (line length), extra space before and after the extract, and/or a smaller typeface. There's usually no need to put it in italic too (italic is usually used for emphasis and to identify titles in bibliographies, etc.), nor should you use quotation marks around your piece in addition to setting it out. If your list of rules tells you that you must set out text *and* put it between quotes (which is what I'll call quotation marks for short from now on), then you can just sigh inwardly and follow their rules (the RTFM principle – always do what they tell you to). When you break off text, that separation takes the place of the quotes and serves the same function. There's no need to do both.

So what is the reason for breaking off longer passages of text? It's to help the reader remember that they are reading somebody else's material. If you simply use quotes, then by the time you've read a few lines it would be easy to forget that you have gone past an opening quote and are deep into another author's content rather than yours, but when text is set out then it is always clear.

Incidentally, I've been talking about text as the familiar example of external material, but of course there are other types of content and they need citing too. Other authors' tables and figures (diagrams and other illustrative material) frequently appear in academic texts, and when they do they need to be referenced properly too. It's normal to do this with a separate source line or section under the table or figure notes, or sometimes under the caption (take advice from your supervisor or look at your course rules to see what you're expected to do). Here, unlike in text citation, it's common to cite the full form of the reference and not use a link to a separate reference list. Finally, there are cases where you're not directly copying another's table or figure but you would still acknowledge an external source. One example is where you draw a figure – a graph or a chart, say – using data from another author's table; here you'd say that's what you'd done, and add a reference to that other author's table.

Coding the source

The simplest way to identify the origins of external content is just to give the full details of the source, there and then, at the point of the text where you are using or mentioning it. Let's take an example of how that might work, using the dreaded Jeremy Evets himself. I first separate the cited text from the main body of text, using the conventional device I mentioned above for longer passages to show that it's from elsewhere; this satisfies phase 1. Then I simply add the source (phase 2) immediately afterwards:

> *Let us turn first to an important point: the mere accrual of opinion tokens is not in itself enough to achieve declarative governmental authority acquisition because there may be other representational or quasi-representational units represented in the framework. To see how this might work, consider a case in which there are two representational units. (Jeremy L. B. Evets, 'A Synoptic Outcome Survey of the Quantitative Accrual of Opinion Tokens in Western Democratic Polities',* The Political Quarterly, *vol. 79, no. 4, 2008, p. 605)*

Job done. Nobody's going to assume it's my text[8] because I've set it apart to make it very plain that it isn't part of my own running text, and also I've stated clearly where it's come from. It certainly works as a method. The trouble is, it's not a space- or time-efficient way of working. It could only be manageable in a very simple text – probably not an academic one – that has only a small number of references. In an academic text with a lot of citations it would create a great deal of clutter and take up space.

Which brings us to the commonest way of achieving phase 2 – by using a code that doesn't take up so much space in the text. This will be completely familiar to everybody. There is some kind of code at the appropriate place in the text that refers to the full details elsewhere, either in a note or a separate reference list or bibliography. It is a more

---

[8] Well, in a manner of speaking, though you may have your suspicions about this Evets character.

space-efficient way of incorporating citations in a text, at the added minor inconvenience of requiring the reader to look up the full details in another place rather than have them immediately available at that point. Besides, the reader does not have to stop to consider the reference if they don't want to so the familiar code system is less disruptive than having the whole source dumped in the text at that point.

Reference systems use two types of codes. First, there are the familiar ones using arbitrary sequences of numbers, letters or symbols, such as 8, [1] or [1]. These simply link that point in the text to the bibliographical details, in the same way that a note cue works – and indeed in a system using bibliographical notes that is what you have. The other type of code is more informative and not simply arbitrary, and is the kind that you'll encounter in the Harvard system. Here, the code in the text is something like Mangold 2008b, so as well as leading you to the right reference entry it also gives you immediate information about the author's surname and the date of publication – hence is more informative but also more intrusive, which is something that a procession of Harvard references can be to the point of irritation.

I'm going to spend a little time looking at these two main approaches to referencing to help explain some of the main details and warn about common pitfalls. I'll spend a little time talking about both numbered and Harvard systems as there are so many ways of getting things wrong in each case, though some details and comments apply equally to each. At times I'll also comment on what you need to do to set up your own reference scheme, in those (probably rare) cases where you have a choice about which scheme you use. In most cases, I expect there will be a reference system that you have to use for your dissertation, perhaps a departmentally required one that's been drilled into you from your very first day at university.

One more thing before I look at number-cued systems. I'll stop talking about *the* Harvard system here, and instead always refer to author–date systems or schemes. This is because talking about the Harvard system suggests that there is just one system that has been set in stone since its creation at Harvard and is always used, which is very misleading. In fact, it's just plain wrong. There are hugely many possible variants on an author–date scheme, which is part of the problem, and using this name for it instead of Harvard is a useful reminder of that. Indeed, there are hugely many systems of references full stop, and as well as the basic variants all manner of journals, publishers, academic institutions and learned societies have their own systems or variants too, so if you're required to use something like the MLA or APA schemes there is no alternative but to look up the scheme, learn the details and use it.

Number, letter and symbol based reference schemes

These systems are simple enough in one respect. Just stick the appropriate cue in the text and list the entry somewhere else; but there are complications that it is well to be aware of. If you are required to use one of these systems and have no choice, the two probable points for getting things wrong are in the details of the reference entries for things like italicization, punctuation and the sequence of items, and in what to do with repeated citations.

First, the details. To be complete, reference entries need at least: the name of the author or authors and in collections of editors too; any appropriate titles (such as of a book, or if a journal then the article title and the journal name); details of editions, volumes or issues; publication details (usually a publisher and place, but can sometimes be one or the other); and a publication date. In this kind of referencing, typically using bibliographical notes or a numbered reference list, the date normally comes at the end of the reference item. (This is in contrast to author–date systems where the date has to come after the author name.) Sometimes there may be a page number or page range too. In addition, publication details must now cover not only traditional publication media but also the many different online variants, so it's common to find URLs in a reference and you should thus find a way of managing those. Internet-based sources can be a headache, and URLs do change, so your system must acknowledge that. It's also common to show when you accessed a particular source or site.

Reference entries: the devil's detail

Whether set up by journals, societies, publishers or others, pre-existing reference schemes normally set out forms for the main kinds of source you can expect to come across in academic contexts. Here's a minimum set of examples:

Wade, J. H. and Boggis, F. N., *Potato, Wheat and Rice: Carbohydrates in the Service of Humankind*, Smee and Glaze International, Heckthorpe, 2012. [example of a book]

Termagant, B. F. G., 'All hail rock and roll: the verse forms of Charles E. Berry', *International Journal of Rhythm and Rhyme*, vol. 13, no. 4, 2013, pp. 14–27. [example of a journal article]

Hildebrand, M. D. F., 'The life of O. M. Reilly, 1903–1987', in Velberfast, M. K. and Nasmold, D., *Lots of Lives in London and Lisburn*, Penniforge, Lulworth, 2004, pp. 134–48. [example of a chapter in a book]

To this you could add other standard types of entry, especially for online sources, and to cover things like unpublished theses and conference papers. I'll just stick with these three for now because even this simple set shows the potential for enormous variation. Most of the detail is arbitrary but uses very common forms. The italicization of titles is conventional and widely followed. I'll list a few of the arbitrary and conventional choices exemplified by these three:

- Book titles and journal names in italic, with 'maximum caps' (capital initials on all main words)
- Article and chapter titles roman in quotes, with 'minimum caps' (capital initials on first word and proper nouns only)
- Items within the reference entries separated by commas
- Publisher and place, in that order
- Author initials after surname, and separated by space (i.e. J. H. not J.H.)
- Page ranges elided (i.e. pp. 134–48 not 134–148).

And so on. It is important to be consistent down to this level of detail, as it is not only more likely to follow your department or dissertation manual's requirements but will also look more 'professional'. The same applies to touches like the 'en rule' (that dash thing, obtainable for example by pressing Ctrl-hyphen in MS Word)[9] rather than a hyphen in the page ranges to mimic professionally typeset material such as you can see in books and journals and in the list above.

The use of capitals can vary, and I've included only a common variant. For example, the journal article title could use initial caps on all main words just like the book title. Notice the lower case initial after the colon in the journal article title. This puzzles some people, and it comes up a great deal because academics are forever[10] using the form 'Fancy or clever title: more descriptive subtitle' for their articles to the extent that

---

[9] And depending on how you've configured your word-processor it will automatically replace the hyphen if you key a word, then a space, then a hyphen, another space and another word, because it assumes you want a parenthetical dash so reproduces the ones that appear in 'professional' publishing. But these too can add a touch of polish to your dissertation if you use them consistently for all parenthetical dashes instead of hyphens.

[10] An aside: as distinct from 'for ever'. That is, I'm distinguishing between 'forever' meaning continually (not to be confused with continuously) and 'for ever' meaning for all time. But this is one of those distinctions that is drifting out of use and that many people don't recognize.

it's become an enormous cliché. You don't need a capital initial after the colon because it's all part of the same 'sentence', whereas in the case of the book title and subtitle in the example above you would need a capital initial after the colon even if you were only using minimum initial capitals, so *Potato, wheat and rice: Carbohydrates in the service of humankind*. That's because for book main and subtitles they are effectively separate 'sentences' and would appear on separate lines on the book's title page; the colon is just a device conventionally used to separate the two in reference entries.

Just to show what I mean about attention to detail, I could rework the sample book entry above using different detail style and changing a few things around, such as:

Wade JH and Boggis FN, *Potato, Wheat and Rice: Carbohydrates in the service of humankind*. Heckthorpe: Smee and Glaze International, 2012.

Notice the way the initials now appear – a common approach in science and technology referencing. Also, I've switched the publisher and place around and changed the punctuation slightly. And isn't the capitalization inconsistent in the title and subtitle? Well, it could be, depending on the style requirements, but I'm assuming here that the style is changed to one that uses maximum capitals in the main title and minimum capitals in the subtitle (yes, people do that). This second version is functionally identical to the earlier version and differs only in the detailed style, but if you were to include it in your reference list when the first version was the required form then you'd have introduced an inconsistent entry, and the general appearance created by a lot of such inconsistencies would suggest carelessness or a lack of attention to detail. This is a particular danger when you cut and paste references from one place to another, such as between different pieces of coursework that you've done. It's possible that the different documents followed different referencing styles so take extra care.

The moral? When you set out your references, make sure that you have a whole range of sample styles for each kind of entry you plan to use, and check each reference in turn against the standard forms when you add them and again later when you do your final checks. It's all part of that 'polish' that makes you look really competent and pleases the marker. These are also the kinds of things that get overlooked when you run out of time because you've not planned your dissertation timings and work schedule properly.

Listing and repeating entries

If you are using a numbered referencing scheme such as the 'Vancouver' variety then that requires a list of the references as a functional part of the scheme. For example, you code citations in the text with numbers such as [1], [2], etc., and then list the references by number – 1, 2, etc. – at the back of the article, book or whatever it is.[11] But what if you are using one of the very many schemes using bibliographical notes, where there are note cues in the text that link to footnotes or endnotes that give the full reference details? That's fine as far as it goes, but as well as having the references in the notes, should you also collect them all together and list them in a consolidated bibliography? You may or may not have a choice for your dissertation if you're using such a scheme, but if you do have a choice then I would say yes, do add a bibliography – it's much more reader-friendly. Imagine you are reading a chapter that has 156 bibliographical notes in it. You get to the end and then decide you'd like to follow up the Moretti reference that the author used and look for it through your library. What was it again? Without a consolidated bibliography you have to wade through all the notes until you find it (it was in n. 71, perhaps), whereas with a bibliography you can go straight to it.

Another question concerns repeats. What happens when successive citations have the same source (for example, you've included a series of passages from a single work). I'm sure you know about devices like the abbreviation 'op. cit.' (*opera citato* = in the work [previously or already] cited) and 'loc. cit.' for the place already cited. They mean the very same source, and not a different part of it (in which case you'd have to say something like 'op. cit., p. 63', to show that it was a slightly different part of the same source). Also, be aware that it's a kind of internal cross-referencing, so as part of your final checking make sure that you still have the original citation in there. It's easy to amend an earlier part of your writing and eliminate the first citation, which would leave all of the subsequent 'op. cit.' instances adrift.

A useful general purpose repeating device is 'ibid.', which like 'op. cit.' takes a point after it to show that it's an abbreviation. It is short for *ibidem* and means 'the same' (the same place). Like the others, you must be careful about its meaning. To see what I mean, look at the following sequence, which can be thought of as an extract from a series of footnotes or endnotes:

---

[11] That assumes the numbers are assigned in order of citation in the text. There are variants that list alphabetically, with the numbers given back to the citations from the order of the alpha list.

12 Wade, J. H. and Boggis, F. N., *Potato, Wheat and Rice: Carbohydrates in the Service of Humankind*, Smee and Glaze International, Heckthorpe, 2012, p. 177.

13 Ibid., pp. 189 ff.

14 Ibid.

15 Termagant, B. F. G., 'All hail rock and roll: the verse forms of Charles E. Berry', *International Journal of Rhythm and Rhyme*, vol. 13, no. 4, 2013, pp. 14–27.

16 Ibid.

In note 13, the 'Ibid.' is followed by page numbers, which shows that it's the same work, but a different page range. If the note had just been 'Ibid.' then that would mean it also referred to the same items as the previous note, namely p. 177. In case you're wondering, the 'ff' (sometimes presented as ff.) means 'and following pages' – one 'f' would have meant 'and the following single page'. That also means that 'pp.' (meaning pages, whereas 'p.' means just page) is correctly used – p. 189 ff and p. 14–27 would both be incorrect. The 'Ibid.' of note 14 then refers to exactly the same page range given in note 13, because it is an unqualified 'the same'. And note 16? Does that mean 'the same place' as note 14 too? No, it doesn't. After note 14 the source changed to the one presented in note 15, so that's the one referred to, with the same page range, in note 16. And so on. It's all fairly straightforward but you need to watch the detail and keep it all under control, and to be especially careful when you cut, add or rearrange the order of notes. You can see how this would create more than merely cosmetic problems. You could even end up with incorrect references and get into trouble.

There's another useful device I should mention before I leave this subsection, one that is used commonly with bibliographical notes in the arts and humanities. It's called the short title system, and is used to avoid spelling out long references in full every time they need to be repeated in an article, chapter, or other document such as your dissertation. With this system, you devise a short version of any source that you repeat in a chapter and then use that shortened form at subsequent repeats. (You would make a note of your shortened version to make sure you always use the same form.) You can also use it with 'ibid.' and other devices, so to show what I mean here's another simulated sequence of notes:

12 Wade, J. H. and Boggis, F. N., *Potato, Wheat and Rice: Carbohydrates in the Service of Humankind*, Smee and Glaze International, Heckthorpe, 2012, p. 177.

13 Ibid., pp. 189 ff.

14 Termagant, B. F. G., 'All hail rock and roll: the verse forms of Charles E. Berry', *International Journal of Rhythm and Rhyme*, vol. 13, no. 4, 2013, pp. 14–27.

15 Ibid.

16 Wade and Boggis, *Potato, Wheat and Rice*, p. 188.

17 Ibid., pp. 191 f.

18 Termagant, 'All hail rock and roll', p. 15.

19 Ibid.

I hope you can see how this works. The 'Ibid.' of note 15 refers to the precise source of note 14, but note 16 switches the source back to the Wade and Boggis book, which it does by using a recognizable short title that you devised – one that you'd use consistently for all subsequent citations in the chapter. Note 17 refers to that too, and then 18 switches back to the Termagant article, again by using a short title. Note 19 refers to precisely the source in 18 (page 15 of Termagant) and so it continues. It's much tidier than using full references. Some nervous people put 'op. cit.' or 'ibid.' after their short titles but there really is no need. It's perfectly obvious that it is a short title, and the implication is that you'll find the full form earlier in the chapter or piece. Or you can find it in the consolidated bibliography, which is another very good reason to have one. The same caveats apply as with 'ibid.' and so on – just make sure that this cross-referencing all works when you come to do your final checks, and be careful when changing your notes around.

Author–date reference systems

Now for a system of referencing that is in widespread use across the humanities and social sciences and beyond. If you remember, I am using the term 'author–date' instead of 'Harvard', but fear not: if your dissertation or project demands that you use Harvard referencing, this is the section of the chapter that covers the system you're interested in. It's just that I want to emphasize that we're dealing with a broad family of systems with hugely many variants, not just one fixed scheme, so part of what I'll do in this section is to remind you of where that variety comes so that you can avoid pitfalls and inconsistencies.

Many of the aspects of reference lists that I mentioned in the previous section apply equally to author–date schemes. As there, you would hope to have a list of the common source types – book, journal article and so on – for you to follow. I can even use the same examples, with one key change:

Wade, J. H. and Boggis, F. N. (2012), *Potato, Wheat and Rice: Carbohydrates in the Service of Humankind*, Smee and Glaze International, Heckthorpe. [example of a book]

Termagant, B. F. G. (2013), 'All hail rock and roll: the verse forms of Charles E. Berry', *International Journal of Rhythm and Rhyme*, vol. 13, no. 4, pp. 14–27. [example of a journal article]

Hildebrand, M. D. F. (2004), 'The life of O. M. Reilly, 1903–1987', in Velberfast, M. K. and Nasmold, D., *Lots of Lives in London and Lisburn*, Penniforge, Lulworth, 2004, pp. 134–48. [example of a chapter in a book]

The change, of course, is that the date has moved to the front of the reference, after the author names, because it's part of the code and is used for the reference look-up whenever the reader finds an author–date code in the text. That means that the date does not need to be at the end of the reference item too, where it would be redundant. There may be some special reason (other editions or translations, for example) for putting other dates in the reference, but they'd almost certainly be different to the date at the front, which to repeat an important point must be there because it is part of the look-up code.

As with other reference schemes, there is any amount of scope for changing the punctuation, capitalization and so on of the reference entries themselves. For example, here's Termagant in a different author–date form:

Termagant, BFG, 2013, All hail rock and roll: the verse forms of Charles E. Berry, *International Journal of Rhythm and Rhyme*, 13 (4): 14–27.

Notice that the parentheses have dropped off the date, the quotes have disappeared from the article title, and the journal volume and issue details have been rendered differently. All variants (except for the date form of course) could have been done this way for the footnoted version in the previous section too. So author–date reference details themselves offer as much scope for variation as any other type of reference, and you need to watch that detail whether you're following a prescribed scheme or inventing your own.

There are some other things to watch, though, and the ones I'll examine here include reference ambiguity and variations in the form of citation.

Creating an unambiguous author–date citation

When you come across a reference code like White 2010 in a text you need to be able to find that reference without any ambiguity. That code should take you straight there. Or, to put it another way, the author–date code should refer to one, and only one, entry in the reference list.

But carelessness or bad organization can create ambiguity or make the process longer than it should be. The first issue is a relatively trivial one, and it is that you should not divide up your reference list using categories such as 'books', 'journal articles', 'websites' and the like under the mistaken impression that this helps the reader. It doesn't, because the reader may have to read through three or four of these sublists before finding the right reference for White 2010. When encountering a citation for the first time the reader probably doesn't know whether it's an article, book or something online, etc. Therefore, *always arrange your references in one undifferentiated alphabetical list* so that the reader can go straight to White 2010 – between White 2009 and Wibbleford 2004.

What's that? Your dissertation rules say that you must divide up your reference list by category? Well, as usual sigh inwardly and do what they say, but perhaps campaign for change at the same time. Subdivided author–date reference lists are not reader-friendly and slow up the reference-finding process.

A more problematic form of ambiguity – and a common one – arises when an author produces more than one work in the same year. In the case of our White, if she had an article and a book published in 2010 then they are both entitled to be listed as White 2010, and hence that code in the text would be ambiguous and fail. You must make sure that there are none of these ambiguities. In case you don't know how to handle them, here's an example. Imagine that Dr Billy Gruff of Mimsborough University produces several works during a busy and typically interdisciplinary 2012, from which you select three examples:

Gruff, B. G. (2012), 'Cheese fondue in Imperial Rome: an analysis of recipes implicated in poisoning', *Proceedings of the Danish Fondue Society*, 23 (3): 210–22.

Gruff, B. G. (2012), *Boiler Design for Gas-fired Peak Power Stations above the Arctic Circle*, Fleischmann, Billericay.

Gruff, B. G. (2012), 'Through a dark mesh: tatting as a preferred method of dreamcatcher manufacture among the Hnung', *International Weirdness Journal B*, 142, 1: 23–9.

This naturally creates three instances of Gruff 2012, which is unacceptable because the instances are not unambiguous and hence must not be used as a code for text citation. What should you do? First, you need to fix the order of these three items in the reference list, based on some principle or other. It's tempting to look for temporal sequence but you only have the given dates, and they're just a reflection of the accidents of the publishing process – you don't know which was written first or published first. It's safer to go for alphabetical order by title, which is the first part of each item to appear after the author and date, and the first part that varies. That would put the boiler book first, then the cheese article, then the dreamcatcher piece. After that, we need to identify each item uniquely and, as I'm sure you know, the conventional way is to use a letter after the date. Hence, in the reference list the reordered Gruff entries would appear as follows:

Gruff, B. G. (2012a), *Boiler Design for Gas-fired Peak Power Stations above the Arctic Circle*, Fleischmann, Billericay.

Gruff, B. G. (2012b), 'Cheese fondue in Imperial Rome: an analysis of recipes implicated in poisoning', *Proceedings of the Danish Fondue Society*, 23 (3): 210–22.

Gruff, B. G. (2012c), 'Through a dark mesh: tatting as a preferred method of dreamcatcher manufacture among the Hnung', *International Weirdness Journal B*, 142, 1: 23–9.

And that's the problem solved. In the text, the matching citations have to be to Gruff 2012a or 2012b or 2012c, not just 2012, and hence are completely unambiguous.

This is all straightforward when you have included all the different sources from the start and can produce the right text citations to match, but errors can creep in when you add references during the course of your dissertation. Imagine that in the first three months of your dissertation work you had only one Gruff source in your draft bibliography – the cheese one, say. As you start to create your text, perhaps including an early version of your lit review, you will refer to Gruff 2012 because that's all there is. But then you decide to add another Gruff reference because you've just read his majestic study of dreamcatcher manufacture among the Hnung and were bowled over by it. It genuinely enhances your own theoretical musings – somehow. Now you have two Gruff 2012s, so first you need to arrange them in the list and recode them in the way I suggested earlier, and hence create Gruff 2012a (cheese) and Gruff 2012b (dreamcatchers). You'll add references to the dreamcatcher source to the text as 2012b, but before you do that I strongly recommend that you go through and change all the existing instances of 2012 (cheese, first draft) to 2012a (cheese, new version). Then you can add the new 2012b references to the text. Whichever way you approach it, do it methodically, perhaps using search and replace if you're careful to avoid altering other things too. That way you don't have any stray unqualified references lingering in the text.

Then of course you decide to add references to Gruff's boiler design book, which adds another complication because with all three in place they need a further reordering as a (boiler), b (cheese) and c (dream-catcher). All the existing references in the text need changing again. As before, do it methodically. Before you add any text references to the boiler text, rename the existing codes using search and replace: first, replace all Gruff 2012b by Gruff 2012c, which gets rid of the 2012bs, then replace all Gruff 2012a by Gruff 2012b, which gets rid of the 2012as. At last you can safely add Gruff 2012a to refer to the boiler book.

The only other likely source of ambiguity you will encounter is when two or more authors share the same name. Thus, if you want to cite 2010 studies by both T. Bungay and H. Bungay – who coincidentally wrote in your field in the same year, and it does happen – then you'd need to introduce an initial into your author–date code, and distinguish T. Bungay 2010 from H. Bungay 2010.

I included the Gruff example because such changes are a frequent source of errors in reference lists, along with authors cutting and pasting references between different documents or from their stock files of references. Nowadays you can also include authors importing reference entries from reference management software, of which perhaps the best known is EndNote.[12] Do check your reference list carefully for both stylistic correctness but also accuracy – does each citation in the text correspond *unambiguously* with the right entry in the reference list? It's worth mentioning that over decades of editing many hundreds of academic texts I never once encountered a reference system that was free of errors.

Varieties and subtleties of author–date citations

At first sight, the text mention of an author–date code is simplicity itself – just the author's or authors' surnames plus the date of publication, perhaps with a letter to distinguish different publications in the same year. But commas, semi-colons and parentheses, plus positioning variations, can alter things greatly. Some of this is style variation, so you need to be aware of the required style of text citation (or create one), but other

---

[12] This kind of software stores your references and can output them into your documents in preset styles. The more elaborate versions are more powerful and can perform other functions, like gathering blocks of references from online sources and importing them. Whether you need something like this or would find it useful depends partly on the number of references you plan to use in your dissertation and perhaps in other coursework or later academic studies. You should be able to get EndNote at an academic discount and there is also a Web version. Or you can use one of the low-cost alternatives in 'lite', shareware or freeware forms. It's up to you.

changes can alter the implied meaning of what you're doing. Here, then, is a review of some of those variations. It should help you to say what you want to say, rather than unwittingly say something unintended.

First, some of the simpler variations. Look at these three sets of alternatives for author–date citations that might appear in a text.

- Johnson 1985 *or* Johnson, 1985?
- Wade 2000a, Wade 2000b *or* Wade 2000a, 2000b *or* Wade 2000a,b?
- Hintikka 2010, Stamp 2001 *or* Hintikka, 2010; Stamp, 2001 *or* Stamp, 2001; Hintikka, 2010?

The first example is an easy one: do you use a comma between the author and date or not? If I have a choice I don't, because it doesn't do any useful work and the code works perfectly well without it. Besides, the comma can appear to interfere with the sentence punctuation, or at least can look odd.

The second example shows three different ways to show a pair of a and b variants for the same author – full form, or with single name but full dates, or with just the a and b repeated. Clearly, the last version takes up the least space, though it's easier to miss that it includes two citations and not just one if you're reading in a hurry. These are minor stylistic choices and like all such choices are at base completely arbitrary. The style guide you're working from may or may not go to this level of detail, but if it doesn't you are free to choose a style for yourself. As with all such minor variations, your care and consistency will help to create a polished look for your dissertation.

In the third example I'm displaying two sets of variations. One variation concerns the punctuation between different authors' works. In the first case I can use a comma between the Hintikka and Stamp citations because I'm not already using a comma between the author and the date. In the second case I am using the comma, so I really need to use something stronger to separate the different authors' works and the semi-colon is a natural choice. So what's the third case exemplifying? It simply shows the two citations in a different order – Stamp before Hintikka – and thus contrasts with the second case. Perhaps you can see or already know the principle here. It's to do with how you order a sequence of citations in the text. In this example, Hintikka 2010 before Stamp 2001 orders them alphabetically by surname, whereas putting

Stamp 2001 before Hintikka 2010 orders them by date. As with the other details, either follow the prescribed sequence or decide on your own and stick to it. Some authors may want to order the citations in order of their significance to the discussion at that place, but this is not likely to be evident to the reader so it's not a system I can recommend. If you want to do that the best way is to cite the main reference, then use something like 'see also' to introduce your less significant sources.

While I'm talking about sequencing citations I should remind you about the dangers of overdoing this, which connects with what I was saying in Chapter 6 about the 'excess' view of academic writing as exemplified by Jeremy Evets's approach. It does not make your work more 'academic' to string together vast arrays of author–date citations at every opportunity. Beware the temptations of using the author–date system as the basis of some kind of credibility code, as if to say 'Wow. Look at all this stuff I have read. I must be really clever.' The kind of defensive annotation and referencing that I've already mentioned in cautionary tones looks so much worse when it's expressed through an author–date system.

Parentheses and position

You may be wondering about parentheses, which I haven't mentioned so far. When you look at academic writing that incorporates author–date referencing it is full of parentheses, so what is their function? I'll mention two main ones: first, they are used to mark a parenthesis (surprise!) to separate out the citations from the rest of the sentence; second, they are used to distinguish the work itself from the author *in* that work. I should say that authors often misuse parentheses or spray them about unnecessarily. As usual, if your rules require a system that has some particular approach to parentheses then you have to follow it, but otherwise I'll present the two cases and you can work with those. First, straightforward parenthetical usage:

> Several researchers in the early 1990s investigated the colour perception of dolphins (Mumford 1990, Mumford and Bellpot 1992, Hailstorm 1993, Fludger and Klamb 1994).

The parentheses here simply list the citations – in this case styled with minimal punctuation and in date order – in the context of the discussion. The list in the parenthesis is saying 'Here they are [or Here are some / the main examples] and you can look them up if you want to'.

To see the other, more subtle and varied uses of parentheses compare these examples:

1. Halverley (2001, 2007) discovered that fizzy drinks significantly increased the libido of persons aged between 29 and 37 who were immersed in pools of 10% calcium phosphate solution.
2. Halverley discovered (2001, 2007) that fizzy drinks significantly increased the libido of persons aged between 29 and 37 who were immersed in pools of 10% calcium phosphate solution.
3. Mope and Draxo (Mope, 2009; Draxo, 2010; Mope and Draxo, 2011) re-examined Halverley's findings (Halverley, 2001, 2007) in the light of several subsequent studies collected in Speenhamland, 2008.
4. Deirdre Ponderous has argued (Ponderous 2005) that Shakespeare was probably a Bulgarian farmer who never set foot in Stratford.
5. This work disagrees with the view of Deirdre Ponderous that Shakespeare was a Bulgarian pig farmer (Ponderous 2005).

They're all quite similar, and in the case of 1 and 2 virtually identical, but the different arrangements of parentheses around and position of author–date citations can create, or imply, subtle shifts of meaning.

Take examples 1 and 2. You could read them to mean the same thing: Halverley has made a discovery and you can read about it in Halverley 2001 and Halverley 2007. That's fine, but the shift of the dates to follow the verb 'discovered' in the second instance could imply a closer link between the discovery and the dates than is implied in example 1, where you know you can read about it in those two works but there's no link between the discovery and those works. They could, for example, be general surveys in which he reviews, among other things, work on libido and calcium sulphate including the one mentioned – which could have been conducted in 1974 for all we know. It's not a strong link in each case, but more of a suggestion.

In case 3 there are two parenthetical uses of author–date sources for Mope and Draxo and Halverley's findings (where the position of the citations implies they are reports of findings and more closely links them to the dates). In this example I've used commas and semi-colons, notice. But my main reason was to contrast their treatment with that of Speenhamland at the end, which has no parentheses. Why? Because the reference is to the source itself – the book or whatever it is – not as in the others in this sentence to the author(s) as represented in or by those sources. That's a major distinction and one that people do get wrong: if that sentence were to finish 'in the light of several subsequent studies collected in (Speenhamland 2008)' the parentheses would be unnecessary and also strictly incorrect. If you're not convinced by the other subtleties I'm mentioning for these five examples then at least remember this one associated with parentheses, as exemplified by these two different endings:

'. . . in the light of several subsequent studies collected in Speenhamland 2008.' [an example of reference to the work]

'. . . in the light of several subsequent studies collected by Speenhamland (2008).' [an example of reference to the author in that work, or at least as reported in it]

So what of sentences 4 and 5, with Deirdre and her Bulgarian bard? Well, it's back to my subtlety claims again. In sentence 4 the author is saying pretty directly that DP argues this in her 2005 work. But in sentence 5 the author is not saying that so clearly, because the citation has been moved to the end of the sentence away from the main verb; here, an interpretation could be that the author is alluding to something that Deirdre has argued all her academic life, but if we want to find out about it the 2005 work is a good place. In sentence 4 we only know for sure that she expressed this view in the 2005 publication; she may not have held the view before that, and perhaps now has evidence that Shakespeare was an extra-terrestrial (the Globe Theatre was actually a torus, a precursor of the LHC, and so on). So do you see my point? No? Not to worry. I think the moral of this is that you should check the position of your author–date citations for any unwonted implications. In most cases this won't happen, but just occasionally a citation position will carry an implication that you didn't intend.

One final thing: if you are using a system of bibliographical footnotes then you should not combine that with an author–date referencing system. It's fine for author–date citations to appear in substantive footnotes, but to use them in bibliographical ones would create a double look-up whenever the reader wants to discover the reference – first they need to look up the note, then they have to look up the reference from the author–date code they find there.

Producing your own reference system

Perhaps your department or your course manual does not specify any reference system for your dissertation or project work. This would be unusual, and you can see from the rest of this chapter that having the details tied down can save you a lot of worries, but if you do have the freedom to choose you should take time to think about the options. Your decision process would look something like this:

1. Choose an overall scheme (e.g. note based, author–date, etc.)

    ▪ Look at other work in your field, such as journal articles and books, to see whether there's a predominant or favoured system

    ▪ There are hugely many systems, some of them strongly preferred in various disciplines, and some fields make a particular system all but mandatory

    ▪ If you use EndNote you have many schemes built in and can add more

    ▪ Remember that all systems are arbitrary – somebody made them up.

2. Write down examples for each of the key categories of item – books, articles, chapters, unpublished materials, online materials, etc.

3. Sort out all of the other detail for both text citations and reference entries and write down what you decide so that you can refer back to it.

    ▪ Even for the text citation component, author–date schemes offer enormous scope for variation (see the previous section of this chapter).

    ▪ For footnote and similar number-based systems the possible citation variations are fewer but are still there – e.g. [2], [2], or ^{2}, etc. Also, there's variety in positioning next to punctuation, so this^2, or this,^{2} – with the latter usually preferred in most styles.

4. Be consistent: once you have chosen a detailed style for your reference system, stick to it throughout.

    ▪ That means using the same style of text citation everywhere, and applying the same style to every item in a reference list.

When you are deciding on a system you may find it's easier to pick an 'off the peg' scheme than to make up your own from scratch because there are so many things to remember and so many details to pin down.

Some further reminders

Make sure that you clearly sort out your treatment of online materials so that you know how to incorporate them in your reference lists. This usually means including what is generally known as the URL and probably also the date when you accessed it.

There are two common problems with URLs and other website identifiers. One is that they go out of date or change – possibly with each time you access them, depending on which way you reached them – and the other is that the URL string can be very long, especially when you are accessing web content that has been generated dynamically. These strings, which you can pick up from the URL window at the top of your web browser, could take up several lines and appear to be full of random characters and gibberish.

As far as the transience of web content is concerned, your access date information and the other standard reference details (such as author, title, etc.) that you provide will give your reader a fighting chance of searching for the content in future if it disappears from the original place.

For those long and unwieldy URLs there are two main approaches. One is just to give the details for the main elements of the site via the top levels of the domain name and leave out the rest – the reader can then search for the content within that domain using the other reference details you have provided. So, for example, imagine the actual details when you accessed the item were:

http://www.frabbledash.org.uk/articles/#pr=asdfjubhdsfjb=sdfjonasdf niuncvuind&asdcjkn&asdincionreind=sdfin&&=efsjubnsdfjbne

When you came to include the details in your reference list you'd simply give the standard details and perhaps only this much of the URL:

http://www.frabbledash.org.uk/articles/

The other main way to avoid overlong URLs is via some kind of aliasing or redirection systems, of which TinyURL is one of the best known. You simply enter your enormous and unwieldy URL at their website (TinyURL.com if that's your choice) and you will receive a short and neat alternative that you can include in your reference list and that it is claimed will never go out of date. It's a good idea to talk to your supervisor about this and other aspects of internet sources in your referencing.

And lastly, what's the correct term to use for your reference list – References, Bibliography, Select Bibliography . . .? As with other details this may be specified in your handbook or by your department, but if not then one way to choose is to use 'References' as the heading for a single list of all of the references cited in an author–date scheme. 'Bibliography' is often used to head a list of sources that is more extensive than that, or not simply tied to the references cited in the piece, though on the other hand these terms are not always used systematically. 'Consolidated bibliography' could be used for a collation of all of the sources appearing in a note-based referencing scheme, though you could equally call that 'Bibliography'. You are unlikely to have elements like 'Further Reading' or discursive bibliographies where you talk about the entries as well as just list them. I would choose something simple, and if in doubt or there is nothing specified in the small print of your dissertation manual, then a quick word with your supervisor should help to sort it all out.

8 When things go wrong

The original title for this chapter was slightly longer: 'When things go wrong – and they will'. It reflects the very high likelihood that over a period of several months, perhaps more than a year, that complex project involving you and your interplay with libraries, experiments, interviews, various other people, theories, methods, ideas and so on will hit some kind of problems. I hope that any problems that arise will be small ones, and that earlier parts of this book have helped to anticipate and prevent many problems, and put contingencies in place. I'll come back to some of that at times in this chapter, but here I've used a slightly different emphasis, one that tries to respond to somebody who says 'Yes, we know all that, and we should have taken precautions [or we did and they didn't work] , but now we have this problem. So what do we do about it?' As far as I can I'll deal directly with that question, though I will have to refer back to preventative methods. You'll probably be reading this before you start your dissertation, so these observations and comments may still prove useful. They're certainly not meant in an 'I told you so' spirit, and the most I would say in that direction is better represented along the lines of the old joke:

Lost person in car: 'I say, rustic person. Could you tell me the way to Frothton from here, please?'

Stereotypical rustic leaning over gate: 'Arrr, I can. But if I was you I wouldn't have started from here.'

I thought the best way of organizing this chapter was simply to list the various kinds of problems, and then discuss tactics or even strategy for dealing with them. They are fairly generic problems, but I hope that if you have one that's not dealt with here, one of the others will be similar enough to suggest a solution. I've also collected them into four groups: problems stemming from you and your circumstances; problems associated with other people's contributions; problems from technology and other resources; and finally problems lurking in the research or dissertation itself. Naturally, these kinds of problems can overlap.

Other people

'I don't like my supervisor'

I have said more than once in this book that your supervisor is a vital resource, the more so because you are running on very limited resources (just you, most of the time) so you need all the help you can get. And you may have never done any kind of dissertation or major project before. So what happens if you don't get on? Do you feel that they're not quite right for your subject area? Though it's likely there will have to be compromises because there will never be enough staff to provide a perfect match for all the different interests and research areas that students follow. Maybe it started out all right, but you don't like what the supervisor asks you to do, or their responses to your problems or queries, or how they work with you at meetings. Or is it more personal than that? Do you simply not like them, even though they were allocated as the best person for your topic? Is there a carry-over from some other aspect of your course – they gave you a low mark a couple of years ago and you thought it was undeserved, or you don't like their lectures or something? Or there's a strange smell in their office (what – drains, weed, farts . . .?).

This dislike or unease can affect your work, with some people more sensitive to such things than others. What can you do, then? First, you need to make sure you're not just being thin-skinned or blinded by vanity (maybe that 43% essay 18 months ago wasn't that brilliant when you come to think about it), or generally less robust than you could be. People in all workplaces need to be able to get on with others they don't like or find difficult; it's part of the real world. Can't you 'move on', to use the familiar soap opera homily? ('Lighten up, Louanne. Maybe he did run over your legs in his pick-up and now you can't walk. And the explosion in the illegal distillery he built in your kitchen did burn your house down and it destroyed your priceless art collection, not to mention your pets. And, yes, he killed your brothers and sisters when he was fooling around with the guns he uses for drug dealing . . . But, hey, it's time to *move on.* You know you two are made for each other.')

No? But consider that possibility first: reflect on what you're trying to achieve with your dissertation studies, and don't immediately go into 'OMG. I've paid all that money and they're going to ruin it for me.' By the time you are a dissertation student you should be an independent, self-directed learner and researcher: your supervisor has a supporting function but is not the one and only thing standing between you and a great dissertation. After all, if you get a great mark you'll want to take the credit, so if you get a poor one be prepared to shoulder the responsibility. Try not to divert the very real pressures and tensions of independent study in the final part of a degree course into some external object or person. Don't look for people to blame when the going gets difficult, or where there are problems. That is a background factor that applies to many of the problems that I'm listing in this chapter. At the risk of sounding jargonish and being consigned to pseud's corner:

> Don't externalize or offload the problems or normal stresses of dissertation or research work into external equipment, processes, events or people. If something's not working then it's probably related to what you're doing and you need to look at it coolly and sort it out.

All right. You've looked at that option and there's still a problem. What do you do about it? One obvious solution is to change your supervisor, and how feasible that is depends on your university's systems and the availability of another person with the same specialism or equivalent expertise. In today's student-focused colleges and universities it will be easier than it used to be in more authoritarian days to change supervisor, and there may even be explicit procedures in your course regulations or documents. Perhaps there is a deadline for doing it, but even if there isn't it will be wise to apply to change early in the process rather than later – which in turn means that you should have your first supervisor visit as soon as you can. If you're not going to get on with each other then it would be good to find out early. It should be evident here that somebody who doesn't get around to meeting their supervisor for the first two months of the dissertation period may find it harder to gain sympathy if they do find they want a change later.

What happens if you can't change? Maybe Dr Caligari is the only suitable person for your topic in the whole university, let alone your department. In exceptional cases it may be possible to look to another university, but this would be a rare option for a Masters and highly unlikely for a first degree. So let's assume you're stuck with Dr Caligari (weird office, smells, leers, prone to sudden outbursts). Is there nothing you can do? My suggestion would be to approach another member of staff, either via the course leader or through your personal tutor, to ask for a second person to work with. The second person can be there for your everyday and general dissertation support, but you still go to see Dr Caligari for the technical stuff. You may not even have to make this a formal arrangement if your tutor or course leader is willing for you to visit them in that role. It depends on the system that operates in your college. It's probable that Dr Caligari would need to know about the other channel, especially if you choose a formal arrangement, but again you can talk that over with your favourite staff contacts to see how it will all work out.

Another remedy is to change your topic (see below) away from Dr Caligari's area, but I'll ring alarm bells here. If you do this you must be careful that you're not cutting off your nose to spite your face. If you find yourself saying 'I would love to have stayed with my old topic and I'm only doing this to get away from Caligari' then you risk being seriously demotivated. Doing a topic you don't really like will cause you far more problems than the occasional visit to the wild and smelly Doctor. Or, to change the metaphor, changing the topic just to dump the supervisor is a case of the tail wagging the dog; you are making the choice from the wrong side. You should only consider the topic-change remedy for supervisor problems if the new topic is at least as stimulating, interesting and researchable for you as the original one.

Here's a summary list of possibilities if you have some kind of supervisor clash.

- Reflect on whether your current dissertation problems really are to do with your supervisor.
- Apply for a change of supervisor (and do it early).
- Change your topic to a different area (risky!).
- Talk about the problems with your supervisor and perhaps change the way you work together (yes, not easy – but some students may be able to do this).
- Apply for or arrange a second supervisor or tutor, visiting the problem supervisor only for technical aspects of your work.
- Use and visit other staff – tutors, support staff, etc. – informally to provide support, again only using the supervisor for technical aspects.

The one thing you should never do is hide or stay away from a supervisor you don't like and not meet at all. That means no supervision, which puts you at a serious disadvantage and possibly in breach of your course requirements (RTFM). Although it may make you feel better while it's happening – and is an example of the venerable and important survival tactic 'Run away!' – it simply replaces a potentially soluble problem with another one, no supervision, that could result in a low or even a fail mark.

'They said they would do it, but they let me down'

It's not uncommon for arrangements with other people to go wrong for one reason or another. This may leave you without some crucial source of data or access to a facility or person. Here are some variations on the theme to show what I mean:

'These firms all said they would send me samples but only one did.'

'I sent out 100 questionnaires as agreed but I've only got six back.'

'For my case studies I'm going to interview Angelina Jolie, Wayne Rooney and Vladimir Putin . . .'

'I arranged interviews with Ned Curtin and Eliza Warmback but they've both pulled out.'

'My Ned Curtin and Eliza Warmback interviews are crucial but they can only do them two weeks before I have to hand it in.'

'They were friendly enough at the beginning but now they won't let me have the transcripts because of some confidentiality problem.'

'Cyril said he could get me a day on the Large Hadron Collider but it didn't happen.'

'The health authority has changed their mind and now they say I can't have access to that group of people.'

'I was all set to examine her letters after my talk with the archivist, but now her family has been in touch and said they won't let students access the archive.'

'They have never answered my emails and phone calls and I'm desperate to talk to them.'

'They were very chatty at first, but now they don't answer my emails and phone calls and I'm desperate to talk to them.'

In other words, the actions and decisions of other people in cooperating or not cooperating with your studies can have a profound effect on your dissertation. Some of these issues are to do with having unrealistic expectations of the access you will gain to busy people or expensive facilities (even ones that are far less exotic and expensive than the LHC). Perhaps most problems arise when people say they will do something but then don't – they either go quiet and you can't reach them, or they plead some change of circumstances or claim to be too busy. These are perhaps the most troublesome kind because your first encounters with them will have encouraged you to build them into your plans: they looked reliable.[1] They cause particular trouble because the problem typically emerges some way in to your studies and you may have built the dissertation around them. Change at this stage can be very disruptive and stressful; you may feel that it has undermined your work and you can begin to feel disheartened.

What are the lessons to be learnt from these examples, apart from the obvious one of not believing anything Cyril tells you? Any that involve early failures to make contact with somebody should suggest that they are not a promising line of investigation for you, so you should change your focus to other people while there is still plenty of time. Also, the ridiculously implausible plans to interview unreachable celebrities or to seek access to international research facilities are things you will discount early on or never entertain, or that your supervisor will discourage – unless you have some really special connections.

Your supervisor and other staff and department will have contacts, connections and goodwill that you may be able to plug into, but when you are contacting the world beyond that, as you may well be doing if you're doing new research, you must expect to find that busy people have very limited time for you. Look at it from their side: if you're working in a stressful and busy environment in which there is never enough time to finish everything, requests from students come a long way down the priority list, and may even not register. Or they'll be filtered out by somebody else in that person's organization or entourage. Emails in particular go out of date very quickly. Most of us receive a large number every day, so if something isn't answered in a day or two it's likely that it has scrolled down the inbox and will be forgotten.

I also added that example of only six replying to your questionnaire, which you may have posted, emailed or set up online using SurveyMonkey or something similar. It's slightly different in that the lack of response is to do with inertia and lack of interest across many people rather than in individuals, but once again it's something that you should *expect*. That means you have to build in what you will do if you get a poor response – though in many cases low response rates are standard. Or you may be able to set up something that ensures a much better response.

---

[1] Take care to distinguish genuinely positive responses from those that are half-hearted or just fobbing you off. If somebody engages you in an exchange and sounds interested, that's good; but if what they're saying is effectively 'Yeah, whatever', then perhaps you should exclude them from your plans at the outset.

This brings us back to the troublesome category of people who promised much but delivered little. In some ways, this is not entirely avoidable because there may well be key people who are important to the course of your dissertation or project. Take the archive example in my list: if your dissertation is about Imelda Pratt-Bingley's 1930s correspondence with Tiffy Bumple and they won't let you look at her archive then you've probably had it for that topic. The timescale of student dissertations won't allow you to track down alternative routes to any surviving letters, and we know that Tiffy didn't keep his side of the correspondence because all was lost when his Tiger Moth plunged into the Adriatic in 1936. (He was trying an Immelmann turn for the first time, but the rudder pedal jammed on the box of her letters that he kept underneath it. So poignant!) What can you do?

One possible first step, and only then with care and in a minority of cases, is to make some kind of plea or appeal. Perhaps you would consider it for Imelda's archive. But this is best done with your supervisor's help, and you should take their advice as to whether this is worthwhile and likely to make things better. If it risks making things worse, then don't do it at all, and – yes – *move on*.

Much more likely is that nothing can be done to recover the lost person's input, whether they were potential sources of access, data or interviews. If that avenue has failed then you must devote your time and energy to looking at the alternatives. One thing you should never do is write some kind of complaining email or letter, whether it's outraged and abusive or of the pompous and sniffy 'I am disappointed' variety. Let it go. You may be enraged and feeling betrayed, but nothing of value will come from a riposte to a person who may even have forgotten about you; instead it may make you look foolish or 'studenty'. You'll probably feel that too, after the initial glow of satisfaction at making your feelings heard. There may be an issue of goodwill or your department's reputation here too. Although a dissertation is a very self-directed piece of study, and it may feel like a very personal affront when somebody lets you down, you are working as part of the wider research environment. If your outburst wrecks future cooperation between your department and an important individual or organization, then you may do a lot of harm.

This leaves you only one serious option, which is to do something else instead. Except in the most dramatic cases, where a crucial failure comes late and there is no time for an alternative, this is much less of a problem than it sounds. And the reason is that you simply must build in alternatives when you plan your research, so-called contingency planning (Chapter

2). During your planning, you must always ask of each stage, input and person associated with your project 'What do I do if that doesn't happen?' and produce an answer. That is your plan B. It is part of establishing the feasibility for the whole research enterprise. In the case of Imelda's archive, the access issue is one that you would have hoped to sort out in the period before your dissertation starts, so that if it goes wrong you think up a new topic: disappointing, but a sensible course of action.

Hence you should consider alternative means of access to facilities or equipment, and a much larger pool of key people and other unpredictable elements. When you sort out your interview targets, also make a list (with contact details) of reserves – say, you want to interview six so make a list of 20. That reserve list may be even bigger if you're interviewing across quotas. If you wanted to interview six people in each of four categories, for example, you'd need a good number of reserves in each group and not just for the total. Elite samples can be a problem too: there may well be only a few people who can answer your questions authoritatively, which means that you can't set up a pool of reserves, and some elite samples are by their nature difficult to get to, which will make it worse. Here your scheduling and contingency planning should be more to do with the expectation of a very low response rate, and building that into your dissertation plan. You may have to use their contributions illustratively and not expect a neat and reliable dataset from which you can draw extravagant conclusions.

So here is a summary of ways of coping with people problems.

- Always allow for contingencies in your project planning (that is, always have at least a plan B, and probably Plan C too).
- If you can avoid it, don't make your dissertation too dependent on the activities of a small number of people, still less one key person.
- Be realistic about response rates to questionnaires, surveys and interview requests.
- Make sure that your plans for other people's involvement are realistic and feasible.
- When a problem occurs and a person doesn't deliver as expected or promised, don't dwell on it; immediately turn to your planned alternatives and *move on*.
- Always ask your supervisor's advice when these problems occur, especially when they come late in your dissertation studies.

You

Yes, the primary resource – a frequent source of problems that can undermine your dissertation or project progress. Most of these are the ups and downs of everyday living, which I said I wasn't going to dwell on in this book for fear of producing a series of tiresome homilies about efficient working routines, early bedtimes and clean socks. Such problems affect all kinds of coursework and examinations, of course, but seem to have a particular currency for dissertation work. This is no doubt partly to do with its prominence and importance for your whole course – it's usually crucial for a good degree – and partly because you're running the whole show. It's not like an ordinary taught course, where somebody else sets up the objectives, provides the core material, compiles reading lists and so on and then delivers it all for you to engage with as you choose. It's all down to you, and whereas that's exciting and inspiring it's also stressful. I've divided this section into three groups: traditional 'personal' problems, freezing (you'll see what I mean), and other demands on your time.

'I'm ill'

During the course of your dissertation studies you may encounter health problems, probably in a small (cold, tummy upset) way but if you're unlucky something more serious, perhaps requiring hospitalization. Your university will have long-standing procedures in the regulations for dealing with this, and there may be other specific rules in your dissertation course manual. Whatever they are, you'll know them by now. Once it was common for students to apply to individual staff members for extensions and to ask for health issues to be taken into account, but that is changing and course tutors' discretion is disappearing. There appears to be a movement in higher education towards centralized systems, amid claims that they are fairer and more efficient. They are designed to prevent situations where students in different parts of a university are treated in different ways – in the Department of Fish Gloxinia gets no extension even though she was run over by a tractor, twice, whereas in the Department of Fowl Armandino gets a two-week extension for a broken fingernail. All I can say here is that you should invoke your procedure as soon as it appears necessary, as not to do so may have repercussions later. This does not mean applying for an extra week every time you have a cold or do an Armandino, but nor should you be stoical and suffer in silence. Nearly all systems will refuse to grant you an extension if you apply after the fact. Never just hand something in late and wait until afterwards to say that, oh yes, you fell out of a hot air balloon and then caught plague and couldn't finish on time. (You know all this, I hope.)

Beyond straightforward health issues there are of course a great many other personal issues that can affect your ability to work well or work at all. The ones that come up frequently are to do with personal relationships, family circumstances (especially death or illness of close family members), house and flat mates, landlords, work, and for an unlucky few involvement with legal issues as result of robberies, assaults and so on. Some of these are external so I mention them again below, but all are real and can nag away at you so don't belittle their effects or allow them to undermine your dissertation progress or – and more often – its quality. Students can struggle on in fairly unpleasant circumstances and still hand in something adequate, but it will often be of a far lower quality than if they'd been in a better place. So . . . (and here the sanctimonious homily warning light begins to flash) make sure you tell somebody. My suggestion would be that you sketch in the problem for your supervisor, or maybe your tutor if your supervisor is Dr Caligari[2] and you'd rather not say. You don't need to go into detail, especially if that's embarrassing ('My housemate steals my clothes and gave my partner an STD and now I've got it, and they put it on Facebook too', etc.), and instead just flag up that you have some stressful things going on in your life and that they could affect your work. If necessary you can then go through the official procedures, but your supervisor is already aware and may have been able to give helpful advice to help you through. It's tempting to be independent and not seek help, which in a sense is commendable, but we all need help sometimes (though I hope that statement hasn't caused your platitude light to flash). Your supervisor will be aware that you're not one of those students who's always making excuses and wants to play the system, as they're normally easy to spot.

'Aaagh. I just can't do it'

Here I'm referring to that rising sense of fear or perhaps helplessness that stops you writing anything at all. It may be with you at the beginning or creep up on you in later months, but the effect can be the same either way. And it's one of those feedback loops, too, in that the lack of (especially) written progress feeds back into your general stressed state and makes it worse.

Certainly, this is one of those factors that you should tell your supervisor about, and if it is a real problem you can talk to support services at your university or college. It may be a response to the sheer stress of it

---

[2] But all those years of being shunned by society may have given Dr C. rich insights and understanding about personal issues, so don't rule it out.

all or it may be more like the fabled writer's block (which you can look up online) though it's unlikely that anything you experience will be as grand as some of the famous stories. When involved in a long writing or research project we will all experience some periods that seem to be going well and others that do not.

Part of the problem, if it becomes one, is our perception of what's happening. At the risk of giving yet more general advice, it is important not to assume that a sticky patch, or a period when you're demotivated or perhaps having doubts, is a sign of being completely stuck or frozen with no way forward. Keep it in perspective: talking about it with somebody else is a good way to avoid the perception that you've hit some kind of disaster. Your fellow dissertation students may also help when you swap stories, possibly with dramatic overtones.[3] There's a risk that you may feel less successful than those one or two people who may claim to have done everything wonderfully well and have no problems at all. They're probably being less than completely truthful; or perhaps they're deluding themselves in the opposite direction.

Preparedness helps with this just as with everything else. Good planning, keeping broadly to schedule, and having alternatives ready if things go wrong, all contribute to keeping the stress levels down and in turn make you feel less anxious and driven. Also vital is just to keep writing. Remember the imprecation in Chapter 6, which your research methods texts and tutors will also recommend: just write stuff. If you're going through a difficult phase in your research it may not be the best stuff you've ever written, but it will be text in the bank. In fact, don't worry about it not being absolutely perfect, because that may be contributing to your feeling that you can't write anything down. You can always return and improve or cut it later. But having thousands of words already on the page will also help to reduce that feeling of pressure and stress that contribute to rising panic and perhaps a seeming touch of writer's block.

'I've got this job now'

Here's another factor that I mentioned in Chapter 2, and it's one of ever-growing importance. As the bills for higher education get bigger, students are under correspondingly larger pressures to take jobs and

---

[3] Professionals and other groups like exchanging horror stories when they get together. These are often about terrible things that have gone wrong or might go wrong, and exaggerations aren't unknown, so don't be too alarmed if you find a few circulating among your classmates (dissertation mates?) too.

for longer hours. The job inevitably steals time and energy from your dissertation. This applies equally to work taken as soon as a taught course finishes though there are still some months of dissertation work ahead, and to work taken during the currency of an undergraduate or postgraduate course itself. There are different kinds of jobs too, by which I mean not the obvious differences but how the job relates to your future ambitions.

The simplest case is where you work just to get money to support your studies, which is probably the case for the overwhelming majority of first degree students. It's more complicated for jobs that students take at the ends of their courses, because these may be the first steps in their career, jobs that are not trivial or incidental and hence ones that they care more about.

For basic 'anything legal to get money' jobs, the key thing to remember is that you are doing the job to support your studies, not as something important in its own right. Or to put it another way, your studies are more important than your job so always try to prioritize things so that the balance is that way round. How many days a week do you work? Is it every evening, for example, as it would be for bar work, or at weekends or on whole days (chosen to avoid your days in class) and so on? Whichever it is, try to keep clear days for your dissertation if you can.

The amount of your course that the dissertation represents will vary enormously, but it could easily be a quarter or more of what you are doing in an academic year so give it enough time. That means at least one clear day and part of another each week, and perhaps two clear days in some weeks and some other smaller snatches of time elsewhere for library visits, etc. Does the job allow you to do this? If you're working in a bar every night until late and don't get home until 2 a.m. it's likely to make the mornings challenging and affect the following days. On the other hand, if you're working in the day you may have the time in the evening but will you have the energy? And so on. You can work all this out for yourself. But make some clear time and say 'this is for my dissertation and nothing else'. Keep the days clear, and make sure there are dissertation days in every week – so there are no momentum-sapping breaks of a week, or a month. Restarting is difficult after a long break and won't be an instantaneous process either.

If you're looking at a 'real' job, though, one that you see as a serious start to your future career, it's harder to make that clear priority. The MA students in my department face that problem because when they finish their class-based teaching they still have another three months of dissertation work before they submit. Few of them can afford to run for a quarter of a year with no income, so they take jobs, and that normally means 'serious' jobs that will follow on from their MA studies and found a new career. This does mean serious planning to stop the dissertation from being squeezed out. We do advise them to tell their prospective employers that they are finishing an MA and to ask for at least one or ideally two free days per week until they submit, with the expectation that this will be unpaid, but understandably many people are reluctant to set conditions or ask for favours at job interviews or on their first day in the job.

There is no easy way round the job time problem. If you face this yourself, then you must set aside clear dissertation time each week, and if you're holding down a full-time job by that time then those clear days may well be at the weekends. Be prepared to have no social life for a period, but hey, it's only for a short time. In case I seem to be setting up conditions that will cause you to burn out and raise stresses of a kind that I've said you should reduce, I don't mean that. Take a week's break during that period, use the evenings to relax, and don't get locked into 'all work and no play' syndrome. And when you finally finish the dissertation, I suggest you then drop these habits and try to get back to a normal work–life balance otherwise you'll carry them over into your new job. In these market-worshipping times there are plenty of employers who seem to think that buying your time is equivalent to owning your life, so don't encourage them.

Oh yes: the internship problem. The phenomenon of people entering professions by doing unpaid work is not a new one, but it's now becoming entrenched in some areas – law, politics and across most media businesses to name but a few. The relative scarcity of good jobs makes it more likely to continue and spread and there is no shortage of young people willing to take it up. The practice is controversial, as you know; some employers pay something to cover subsistence, travelling and a little else besides, but others pay almost nothing, bringing justifiable objections that it is a fundamentally exploitative practice. Critics also point out that it selects in favour of people who come from wealthier backgrounds, as they're the only ones who can work for up to a year for nothing. The point for us is that internships and jobs are more or less equivalent in their effects on your dissertation – they are both threats to the time and energy that you can give it, so they need managing in the same way.

Technology

This category could be summed up in one short statement, really – 'See Chapter 5'. Most of the preventative and management measures that I talk about in that chapter are designed to obviate or lessen the problems that technology can cause. But they will not eliminate them entirely. We've all forgotten to do backups, and anybody who has been computing for very long will have experienced standard breakdowns and problems like hard disk failures, lock-ups and corrupt files.

Actually, computers and ancillary equipment, extending to audio-visual and other electronic gear, are now hugely reliable for all sorts of reasons – such as better and less stressed designs, more reliable components, more consistent quality, a better understanding and control of quality (usually), and a changed attitude to consumption and repairability.

In the 1960s (ah, that decade again), televisions broke down relatively frequently. Valves (tubes) and other discrete[4] components needed replacement as they wore out, and the picture tube was a major and expensive component whose failure everybody dreaded. Repair was performed at the component level by technicians brandishing soldering irons, and many people rented their sets to avoid both the capital outlay and the repair bills. Nowadays televisions rarely break down and many people use them without problems throughout their design lives, and they often become obsolete before any breakdown threatens. Nobody repairs them at component level. If they are repaired at all it is by plugging in replacement sub-assemblies on a modular basis; or they are simply thrown away. And relatively few people rent televisions.

The same is true of computers and peripherals. They used to be big and impressive, cost a small fortune, and were wildly over-engineered to last vastly longer than their useful functional life, which constant innovation and updating has made very short. Now they're just familiar lumps of stuff, like TVs and washing machines, and they just work. Some people understand what happens behind the screen and inside the box, but most don't. People buy them, run them till they're obsolete, then junk them. Hardly anybody rents them, apart from in commercial leasing. They are ultra-reliable, and even weak spots like the hard drive are much better than they used to be. All of which gives rise to complacency, a well observed phenomenon that troubles people who

---

[4] Yes, 'discrete' as opposed to 'discreet' – one of those confusable pairs of the kind that I list in my spelling reminders for Chapter 6.

investigate air, sea and rail accidents. That's mainly why I included Chapter 5. When things work in the same way time and time again, we can drop our guard. We become casual about backups, for example, and then one day the hard disk fails. As they still do. We are mortified. It's tempting to think of hardware as extremely disloyal at times: why does the printer choose to break down just when we're about to print out that piece of coursework that is due in two hours' time? Or that dissertation? What follows are a few more brief observations to add to what I said in Chapter 5.

'An alien ate my laptop'

Did it? What monumental bad luck. It's probably something to do with the Geminids (or substitute your own favourite meteor shower) or a misdirected reply to SETI transmissions that hit your laptop instead. So what now? You have backups, so that's all right, and you've probably got access to other computers at uni, so you can recover what you've done and carry on. Perhaps you have a kind relative who can give you a new laptop, or you've earned enough to buy an inexpensive netbook. And so on. All is well, apart from the tinge of annoyance at the extra expense or the bad manners of people in the Tau Ceti system.

But what's that – you haven't got a recent backup? You meant to do one but you've been very busy? Ah, you do have a backup but – oh dear – it's from two or three weeks ago, so you have to re-create everything from that point onwards. It's like forgetting to do a recent save in a computer game. Your last save was on this level, so at least that's all right, but you've lost all of that sequence where you defeated the Ur-Myrmidons of Thrag to reach the dragon, and took several goes to get past those tricky quick-ghasts in the reactor corridor. In other words, it's not a disaster but it's an absolute pain, a real nuisance, and represents days of lost work.

So, to return to the theme of this chapter: it happened, so what do you actually do about it? Everything depends on the nature of the break-down or fault, which you should investigate as soon as you can. For example, a hard disk failure is bad news, and only hugely (prohibitively) expensive data recovery procedures can get your stuff back. But much else that goes wrong will leave your hard drive unscathed, in which case your data is still there and recoverable. Laptops get a lot of physical damage through being dropped, knocked or sat on, so broken screens are common. Or something comes loose inside and there's no activity on the screen. Batteries and power supplies die, motherboards fail, memory chips work loose, etc. Take it to your local computer support people – university-based services should turn out to be more student focused than high-street ones – and ask what's wrong and also if you can have your data recovered and transferred. It's actually not difficult if the disk is still working. If the machine's completely dead you can slip out the drive, pop it into a special free-standing case, and copy over any relevant files to another machine via a suitable cable. Unless you have a very trustworthy friend – see Chapter 5 – I'd recommend you take the professional option though it means spending some money. For one thing, the receipt they give you – especially one from your university's own computer services people – may be useful if you have to talk to somebody about a delay to your dissertation.

If none of these things works and your latest saves really are lost, try not to despair. Yes, you should have backed it up and no you didn't, but don't bash yourself too hard about it. It's done, and now you have a practical problem so what's the solution? If you just sit there hitting yourself you risk falling into one of those two problem modes – freeze or run away. Unfortunately, the solution does mean recreating the lost material, but there are better and worse ways of doing that. You may be able to do it in convenient slices rather than put everything else on hold while you build back the text. By all means immediately make notes on what you remember in the lost section, or consult any rough notes that you used to create it the first time round. Then I suggest you rewrite it a bit at a time, using a small part of your regular allotted dissertation time, but for the rest of your time keep the main thrust of your dissertation going and write up the new material that you were planning to do at this stage. This way, you reduce the chore of replacing lost material by breaking it into manageable chunks while at the same time keeping your overall momentum going. It should help to prevent you falling into gloom and 'what's the point?' inertia.

This time, of course, you'll remember to keep those regular backups. You should also tell your supervisor immediately, so that if there is an IT-related problem with your dissertation they at least know about it early.

'It broke halfway through the experiment'

At one end of the scale, it's easy to replace a failed Bunsen burner or stopwatch or voltmeter, probably from the managed stock of the institution you're studying in; at the other end, if a major component of the LHC or the Hubble has a breakdown, you're unlikely to be able to build in contingencies for that kind of gear ('Note to self: remember to include spare space telescope'). But you're not working at that exalted end of the spectrum. Hence when you plan your resource needs and ask 'What happens if it goes wrong?' you'll probably have more of the former kind of gear.

Whatever the replacement regime or feasibility of using an alternative, your problem is the effect it has on your dissertation schedule. If something goes wrong late in the day and there is no time to deal with it, then I'll pick this up again in the next section. If the problem happens earlier then the new or replacement equipment is presumably something that you can accommodate in your experimental design because when you originally made your research plan and schedule you made allowances for some things not working out as planned. Um, didn't you?

In some ways, the 'key equipment' provision resembles the 'key person' provision I mentioned earlier, and the same pros and cons apply to that. It may be that you have to use certain equipment in order to carry out particular experiments or tests, in which case you will no doubt build enough time into your schedule to allow for repeats or setbacks, as I suggested in Chapter 2.

'Oh no. It didn't record'

You don't have to be working in audio or video fields to use recording devices for sound or vision. Audio and video recording are common ways of preserving interviews, performances, observations or the progress of experiments, for example. And don't forget good old photography, which is now almost certainly going to be digital but in a few cases may still be on film. These technologies do go wrong in various ways, of course, and when they do you may lose everything – and not immediately be aware of it. What you lose could be irreplaceable – if it wasn't something transient that vanishes on the wind you probably wouldn't be recording it in the first place.

This is a rather special case of equipment failure that may stop you dead in your tracks, so what are good ways to reduce the likelihood of prevent problems or sort those that may have occurred? The answers are once again to do with preparedness and planning.

Let's take one of the most likely sources of despair: recording or videoing a one-off event like an interview and then finding the recording didn't work for some reason. The awfulness of this happening varies with where and when you discover the problem: if it's immediately then you may have a chance to do another recording (though the people being recorded may be less than thrilled by that); if it's only when you've returned to base then naturally that's much worse. If you are unable to repeat the session then you may have to write off the interview, observation or whatever it was and either substitute another or do without. The problems could have a number of causes, of which the main ones are:

- equipment failure
- power supply failure
- corrupt or full storage media
- operator error.

Just listing them in this way should already suggest how you can prepare for recording sessions and avoid the worst. For a start, you must make sure you test everything fully before you take it to the recording session, and that means testing you too – are you really familiar with those controls and that menu system? This applies particularly to other people's equipment, such as that you might hire from a studio or from your university's AV services. If the equipment is unfamiliar and strange, make sure you have the manual and study it beforehand; if there is no manual then there is usually one on the internet somewhere, whether on the manufacturer's site (look for areas like 'downloads' and 'support' or 'documentation') or on specialist manual sites. Search on model names and numbers to find the right ones.

For battery-operated equipment always take a supply of fresh batteries, and take the power supply and if appropriate the charger too. For rechargeable equipment never say 'There should be enough charge in that battery pack so I won't take the charger', because that allows for no changes of plan (say, having to do another take) and assumes an unfeasibly precise knowledge of the available running time. Always take the charger. It's a variation on the theme of backup – have multiple and reserve power sources with you at all times.

Do a test run before you go (a quick record and playback) and also when you arrive and set up at the venue for the recording. Don't leave out the playback check, because it's easy to think you're recording when you're not. Also, if there are other pieces of kit in the system like mixers or laptops test them too, and do it in the set-up you'll use when you get there. Do you have a plan B if one of those supporting items fails? Include cables in your checks and backup planning too, of course, because cables and connectors can fail in ways that are difficult to repair in the field.

Now here's another suggestion that's frequently followed by academics and other professionals who need to record people on a regular basis: take a spare device. You may say that's impractical and ridiculous if your equipment is based on a near broadcast-quality video camera that you've had to hire at great expense. How could you afford to take another? But it's much more practical if you're doing audio recordings, especially where you're not seeking high fidelity and just want to capture what somebody is saying: this can be accomplished using cheap digital recorders where having a second one is not implausible. Perhaps you can use your own and hire a backup from the university, then when you do the interviews or observations run both at the same time so that you have two recording devices running. This is the way to use the backup device, rather than using one and leaving the other one in your bag in case the first one breaks down. To come back to the first example of a vastly expensive piece of video equipment that you couldn't possibly duplicate, well, fair enough. But you can still back that up with a cheap digital video camera or even digital audio, because if the main gear fails at least you've got something to show for the session.

Most media you'll be using these days will be digital, in the form of built-in or removable cards or disks. Naturally, you should take backups of these if that is practicable and expense is not a factor – disks are cheap even though some solid-state media, such as higher-capacity SD cards, can be quite pricey. Small recorders often use their own built-in storage, and there the problem is more about what to do when they are full. To free up the space you need to upload or transfer the content to another location, perhaps a laptop, but that's an operation that has potential to go wrong. I strongly advise that wherever possible you transfer the material using a *copy* function first, because if the transfer fails or the copy won't play back (and you should test it) then at least you still have the original. If you use a *move* function you don't have that safeguard because you wipe the original when you make the copy – very risky. Even if you use the copy function and it has been successful don't immediately rush to erase the original. Remember: never have just one copy of everything, so before you erase the original and free up the space, make a second copy from the original, ideally on to a separate device or storage medium such as a USB stick. It's preferable to make the second copy from the original again rather than from the new first copy – tempting if you're using a laptop. This provides better insurance against the first copy having a corrupt portion somewhere later in the save, and also harks back to analogue days when making copies of copies introduced progressive quality degradations.

Analogue media create different problems, and if you're using them these days it will probably be because of some intrinsic property that they have. That means you've had training and know the strengths and weaknesses of the medium, and also how to look after it. You'll know that tapes should be kept away from magnetic sources, for example, and that 35mm film cassettes and 120 roll films are not light-tight enough to be casually taken out of their containers or foil wrappings and left lying around under a desk lamp; some brands use translucent containers for film so you can't do this even when it's in the container.

Film is perhaps the main candidate for not knowing how things have turned out until you get back to base. That's part of its appeal, and one of the reasons why film photography presents a completely different experience from its digital cousin. It needs processing, and until that happens you don't know whether the quality is adequate or whether there is anything on the film at all. By that time it probably is too late to go back and redo it. Once again, consider the backup options. Take a spare camera body of the same type with you, for example, which is the only way of preparing for shutter or electronic breakdowns. Naturally, this is easier if you're deliberately using cheap equipment, such as single-use throwaway cameras for a lomography project. Even lenses fail, usually mechanically – something jams or breaks – but are you prepared for that? Don't forget that many film cameras use batteries for anything from powering the meter to running the whole camera, so the power supply caveats apply here too. Or take a digital camera too to take matching shots. As with the digital video case, the backup may be of poorer quality or not what you really wanted, but it may save the day.

The research itself

This final section concerns problems that come out and bite you from the research or dissertation itself. They're not down to you, or other people, or the equipment you're using, but stem from the choices or discoveries you make as you work through your programme. They are common, and most people will have to cope with at least one. I'll group them under some arbitrary heads and say a few words about each.

'I've found some fantastic stuff that I didn't know about before'

Very interesting, that, and it can be a real stimulus; but it can also be a curse. Why? Because a new avenue opening up halfway through your project may lure you from your chosen path (sounds as though I'm moralizing again). Yes, it may be fascinating, and you should follow it up for your own interest and in your own time, but the later in your dissertation sequence it comes, the more likely it is to distract you and pull you away from your main focus. Is this really a fascinating new angle on your main theme that you can integrate into your current work as a genuine enhancement? Yes? Brilliant – it may gain you some marks too. But do be careful, as you can so easily end up diluting your main argument with new material that really ought to be the subject of a separate dissertation. Always talk to your supervisor about exciting new directions: they will help you decide whether it's an opportunity or a threat.

'I've changed my mind!'

Here's a venerable problem that probably raises its head for most people at some stage in their dissertation studies. If your change of mind comes early in the sequence then it may well be possible to change, but the further on you go the less chance there is making substantial changes to your topic or your approach. In both cases, it's essential to talk to your supervisor.

If you're close to your final draft and you read an article or book that suddenly transforms your ideas, well, that happens. For the most part, you just have to grit your teeth and carry on with what you're doing because there is no time to go back and redo things. It may be possible to integrate something of the new ideas into your discussion, or at least mention them to show that you're up with the latest developments in your field, but be very cautious about doing more.

Imagine this scenario: you're just finishing off your first complete draft and your investigations are complete. As all current researchers in your field are doing, you have based your analysis of the Wildboar Conjecture on the strength of recent work by Glup (2008) and Moribundia (2010a). It's all come together nicely, and you have been able to demonstrate a splendid van Striethen curve. Then while leafing through the latest number of the *Journal of Enormous Bangs* on the bus back from London you come across an article by Jeanette Poog and Nathan d'Eath. They, radical souls that they are, have applied Hogbeach's (1994) disintegration theorem to Wildboar – neat move, guys – and claim that this renders the Glup and Moribundia approach obsolete at a stroke. Oh no! What do you do? Well, you may well have time to mention this new approach in your discussion or conclusions, but you can't fully integrate it at this stage and redo your work. And why should you? It's not what you did, but what's wrong with that? What you did was very good, and entirely consistent with the most recent theory and analysis in your field.

At this late stage it could well be a serious mistake to dash back to your room and spend three days reworking your entire dataset and findings after the manner of Poog and d'Eath. Hmm. Well, the van Striethen curve is still reasonable, sort of, though what's that nasty bump in the middle? It's unlikely that you would make a good job of this major revision, and that's mainly because there isn't time for thinking and reflection on the implications of the new approach. Let's imagine you rework everything in the nick of time, dash to get the thing bound, and hand it in at the last minute. Phew. What an ordeal. Then, four weeks later, you find Hogbeach writing in *Bang Notes and Queries V* that Poog and d'Eath have made a foolish mistake, and besides he revised his disintegration theorem in 2004, which they should have known. Within days, Poog and d'Eath respond on the Bangform.org online forum, and agree that they overlooked a crucial factor. They are grateful to Professor Hogbeach and will be publishing a new article in the fall.

You would be very depressed because you allowed yourself to be rushed into changes that you had no time to consider. You had abandoned your first-rate work using accepted approach A and substituted a very hastily put together and ill-considered replacement using raw and undiscussed approach B. As always, talk to your supervisor. They can help you decide what and how much to change, or whether to change anything at all. Beware of being dragged along by the latest fashion, and instead stick to established principles of rational academic inquiry in a shared environment. Sometimes game-changing developments do crop up in academic investigation, rendering everything else obsolete or obsolescent, but that's unlikely to apply to your dissertation work. You are going to be evaluated on the process and evident learning as much as the outcome – though a good outcome is naturally a pleasant achievement and may be genuinely informative and useful to others.

'This doesn't work, and is not what I expected'

This heartfelt cry is a representative of many different types of problem, such as 'I can't find what I want' or 'The data doesn't exist'. This time, it's not that you've changed your mind about your topic or the whole approach, which you're still happy with, but that some key aspect of your project or inquiry is not working. What do you do? There are some obvious links here with earlier parts of this chapter, not the least of them being that you should have planned some 'What if it doesn't work?' scenarios at the very beginning of your dissertation work. I always try to talk through issues of feasibility and data availability with students as early as possible, and often at our first meeting. I'm often saying something like 'That's a fantastic idea, and it would be great to know that. But how are you going to find out? Where will you obtain useful data?' When discussed at this stage, there's usually plenty of opportunities to rework everything and either seek new data or recast the question or hypothesis to make it doable in the time.

Don't forget that you may be able to incorporate the problem into the discussion. I said in an earlier chapter that you should not imagine that hitting problems, or finding that something you thought was the case is not the case, is a 'bad thing'. It may form a very good discussion topic that will form the core of a good dissertation but may help others later. Again, talk to your supervisor. Or, to look at it another way, you can think of it as turning features into benefits. Marketing people know all about this. It means taking some characteristic of an item or event – something that is neutral or even potentially negative – and turning it into something positive.

Here's a gentle example: you want to sell your much sought-after Thrupp Gleamball washing machine on eBay (you need the money to put towards the Thrupp Auto-Emperor II, which you've coveted for 15 years), when all of a sudden it breaks down. You take it to the repairer who smiles wistfully but declines to do anything. It needs a new flub motor and it seems they're made by hand on a small Pacific island out of bronze and albatross feathers. It'll take ten weeks and cost thousands. Drat. But you remember your marketing training and realize that the dead Gleamball is nevertheless a wondrous source of other exotic parts. So you go ahead with your online ad but instead of saying 'Broken down Gleamball – not worth much' you present it as a 'Fantastic opportunity to buy Gleamball spares' and then say it's in wonderful nick and all working apart from the mere trifle of the flub motor. In no time you have 132 bidders. As I say, marketers know all about this. I'm not suggesting you produce vaguely dishonest discussions or tell fibs – far from it – but I am saying that when things don't work or go unexpectedly, ask whether there is still something interesting and valuable that you can say about that. As in the change of mind example above, this is far better than being panicked into a complete change of direction that you won't have time to work through properly.

The same applies when you find a genuine fault or problem close to your deadline, one that simply can't be left in the dissertation as it is. You need to do what you can to correct it, and of course talk to your supervisor, but it's unlikely that there's scope for a major reworking of your thesis. Instead, there may be scope to mention the problem and to weave it into the discussion as a valuable lesson or source of insights that will help future researchers. The fact that it went wrong could provide the substance of a good and valuable discussion.

'My ideas and research are wonderful but my supervisor says my draft is crap'

I hope you don't have occasion to say this – and certainly not after you've read this book, which is about turning your ideas and research into a good dissertation. If you are confronted by negative comments when you submit a draft then you need to ask your supervisor precisely how it is crap, because then you can start to do something about it. All of the topics in this book could be implicated in the crapness. Is it the structure, perhaps, or the argument, or your general accuracy with poor spelling and punctuation? Have you included all of the elements that your course handbook, research training and supervisor have said should be in there?

One kind of problem that I've seen before in dissertations across various fields is more subtle than this. It happens particularly when students have little experience of writing formal academic prose even after a couple of years on a degree programme. They don't get 'academic speak', as it were. The problem cuts across areas I've discussed in many parts of this book, including Chapters 3, 4 and 6, and reviewing those chapters, perhaps in conjunction with the checklists in Chapter 10, may help with finding a solution if you're surprised by how your draft was received.

The people affected by this tend to be those whose assessment and coursework history includes relatively little formal writing of longish documents in a sustained academic register. So this would not be a discipline like, say, history, but one in which assessments are frequently based on presentations, visual or aural media, performance and so on; there may be some supporting written elements to go with these, but nothing like as much as there is in disciplines based on endless essays, reports and article-like writing. The problem is even more intense for people who've come back to higher education after many years away from any kind of education. I've also known students who resented having to write like this; they regarded it as lifeless and unnecessarily detached from the complex emotional life of human beings. Well, yes; but that's precisely it – remember Sophie and her Ruston engine in Chapter 6.

As I've said before, academic writing does make certain demands and requires a formal approach, and even though you may hate writing like this, for the purposes of your dissertation I'm afraid you have to. Think of it instrumentally if nothing else: 'I am doing this because it will get me far better marks than if I just followed my instinctive way of writing.' It takes you out of your comfort zone, but that can be a very good thing when you're studying and learning. A dissertation or major project is meant to be a demanding test. *It's supposed to be hard.* You're at a university, so you should not expect the creation of your major assessments to feel like writing GCSE coursework or your diary or your blog.

'I found some really good stuff but I'm not sure how to use it'

Is it really 'good stuff', though? If it is, then it may be a question of not knowing how to incorporate some unfamiliar or unexpected data or its implications into your discussion and conclusions, in which case your supervisor should yet again be your first port of call. My reason for including this topic is different, though. It's about making sure right from the start that what you intend to use as 'stuff', which will be the data, the raw material, you get from your primary and secondary research, is fit for purpose and right for your dissertation. I'm going to characterize this by making a distinction between good data and what I call 'sexy data'.

Sexy data is bewitching and beguiling, and it's usually exciting to get hold of. That's the point, really: by sexy data I mean data that it is really exciting to acquire. It feels a bit special, such as when you achieve some fortunate access to an archive or a person or a facility that would normally be closed to a student researcher. The problem? That this data may not be good data from the point of view of your overall dissertation or project – in other words, it may not serve your overall argument.

'But', you may say, 'surely[5] if I get an interview with the Queen then that is a major coup? How could that be anything other than brilliant?' Well, it could be brilliant, but not if your dissertation is on the decline of the high-street store, or the thermal properties of a new kind of insulating wall block. Yes, a ridiculous example, but you can see what I mean. There are students who have some accident of access in mind – their aunt runs the LHC, for example – almost from the first day they enter the university as an undergraduate: 'In just over two years' time I'll get Auntie Meg to let me use the LHC for a day or two. My diss will be absolutely mega.'

Like Auntie Meg's niece, some students build their entire dissertation around the prospect of such sexy data. Sometimes it works and sometimes it doesn't. I've seen both. If it works you'll feel really chuffed, but there are at least two serious risks: one is that the sexy data doesn't yield any meaningful discussion and you end up with a whole dissertation that is banal or trivial or both; the other is that you introduce the sexy data alongside other ordinary (asexual?) data and it just doesn't fit, whereupon it sticks out as an irrelevance or entices you into losing focus by spreading the dissertation into unwanted new areas.

Sexy data may be good data but it may not. I'm not saying never follow it up or take an exciting opportunity, but keep your critical faculties active when you assess its value. Whenever you find yourself following an exciting lead, such as gaining an interview with a normally unattainable person, ask yourself whether this really feeds your main line of research and serves your argument. You can try to describe this person as an

---

[5] Yes, apply the same gag if you wish.

'elite sample' in your methodology but that's not enough. Figure 8.1 is a little Venn diagram to remind you. It's not to scale, of course, because the categories are not meaningfully quantifiable, so don't try measuring the shared area to work out what proportion of data is both good *and* sexy.[6]

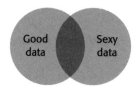

Figure 8.1 A pictorial representation of good *vs* sexy data – not to scale!

'It's far too long – help!'

To close this chapter I'll look at problems of length, which are familiar and arguably universal irritations for anybody who writes academic prose, as there's usually a length restriction whether you're writing a dissertation or a journal article. I suspect all of you at some stage will say of part or all of your dissertation that it's too short or too long. So how do you deal with this? I'll assume in this section that you are absolutely clear about the required length of your dissertation and any other supporting documents, and that you've read your handbook carefully to check whether bibliographies, etc., are included in that word count (RTFM, Chapter 1).

Well, if it's too short then there are a number of possibilities, such as: you have omitted some crucial elements; your discussion, conclusion or other component is insufficiently developed; you haven't spent enough time or effort on the dissertation as a whole or some part of it; you may have selected a weak topic that doesn't sustain a whole dissertation, and so on. In the case of the last possibility – a weak topic – this is something that should have been weeded out very early, perhaps in your first meeting with your supervisor; so have you had regular meetings or did you neglect them? It may seem that I'm glossing over this aspect – not long enough – which is true. Quite often, I think, drafts that are far too short come from students who have not worked consistently on their dissertations, typically starting everything really late and then rushing to finish what little they can do in the remaining time. If you start

---

[6] Or compound the felony by citing the 'number' (say, 31.338%?) with appropriate reference (Ball, 2011) in your dissertation. Unfortunately, some people's use of sources is like that: properly cited and fully referenced nonsense is still nonsense.

early and see your supervisor at the first available opportunity you are highly unlikely to produce an under-length draft. The worst dissertation I have ever received was like that: the student had clearly written it the evening before the deadline. It was bulked out with spurious title pages and blanks and the text had hilarious multiple line spacing so that there were only about eight lines of text on each A4 page. The whole thing was about 1,200 words. It was of course an instant and devastating fail. I can't show it to future students as a horrific example because it is confidential to the student perpetrator, but I still keep it on my shelf as a source of wonder.

I think by far the majority of length problems are to do with excess. People find that their draft is over-length and by a few thousand words, or – another very common happening – a student will write a couple of chapters and find that they've already used up two-thirds of their word allocation with four more chapters still to write. What can you do?

The short answer is of course to cut. Once again, talk to your supervisor if you're worried about the relative length of different parts of your dissertation. As I've mentioned earlier in the book there's no right answer to the relative length question. Your dissertation rules may have some stipulations about the lengths of certain formally required components in your dissertation or report, but usually you're in 'How long is a piece of string?' territory. So, first, find out whether there are any constraints, and then settle on your plan for the relative length of the different components. As you progress through your studies this may mean revising a length and structure plan that you produced earlier in the light of your subsequent research.

Actually, cutting text is not a quick and simple business. Experienced editors know that when they have to reduce the length of an author's text there is usually no quick way to do it. Anyone hiring editors will know that they will (should!) have to pay a lot for it. One implication of this is that if you find you are running up a high word total early on in your writing, then start to tackle that problem sooner rather than later. If you leave it all to the end – say, you have 20,000 words for a 15,000 word limit dissertation – then don't underestimate the amount of time you will need to make those cuts properly. Overnight, or even a couple of days, at the last minute is not going to be enough.

Not only is it time-consuming but there are different ways and degrees of cutting that involve everything from tweaking the occasional sentence to hacking out great chunks of text. Which you need to do depends on how much text you need to lose. Here's an example of what I mean. Let's take a sentence from an imaginary dissertation and look at the scope for cutting it:

> *Hiller and Moncrieff (2008a) examined the relationship over nine months between tidal energy consumption in the Severn estuary and the output of table tennis balls from Starping, a factory at Humbury upon Severn, and were unable to discover a correlation using either Bultitude's reduction coefficient or modified nu-sufficiency.*

There you are – 48 words (if you include 'nu' as a word). How would you cut it? Here's one gently reduced version:

> *Hiller and Moncrieff (2008a) examined the relationship over nine months between tidal energy consumption in the Severn estuary and the output from a factory at Humbury upon Severn, and found no correlation using either Bultitude's reduction coefficient or modified nu-sufficiency.*

That leaves the existing structure intact and just removes some of the words and reorders others. It gets it down a little, to 40 words. It took a minute or so to do and saves 8 from 48, so about 17%. Applying that to our 20,000-word problem it would get it down to about 16,700 words, so it is not enough to work at this level throughout. We'd have to cut more drastically, and because the scope for cutting would vary from sentence to sentence we can't assume that we could do this for every sentence. We might find ourselves cutting some sentences fairly hard and leaving others virtually unchanged. Also, notice that the change from 'were unable to discover a correlation' to 'found no correlation' brings with it a subtle shift of meaning, and that we've lost some information by cutting out the factory name (which may not matter). How about this next example?

> *A nine-month study (Hiller and Moncrieff, 2008a) of the relationship between tidal energy consumption in the Severn estuary and a Severnside factory's output found no correlation using either of the two main tests.*

It's a sharper cut compared to the original and we're now down to 34 words, so if we were able to make that kind of more drastic reduction of nearly 30% everywhere we'd be able to get our 20,000 words down to below 15,000. But if we could only apply them to half the sentences then we'd fall short of our cutting target and be back around 16,500 again. Once again, look at the loss of information and keep an eye open for shifts of meaning. Does 'the two main tests' identify them unambiguously? We don't know: it may do in some fields but not in others. Also, is it correct to recast a study of some phenomenon 'over nine months' as a 'nine-month study'? The study may have taken two years, of which only the observation phase was nine months. One more go, then:

> *Hiller and Moncrieff's (2008a) study of the relationship between tidal energy consumption and a local factory's output found no correlation.*

It's down to 20 words now, and that's a significant reduction of nearly 60%, but once again the amount of detailed information is further reduced. How important that information is, only the author can say (or at least, they should be fully aware of what they're doing).

The most drastic cut of all is to leave out the entire sentence, of course, and that's another option. Be prepared to remove whole sentences, paragraphs or complete blocks of text if that's what it takes. If you have to make large reductions, particularly of 25–30% or more of the total, then there must be an element of total cutting to make the target.

In various creative arts there is a piece of advice that is usually expressed along the lines of 'You must learn to be able to murder your babies' – in other words, to put this into the dissertation context, even though you may be very pleased with something that you've written and you admire it greatly, if you come to see that it doesn't actually contribute to your main argument then get rid of it. (Perhaps it was a sub-discussion where you got sidetracked into analysing some sexy data.) What I suggest to students who are disappointed to find they must cut content that they really like is that they should do two versions of their dissertation: the one they hand in, with all of the extraneous bits cut out, and their own 'director's cut', which they can bind separately and keep on their bookshelf at home. If you do this just make sure you hand in the right one!

In practice, your cutting will involve all of these kinds of reduction – minor rewordings, simpler sentences with less information, and complete removal of content. It will take time, and that time is not just the hours you spend making the cuts. It must include your rereading and re-evaluation of the new version to look for lost information or detail that you may subsequently decide has to go back, and for those changes of meaning that may leave you appearing to say things that you don't want to say. The message is, once again, don't leave it too late to start cutting text. Keep appraising the total length and balance between the various chapters and sections, and if you find you need to cut some material do it straight away.

9 The dark side

I am assuming that this chapter is one that you can read with a clear conscience – or is one that you feel you don't need to read at all. I'm sure for the vast majority of you that this is true. Nevertheless, I feel I must include it, not just as a reminder of a set of serious problems facing the academic world, including practitioners and students alike, but also to help some students avoid making errors that could get them into trouble.

This chapter, in short, is about cheating. And although you have no intention of cheating there is one good reason to read on, which is that it may help you avoid making a mistake that could cause you to appear to be a minor cheat. Real and determined cheats won't read this chapter; indeed, they won't read this book or any other book like it. If you can buy your coursework off the internet or otherwise pay somebody else to do it for you – or just steal it – then why would you agonize about the finer points of writing and research? Somebody who does that pays for something worthless in the hope that they can pretend to have done something that they have not done, and thus be something that they are not. They hope that they can succeed and thus carry that deceit into their life beyond university.

So I suppose there is another good reason to read this chapter: you are not a cheat, but you might know somebody who is, or who perhaps is sorely tempted – maybe because they're under pressure and time is running out. You might be able to save them from themselves.

Yes. This sounds out of date and a bit quaint, doesn't it, as if I should say next that cheats never prosper (which is unfortunately false) and then send you off for a cold shower. I'm sorry if it does – I don't want this to come across as a strait-laced Victorian crusade against something vaguely naughty that doesn't really matter. What I'm talking about in this chapter does matter to all of us, and in the immediate student environment it matters to you, because cheats undermine the value of what you achieve.

What kind of cheating?

This chapter looks at two kinds of cheating – one briefly and the other at more length. The brief look is at falsification of data and the longer one is about plagiarism.

Falsification

Making up data, or changing the data that you do have to make it appear to give you the answer you want, is something that unfortunately happens in academic research. It shouldn't, and it's not widespread, but it does happen; and it's not restricted to people at the beginnings of their careers either. Some people caught cheating in this way have been at the tops of their careers. If you want to see examples, just put a couple of key terms such as 'falsifying data' into a search engine and wait for the thousands of hits.[1]

When people give way to this form of cheating they usually do it because of career pressures – the desire to deliver results that match their supposed status – or an attempt to produce something that makes them stand out from others in order to enhance their promotion prospects or prestige. You may have hoped that the academic world is one of calm, reason and integrity and in many ways it is, but ambition, ego and vanity are drivers that have an influence here just as everywhere else. For a minority of people, these drivers are just too powerful to resist. If you add into this the fact that competition for posts is fierce and funding for academic positions and research is more tightly controlled than it used to be, it would be surprising if a few people didn't crack. This kind of cheating does huge damage, though – in the worst case (think of biomedical research, for example) it can affect people's lives, and it damages the reputation of the academic world in the media at large.

So what's this got to do with your dissertation? After all, you're probably not about to apply for a professorship or half a million euros of research funding. You're right that large-scale fraud is not something that affects what you are doing, but there are some real risks at a much smaller scale. These are more likely to apply, at least in their more obvious manifestations, in quantitative research where some kind of countable or other quantifiable data are being sought for analysis using established tools such as statistics and analytic software; but subtler variations can occur in non-quantitative research in the arts and humanities too.

---

[1] Or for an example of a high-profile case that emerged in 2005–6, search on 'cloning' in association with the name Hwang Woo-suk.

An example? All right. Imagine that you perform an experiment as part of your dissertation work, possibly looking for a particular outcome as especially desirable, but as you measure your dependent variables you find that the data is not quite behaving itself and isn't going to produce the significance or probability level that you were expecting, or that nice curve that you wanted. So you round up a number here, tweak another one there, and it does the trick. Maybe it was just the teeniest little adjustment, and no more than that, but it's a small version of the distinguished professor's falsified data. This is not the same as trying to produce the best available interpretation of your data by choosing one set of graph axes or scales rather than another, or by drawing a more favourable curve through a set of points, or by choosing one statistical measure rather than another. (I'm assuming here that these alternatives are all equally defensible.) If you overdo this interpretative massaging your supervisor or marker may criticize you and it may well affect your mark, but that's more to do with good practice, not cheating. The point I'm making here is about changing the data itself (or 'the data them-selves' if you're one of those people who like to treat 'data' as if it were being used as the plural of 'datum').

The temptation to massage the data may come from a desire to please or to get the best possible mark, and that may in turn be linked to one of two different tendencies. We've met both of them already in Chapter 4. One is to have a particular result in mind and to bend everything you do to try to achieve it, perhaps overlooking anything that might produce a different result; the other is the feeling that the result is not what you expected – you couldn't establish your hoped-for significance, for example – that thus you have somehow got it wrong. The first is clearly something to avoid, and is not the same as forming a hypothesis and then neutrally testing it. The second tendency is simply mistaken: research works like that, and if it didn't it wouldn't be worth doing. Often, finding out that something you thought might be true is not the case is just as interesting as finding that it is the case.

At this level it may sound relatively unimportant to you, like being a little bit naughty at school and acquiring a reputation for a rather fetch-ing roguishness, but that's not what happens in academe or higher education. And the environment is getting progressively tougher for transgressors: as universities and colleges adapt their rules to cater for new technologies and new challenges to the integrity of student work, they are moving in the direction of less sympathy for wrongdoers, less patience with misconduct, less inclination to give the benefit of the doubt, and harsher penalties all round.

Don't think that it stops with the marking either: even where a student appears to get away with a conduct offence because it hasn't been spotted, somebody may look at their dissertation in the future – another student, for example, working on the same topic and trawling prior sources for their lit review – and find out what they must have done. And in those cases, universities can retrospectively apply penalties for discovered breaches of their academic conduct rules. Imagine a student finding two years after they leave university that their dissertation mark has been withdrawn – and hence their degree too – pending an investigation.

Just before I turn to plagiarism, the main part of this chapter, let's look at a quieter kind of transgression that has parallels with data falsification and is easily carried out in arts and humanities environments. I'm referring to *false citation*. In other words, if you are carrying out secondary research in any field and cite anything that you haven't read, then strictly speaking your calling up the (secondary, etc.) data or discussion is dishonest. It might sound less of a problem than falsified data of the traditional kind, but it certainly lacks integrity: you are claiming to use data that you do not have. How significant it is will vary, depending on whether the unused reference is inserted just to make up the numbers – perhaps on the silly 'more references means it's more academic' principle (remember Jeremy Evets in Chapter 6?) – or is crucial to the argument of the dissertation. In the former case, the practice is just misguided; in the latter it's reckless and risky because it could be found out. If you are being interviewed or vivaed on your dissertation then it's even more likely that you could come unstuck.

All right, in most cases this kind of thing will go unnoticed and unremarked, and I think it may be a habit that grows up in the early part of people's studies – such as first-year undergraduate – when they seek to pad out their references or bibliography in the belief that this will add credibility. But the next time you, say, insert a reference to the original source article for a core theory in your discipline – an article that you have never read or even seen, because your knowledge of the theory is only second-hand, via interpretations in lectures and textbooks – take a moment to reflect on what you are doing. Perhaps a simple expression of this principle could be:

If you haven't read it, don't cite it.

Collusion

I said I was going to talk about plagiarism for the remainder of this chapter, but before I do here is another brief stop-off on the way. I want to take a quick look at collusion, which is an academic offence in most institutions but can be easy to fall into. It means, of course, working with another person or persons when the submitted coursework – your dissertation, for example – is required to be your own unaided work. But it doesn't have to mean out and out sharing of the same content between two people, in the same way that old-fashioned 'copying' at school takes place.

The notion of unaided work may lead you to wonder what kind of 'aid' it is that is forbidden here. Perhaps this conjures up images of schooldays – getting your parents to help with maths homework, working with schoolmates on a piece of homework before going off on your own to write it up, having your teacher's help to shape a piece of GCSE coursework and so on.

For ordinary coursework, collusion would normally involve somebody in the same class or module who is working on the same assignment. When two people pool their resources to share the load of the research or reading behind their written coursework, they not only save time and energy, but gain thinking and problem-solving power. Although this cooperation is beneficial in workplaces and research teams, in the case of an individual taking an examination or submitting assessed coursework such benefits give them an unfair advantage over other students. It's not surprising that the practice is not allowed. Think about exams, for example: in the examination hall nobody expects to be able to lean across and chat to somebody at the next desk about a problem. That is why collusion is usually expressly banned in university regulations. If it isn't stated as a forbidden practice in the handbook for your class or for the dissertation, there will be a general university ordinance or regulation preventing students from getting together – colluding – on individual coursework.

Dissertations are slightly different from conventional coursework because it is less likely that two fellow dissertation students are working on exactly the same thing – though in some disciplines they may well be investigating topics that overlap. Even if they are not, there could be some early stage of research where two or more students could benefit by, say, sharing reading for their secondary research. If this looks like a possibility for you then you should regard it as probably forbidden. Do check with your supervisor early in the process if you think something like this is a risk for you. Notice that you could still technically be regarded as having colluded if you do this even if the dissertation you submit is completely different from the one submitted by your study-mate. As I say, do check.

Before I get back to plagiarism, you may be wondering where this 'no collusion' rule leaves you if you get other people to proofread your dissertation, or ask somebody to copy-edit it – especially if you are not a native speaker of the language used in the dissertation. These kinds of services are often advertised on university noticeboards. How about when you ask friends, or your supervisor, to read your dissertation in draft form? Does that constitute illegitimate help? Generally, no – and in the final chapter (10) I'm going to suggest that it is valuable and impor-tant to have others look at your dissertation before you hand it in. But these are *checking* phases – where you've already substantially done the work and written it up – and not *creation* phases where somebody else who was involved would be doing some of the research, thinking or writing up for you. Similarly, when you talk to your supervisor about the stuff of your project and research, or ask them to read your drafts, this is not collusion but part of the legitimate and essential support that is built in to all dissertation and project work.

Although when you do a dissertation you are working on your own from start to finish, this doesn't mean you are supposed to be abandoned in some kind of void to sink or swim; it's not like being dumped in an inhospitable jungle or desert as part of a survival course.[2] And of course it is also perfectly proper to use any university support or study serv-ices that you may be entitled to – if you are registered as dyslexic, for example. If you have even slight doubts about any help with your stud-ies, checking phases or other aids then do talk to your supervisor.

Plagiarism

This is the area that causes most problems in academic life in the modern era. When I was an academic conduct officer most of the cases that came my way involved charges of plagiarism in one form or another, from the almost inadvertent to the villainously deliberate. As I said at the start of this chapter, I neither want to dwell too long on this topic, which is rather an unpleasant one and is difficult to be light-hearted about, nor do I want to suggest that most if any of you will indulge in this kind of thing. Anybody who wants to avoid the long and evolving sequence of thinking and

---

[2] Or it shouldn't be. I can remember feeling it was a bit like that when I was a student.

learning that characterizes a dissertation has probably already visited one of the online sites that sell or give away essays and dissertations. Usually, these sites claim somewhere on their home page that their downloads are intended merely as examples or for 'study purposes' only. Oh yeah – very convincing. The owners of these sites couldn't *possibly* suspect that their cynically recycled content would be submitted as coursework by naughty students, and they'd be heartbroken if they ever found out that anybody had done such a thing.

But we can ignore all of them – the dissertation downloaders and the degree buyers. They are not part of any process we're interested in. You, on the other hand, are reading this book; you're not one of them. So here I want to point out some pitfalls that could cause even the best students to drift into the fringes of academic malpractice or lure them into borderline plagiarism without realizing it. To be frank, these aren't the kinds of things that you should be doing by now if you have the normal kind of university or college career: if you're doing a dissertation then you probably have at least two years' academic experience at degree or equivalent level, and possibly more. Yet the nature of that experience will vary; some students will have written many reports, essays or other formal documents, perhaps under the aegis of a very strict referencing regime; but others may have done far less of this even though they may be two or three years into their degree level studies. For example, it is possible that students who have come back to academic study after a number of years away, or who are in fields that use a high proportion of practical coursework (involving, say, artwork, presentations or performance), have done relatively little formal academic writing, and not enough to develop the habits of good academic practice.

All of this means that a small number of dissertation students may still make mistakes in the use and proper citation of other people's material. It is mainly those people who may find the rest of this chapter useful, but it's not a long chapter so even if you aren't in this category it won't take you much time to finish it.

What is plagiarism anyway?

In case you're unsure, it's the unacknowledged use of other people's text in your own work, and hence the passing off of other people's text and writing as your own. It's a bit more complicated than this simple statement would imply. For example, it doesn't follow that you plagiarize only if you use exactly the same form of words as the 'victim' (I'll use that rather dramatic term to avoid having to talk about the 'plagiarizee'[3] or something equally ridiculous). It's easiest if I give some examples to show what I mean. My emphasis will be on unwitting or careless plagiarism rather than full-on deliberate plagiarism – so it's the kind that could end up in your text if you are not paying attention, or where you are rushing and don't have a checking stage before your final submission.

Let's imagine that there is an author called Francesca Treen and that she wrote the following somewhere in her 2009 book *Thrupton: Anatomy of a Steel Town*:

> *By 1963, Darble Road and the adjoining terraced streets between Clutch Crescent and the gasworks had been demolished. Local councillor Ewart T. Blacklock, later imprisoned for accounting irregularities, had proposed the building of a new high-rise estate on the vacant land, and within two years it was virtually complete. The contractors were Huckle and Flume, Blacklock's own building company, but it was to be another five years before formal complaints were made about the objectivity and transparency of the planning process that allowed it to happen, with Blacklock's position as chair of the planning committee a major source of embarrassment to the local Independent Urban Unionist party. Within twenty years all but one of the new blocks on the Clutch Crescent estate had been demolished following major structural failures. By 1990, the plot was derelict and earmarked for a new park and civic amenity site.*

Now let's imagine that fearless student Chesney Munn is writing his dissertation ('Aspects of Change in the UK Steel Industry, 1950–2010'), and that he read the Treen book as part of his original research. He has borrowed it for the vacation and kept it on his shelf for reference while he wrote the bulk of his study. Later, we come across the following somewhere in his dissertation:

> *By the end of the 1950s the British steel industry was facing major competition from overseas, and both it and the manufacturing base it supplied began to decline. As the steelworks in northern cities lost contracts and their output fell away, so the unthinkable happened and works began to shut down. Workers moved away in search of other jobs. As this process got under way, so the residential areas that supported the industry declined too. Several cities saw large*

---

[3] The use of this '-ee' suffix is spreading into bureaucratic language. Have you noticed how people at a meeting or conference are now described as 'attendees'? It seems to have stuck, but like some other modern '-ee' uses would seem to be a bad choice: think of older forms like 'employer' and 'employee': here, the '-ee' person is the one who is on the receiving end whereas the one doing the action (employing in this case) is an '-er' person. So what can 'attendee' possibly mean – somebody who is attended upon? It should be 'attender', shouldn't it? They're the people doing the attending. But there we are. That's the evolution of language use for you.

numbers of old streets demolished to make way for new developments, ridding the centres of substandard housing but creating new problems where their replacements were poorly designed or built. In 1963 in Thrupton, for example, Darble Road and the adjoining terraced streets between Clutch Crescent and the gasworks had been demolished and replaced by the building of a new high-rise estate on the vacant land that was virtually complete within two years. But within twenty years all but one of the new blocks on the Clutch Crescent estate had been demolished following major structural failures.

And so Chesney continues. The question is, did he plagiarize in this passage? Your answer may be 'Well, it depends on whether he cited Francesca Treen's book in his bibliography. If he did he's OK, and if he didn't he plagiarized.' Is that right? I have had students say very much the same thing over the years. The answer is *no*, that's not right. Chesney has plagiarized Francesca regardless of whether her book is included in his bibliography or not. We'll come back to the correct reference point later (and you may want to refresh your memory with a look back at Chapter 7 afterwards, which is where I talk about referencing). But this is a blatant case of plagiarism. Why? Because when we read Chesney's text we assume that it is all his – in just the same way that when you read this book you assume (not surprisingly) that I wrote it. It's an almost universal convention and it's hard to think of exceptions; even where something is written under a pseudonym or anonymously it doesn't change the basic assumption that 'the author' (whoever it may be) wrote the whole text unless otherwise stated. But in our example some chunks of the text are clearly not Chesney's but Francesca's – yet *he hasn't told us that*. I'll repeat the end of his piece and put the copied text in [brackets]:

. . . ridding the centres of substandard housing but creating new problems where their replacements were poorly designed or built. In 1963 in Thrupton, for example, [Darble Road and the adjoining terraced streets between Clutch Crescent and the gasworks had been demolished] and replaced by [the building of a new high-rise estate on the vacant land] that [was virtually complete] [within two years]. But [within twenty years all but one of the new blocks on the Clutch Crescent estate had been demolished following major structural failures].

Perhaps we'd be less fussy about the short extracts 'was virtually complete' and 'within two years' if it hadn't been for the other parts that are clearly the same as Francesca's. It can't be a coincidence that all that text is the same as hers. Hence, any marker recognizing this, or perhaps a Turnitin analysis if one had been used, would flag this up and Chesney would be cited for some kind of academic conduction violation based on plagiarism. Why? Because he allowed us, his readers, to assume that the text was his, and did not show clearly that it was not. How could he have corrected this failing? Here's the simplest way (assuming Chesney is using an author–date referencing scheme):

> . . . *ridding the centres of substandard housing but creating new problems where their replacements were poorly designed or built. In 1963 in Thrupton, for example, 'Darble Road and the adjoining terraced streets between Clutch Crescent and the gasworks had been demolished' and replaced by 'the building of a new high-rise estate on the vacant land' that 'was virtually complete' 'within two years'. But 'within twenty years all but one of the new blocks on the Clutch Crescent estate had been demolished following major structural failures' (Treen, 2009, p. 185).*

I've simply used quote marks instead of the brackets in the previous extract and then added a source that says where the text came from. It's not very pretty at this point (I had to put two sets of quotes around 'was virtually complete' and 'within two years', for example, because they don't occur in that order in the original and hence I can't use 'was virtually complete within two years' which would only be correct if they did). But it's correct as far as it goes. I could have been more fussy and put the Treen citation after the first quoted block (after 'demolished') and then added others after the rest (or more likely used a device like 'ibid.'), but that creates clutter and unless you're working within a very tight citation regime it should be obvious to most readers of Chesney's paragraph that these adjacent quotes are from the same source.

The crucial first step in avoiding plagiarism of others' text, then, is to *show that the text is not yours.* And there are two ways to do this. One is to put the text between quotation marks, as I did in the previous passage, and the other (for longer passages of text) is to break them off, or set them out, as I have done with the passages above that I've used to illustrate this chapter. Of course, in this case I actually wrote those passages too – there is no Ewart Blacklock and no Francesca Treen, and neither is there a careless plagiarizer stalking her called Chesney Munn. Well, I hope not – it will be entirely accidental and pure coincidence if there are. But the point remains that the device of setting out or 'extracting' longer passages is the other main way of showing that text is not yours. (In this chapter it just happens that I'm using this device for another purpose, to display example text.) To see these two modes of displaying others' text in action, just grab[4] a handful of academic books and look through them.

---

[4] Legitimately, I mean. Of course.

As to how many words you can use between quotes and when something is long enough to need setting out, well, there's no rule. Sometimes publishers set guidelines in their style sheets or when briefing editors, and editors and authors can have their own preferences too. Perhaps 40, 50 or 60 words or more? Setting text out provides an emphasis, a contrast with the main text, so it can be used even for short passages to do that. The main idea behind setting out longer extracts is that when you use quotation marks for long passages it's easy to read on for a couple of lines and then forget that you're reading somebody else's text, whereas when it's set out you have a constant visual reminder.

One more thing. Would Chesney have been able to avoid the threat of plagiarism by rearranging the quoted text, something like this (to use just the last part again)?

> . . . ridding the centres of substandard housing but creating new problems where their replacements were poorly designed or built. In 1963 in Thrupton, for example, the Clutch Crescent area around Darble Road, the nearby terraced streets and the gasworks was demolished. Within about two years there sprang up a new high-rise estate on the resulting empty space, yet by about 1983 all but one of the high-rise blocks on the new estate had been demolished for major structural failures.

What do you think? There's some rearrangement, definitely. And some altering of the text here and there – the Darble Road sentence is turned around, 'twenty years' has been translated into 'about 1983' (though without any clear evidence that this is the appropriate date), a few tenses have shifted – pluperfects to perfects, and so on – and there's even a new sparkle to the language with 'sprang up'. Whoopee. But is the result different enough to be Chesney's text, and hence definitely not plagiarism? Alas, no. It's still plagiarism. The changes are only cosmetic. If somebody steals your car, resprays it, gives it new seat covers and wing mirrors, changes the engine number and registration plates and so on, it's still a stolen car – your car. Let's take the analogy a stage further: if somebody steals two cars and 'cut and shut' welds them together, half and half, as two 'new' cars, the result is still a mixture of two stolen cars – mutilated and concealed though they may be.

One bad plagiarism case I had to deal with some years ago (not from a student this time, but out in the wider academic world) was where an author had taken another person's whole article and rewritten it completely such that by the end of the process there were only two words out of the many thousands that still matched the original article – I ran a file comparison and checked. Everything was seemingly 'different' between the two files. But under the surface everything was the same. The structure was the same (though the headings had been rewritten), the definitions were rewritten but essentially the same, the arguments were the same and presented in the same order and so on. The author eventually admitted it and some unfortunate consequences followed. It is a useful reminder that plagiarism doesn't only occur when there is verbatim copying. You can't legitimize copying just by tweaking the text a little.

Notice something else too: whenever somebody does this kind of thing it is clear that they are trying to hide something – honest car dealers don't file down the VIN or number plate and replace it with a false one. People examining academic conduct issues look for similar signs because as well as the evidence of plagiarism there is normally a desire to discover intent. If somebody plagiarizes, then makes cosmetic attempts to hide their tracks by rearranging the purloined text, they are trying to hide something. Hence they provide evidence of an intent to deceive. Worse still, in this 'Turnitin' era, if they interfere with the electronic text files that are submitted to the system, they are being significantly dishonest, and such acts are nearly always taken to be signs of deliberate villainy and receive the harshest penalties. Nobody will believe that these evidence-falsifiers 'accidentally' used somebody else's text.

How to avoid unwitting plagiarism

The first and major step in not plagiarizing is:

> Always, always, always show clearly that other people's text is not your own.

You know how to do this, with quotation marks and devices such as setting out the text separately. The next step is then to apply your referencing scheme (Chapter 7) to say where you found it, using whatever system you have chosen or have been told you must use. This brings us into a separate area, that of using the reference system properly, which you will no doubt be marked on; but if you have marked all the text from others and have tried to reference it properly, then the *quality* of that referencing is not normally a question of plagiarism but of appropriate academic practice, good or bad. Also, although you may have shown and cited all of your passages correctly, if you used loads of other people's text this may still count against a high mark because you have been so unoriginal. Imagine that in a 15,000-word dissertation

John-Louis correctly cited other people's text throughout, but that it amounted to 7,000 words. All other things being equal, such a profligate reliance on second-hand content would not normally be very inspiring for a marker to read. It would be legitimate from the plagiarism point of view, but rather feeble stuff that is unlikely to get good marks.

Keep those notes clean!

There is one other area where, based on my experience as a conduct officer, I think people can improve their resistance to plagiarizing tendencies. When interviewing people who had been referred to me I noticed that some, when I asked them to explain how they had come to plagiarize others' text – and I'm talking about the careless end of the spectrum here rather than wicked folk – would show me the notes that they'd amassed when reading for the dissertation or coursework. Sure enough, they'd read at least what they were supposed to read and often much more besides. Some were very organized about it too, keeping diaries as well as copious reading notes. Then they'd say 'I just copied this passage out of my notes, see?' and, yes, they had. Trouble is, that's not really much of a defence against plagiarism, given that they were just as responsible for compiling their notes as they were for producing their final coursework or dissertation.

But there was something amiss, and it comes down to these students' study methods. Diligent though they were, they had not maintained an appropriate identification and control routine in their research notes and reading notes. They'd identify the book, article or whatever it was, and write that down as a title, then they'd write their notes underneath as they read through the source material. What they didn't do was clearly distinguish what was their own notes, based on their reading, from verbatim quotes taken from the piece itself. Hence they ended up with pages of text that could have come from anywhere, and by the time a month or two had passed it became progressively more difficult to say who created what text.

The remedy is actually quite simple, and I can state it by just modifying my number 1 rule from above to include your note-taking activities as well. That is, when you cite text from elsewhere in your notes, show when you are quoting text from the source you are reading – as before, using quotation marks or extracting the text in some way. Perhaps if Chesney had put things like this in his diary he wouldn't have got into trouble?

Francesca Treen, Thrupton: Anatomy of a Steel Town, *Ravitz and Landauer Publishing, 2009. Borrowed from uni main library Jan to March 2011*

Treen says Ewart Blacklock proposed new estate in Thrupton and then had it built by his own firm after 1963, but all demolished by 1983[?] as badly built.

'The contractors were Huckle and Flume, Blacklock's own building company, but it was to be another five years before formal complaints were made about the objectivity and transparency of the planning process that allowed it to happen . . .' (p. 185)

This gives Chesney a clear statement of the source, plus a statement that is easy to identify as his own, including a question mark by a date that he would have to think about if he chose to use it. Then he adds a verbatim quote that he has put between quotation marks (*show clearly that other people's text is not your own*) and paginated. When he comes back to this again in the future there should be no mistake.

Of course, you could make a case for not having a lot of quoted matter in your notes at all. What is it all there for? Ideally, you should read, think and interpret, and then write your own notes. Yes, there are some good reasons for having a few short quotes in verbatim form. One is if you intend to use them directly in your text (clearly identified as such, of course). Linked to this is another: where the source is hard to get at (say, in a remote archive) and you're unlikely to go back and look at it again, you need a few samples of the original text in case you decide to use them. But other than that, I'd suggest you keep verbatim quotation under tight control during your note-taking and that you keep the bulk of your notes as just that – your notes.

This practice of clearly identifying others' text in your notes is something you should do whether you're writing the notes longhand, keying them into your laptop or other device – or simply block-copying text off the internet into an electronic file (the most dangerous procedure of all – be very careful that you don't end up dumping some of that text into your own work). Then when you come back two months later to see your notes on that book or journal, or to look again at the online text, you'll know where it came from and there'll be no doubt whether it is yours or not. (Needless to say, you wrote down the source at the same time as you made the note, even for those possibly transient online materials, where you should also add the time and date at which you accessed them as I mentioned in Chapter 7.) So here's the note-taking variant of rule 1.

> Always, always, always, when you make reading or other research notes, show clearly that other people's text is not your own, and keep verbatim quotation to a minimum.

Believe me, when you come back to them later you'll be pleased that you can identify the source of those notes. It will help you to avoid one of the traps of working carelessly from poorly identified notes. As I mentioned when I first introduced Chesney Munn's 'extract', it is not enough to list the source in your bibliography and then behave as if this gives you a licence to drop text from that source unannounced into your own writing whenever you feel like it. Always show others' text as not your own. Once again, and put more brutally still:

> If it ain't yours, say so.

Otherwise we shall assume it is yours, and you risk being discovered as a plagiarist.

10 The final frontier

So it's all done? The reading is finished, the primary research is complete, and you've written a complete draft with all of the prescribed elements in place. Now what? Well, you need to do some careful checking before you hand it in, and that's what this chapter is about – the checking and quality control phases from the later draft stages onwards. I thought it would be most useful to present this through a series of checklists and comments, and where necessary to point you back to previous chapters where I've also reminded you about the importance of checking what you do. I'll start with the draft itself.

The checking elements described in this chapter concentrate on those that you can usefully apply when you reach some kind of full draft in the latter part of your dissertation studies. A checklist for the beginning of your work would look very different, and the one item at its head would be *Make time for your dissertation*, which will set different challenges depending on your circumstances – the demands of other parts of your course, whether you have a job and for how many hours a week, whether you're trying to bring up a family (a particular challenge) and so on. Whatever it is, set aside clear time for your dissertation right from the start – the equivalent of at least one day a week and possibly more – and always use it (Chapter 2).

When you check off the following draft-stage items (if that's how you decide to use this chapter), don't just go through and say 'Yeah. Done that. Done that,' and so on. Instead, ask the following question before you tick an item off:

■ Would anybody reading the present version of my dissertation *see* that I had done that?

We're back to the *raison d'être* of this book – the dissertation itself as a presentation of all your research and analysis, and the only evidence of it that the outside world (and markers) will see. Does your dissertation provide that evidence? Does your dissertation do justice to all of that investigating, thinking and writing?

Producing a complete draft of your dissertation

Whatever you have to produce for your study – be it pure dissertation, extended essay, project with reflective report or whatever – you will reach a stage where you have completed most of the writing and all the main parts are in place. You know you will need to spend more time polishing it, but it's a very good point to review what you've done and to involve other people in that process too (in a legitimate way, of course). For simplicity's sake I'll call this 'the' draft, as if there is only ever one draft and it's always a draft of the complete work. In practice, of course, you'll have produced draft versions of chapters or other parts of the text prior to that, and you may well have asked your supervisor to look at some or all of those, depending on what you've agreed between you. It's natural and sensible to do this to get some kind of answer to the question 'Am I on the right track?' or 'Am I doing the right kind of thing before I go on and do the rest of it?'

As to how many drafts you should produce, there's no simple answer, though you'll find that research methods texts will give you a lot of advice on this. My view is that it's more a question of whether your drafting sequence is functionally effective – that is, whether it tests the work you've done so far, and the way you've written it up, to the extent that you can review it, reflect on it, amend it and then go on and finish it to produce the best possible outcome. To this end, you may produce several versions of some parts of the dissertation – possibly ones that have been difficult or troublesome – and perhaps just one or two versions of some of the other parts about which you've been more confident. It depends.

There is another issue here, which is the extent to which students can expect to receive help and inputs from tutors and others at this stage of their academic careers. A dissertation is something that is a feature of the final year of an undergraduate degree or at MA, MSc and similar level. It is designed to test and encourage independent research and inquiry and, as I've said in earlier chapters, you're essentially on your own and that limits what a tutor, even your supervisor, can say to you or feed back to you about drafts. Also, depending on policy, resourcing and other factors, your supervisor may be one of the markers and that would act as a further brake on what they can say about your drafts. I'll just summarize this by saying that this is something that you must talk to your supervisor about and negotiate with them.

As for other people who could read your drafts, there are more or less useful and more or less risky alternatives as I've mentioned in earlier chapters. Asking fellow dissertation students and others of your friends studying the same subject to read your draft is a high-risk activity because it would be so easy to stray into the academic misconduct zone. Perhaps the biggest risk here is one of collusion, where one or more of you could gain an advantage by reading another's dissertation draft and hence breach your institution's academic regulations. Therefore be very, very careful about letting fellow students read your dissertation, and observe similar strictures about you reading theirs. I know it's difficult to avoid exchanging information, especially if you're sharing a house. And I appreciate that they are probably doing a very different topic from you, so it might be tempting to assume that it's all right to read each other's work, but there is probably a shared base of underlying theory and practice that could cross over between you. Just be extremely careful, and err on the side of caution.

What of the less risky alternatives? I suppose these are variations on the 'mum read',[1] where you have somebody read your drafts who knows little or nothing about your topic or your field and is just reading it to see whether it makes sense, as far as they can tell. This is usually less controversial, unless your mum or equivalent figure is an expert in the field you're researching, in which case you're back into the high-risk zone. This more distant class of readers would also appear to include people who advertise themselves around universities as proofreaders or editors for dissertations and theses, though again it depends on the kind of intervention they are offering. Talk to your supervisor and check your university and course regulations if in doubt about any kind of input from others. Provided they are not too close to the topic, an external read from somebody who is interested in whether your draft makes sense is a useful resource because they may see things that you are too close to the work to see. A second or third pair of eyes is always valuable, even if you go on to disagree with what the eyes' owners say, but in this chapter my main purpose is to provide a framework for you to do your own self-checking. And, to repeat what I said at the start, it's not enough to know that you've done whatever it is; it is whether anybody reading your dissertation can see what you've done and how you've done it.

And before we get to the checking stages below, there's one primary check or pre-check that it's worth doing at this stage (as well as just before you hand the whole thing in):

- RTFM again.

---

[1] Or the 'dad read' or the 'great aunt read' or the 'lover read' – whatever you like, though probably not a 'cat read' or 'pet fish read' however much you love them. It's just that I have found that mums are commonly relied on here.

Yes, very tedious, but it's possibly several months since you last looked at it, and it's so easy to forget something crucial. Read through it again from start to finish and pay attention to the small print and detail, such as precise word limits and what you are required or allowed to include in that word count. What about notes, for example? If you have a lot of them and they're included in the word count, that will make a difference to the length of your main text. If (which is highly unlikely) your dissertation structure resembles the Hans Peter Duerr example I gave in Chapter 7 then they could make a huge difference. Is there a stipulation about how the dissertation is to be printed out – precise margins, line spacing, particular fonts? Do you have to submit an online version too? If so, where and in what file format? Anyway, read all the detail and make sure you meet your institution's and dissertation handbook's requirements to the letter.

And when is all this happening? The point about the timing of the checks in this chapter is that I'm assuming you've reached a draft stage where you have a more or less full version of the dissertation, but that there is still some useful working time left. It would be good to have, say, another month left when you're doing all of this, wouldn't it? There's no point in undertaking careful checks and rereading if it's so late in the sequence that there's no time left to act on anything that needs doing. If you do your 'checks' only a few hours before you print out the final version and give it to the binder there will be no time to correct any problems. All you'll do is make yourself unhappy, or you'll make a few desperate last-minute changes that may create new problems. When I used to run courses around the UK for academic editors I would always include a reminder at frequent intervals:

■ Whenever you make a change to a text there is always a risk that you will introduce new errors or problems.

This applies to editors and proofreaders but equally to authors changing their own texts. As I mentioned back in Chapter 6, word-processors allow us to make endless changes all the time, so the scope for introducing new errors is high. Worse, when you check late you do not have time to reread the hastily amended new draft before it goes for printing and binding, so the chances of introducing new problems are further increased if you panic and rush through corrections at the last minute. Hence:

■ Build in enough time after your final draft and checking stages for you to be able to correct problems, make improvements and proof-read the new version too.

Right. Now it's time for some specific checks. I've collected them together in groups of bullet points but that's more to keep the sections clear and avoid long blocks of text than anything else. Also, the sequence of these groupings is fairly arbitrary, so work through them in a way that makes sense to you in the context of your research and the final product – your dissertation. As in all of this book, when I mention 'dissertation' that includes projects, extended essays and other submissions of an equivalent type.

Intentions and arguments

This first group of checks concerns what you set out to do and how, and whether you actually did it. Remember, it's whether somebody reading your dissertation can see this, not just that you believe you've done it.

- Do you set out clear aims and objectives early in the dissertation, and is there evidence in the later parts of the dissertation that you've achieved them – whether explicitly (you actually list them and say so) or implicitly (in which case it should be clear to the reader)?
    - Or, if you were unable to achieve any of your objectives (which may well happen), have you given a good explanation of why this was, and if appropriate what the implications are?

- Have you set out a research question or hypothesis, or some other agreed starting point for your inquiry, and addressed it via your dissertation in a rational manner that allows the reader to see whether you've answered your question, evaluated (or rejected, etc.) your hypothesis, or in some other way resolved your initial intent?

- Are you sure you have not built in bias or come to foregone conclusions – for example through your choice of definitions or methods?

Don't worry about outcomes that are negative, or contrary to expectations, or generally surprising: obviously, talk to your supervisor if you are worried that you may have done something wrong, or that such outcomes constitute a 'mistake'. An unexpected outcome can sometimes lead to great things.

- Does your dissertation exemplify the principles of rational inquiry, using theories critically, gathering and evaluating evidence, and then proceeding via a discussion to concluding remarks in such a way that the whole is held together by a flowing argument?
    - Are your source materials (theories, data, etc.) linked to the discussion and conclusion in a clear manner?
    - In other words, is your dissertation a joined-up piece of work or a bag of unconnected bits?

■ Can you identify logical connections between the parts of your argument(s) – say, between premises and conclusions, and through inductive or deductive reasoning – and have you used key terms with care and not casually? (Including those deceptive little words like 'because' and 'therefore' – see Chapter 4.)

■ Are your discussions and conclusions free of unsupported conjecture and guesswork that is independent of your findings and analysis?

■ And where you have discussed things speculatively (say, when making predictions of future outcomes in your conclusions), have you made it clear that this is what they are, and linked this speculation to your main discussion (that is, it is rational speculation and prediction as opposed to wild guesswork)?

Structure and design

I said in Chapter 6 that it is important to distinguish structure from design. But you need to attend to both if your dissertation is to be accessible and reader friendly. It would be a shame to do good research, write it up well, and then present it in a deplorably cluttered manner that would put off all but the most diligent reader. As part of their job a marker has to be a diligent reader, but it is as well to keep them happy in as many ways as possible. A well presented and clearly set out document can be a joy to read, especially when a marker has just finished wading through one that is just a mass of unbroken text set out in a tiny font.

■ Is the basic text structure clear, using chapters, sections and other elements to support the presentation of your findings and argument to the reader?

■ Have you been able to use other structural elements such as lists, dialogue, tables and figures, etc., to convey your discussion and arguments?
   – But not just for their own sake, of course, or to make it seemingly more 'academic'.

■ . . . And don't break up the text so much that the narrative or overall coherence disappears into a mass of fragments.

■ Have you avoided structural excesses, such as masses of over-complicated diagrams and tables that don't add anything to your exposition or argument, or at the other extreme page after page of solid, unbroken text?

- The 'over-complication' danger may be more prevalent in social sciences, sciences, technology, etc.; some students like to spend time making these pretty objects, and others may add them and complicate them because they feel it makes their work look more 'technical' and hence attractive to brownie points. (So always ask about the function of all those elements: for example, are those tables and figures doing any useful work?)
- The 'mass of solid text' danger may be more prevalent in arts and humanities subjects where the conventional medium is just text, and there is very little scope for objects like figures and tables (though don't forget that genuinely informative illustrations can help). If you do have 'just text', try to employ helpful headings, subheadings and possibly sub-subheadings, and use a clear font and more 'spacey'[2] design to make the pages of text look less oppressive.

A design that supports your structure

- If you have a choice, have you selected a gimmick-free, clearly legible font that is appropriate to academic discourse? (If you have no choice then you have used the typeface and type size, etc. (font) specified in your dissertation handbook. Yes?)
- Have you chosen suitable margin size, line spacing, heading fonts and sizes, etc.? It's a good idea to use different typefaces (fonts) sparingly – say, one in a couple of size variants for the main text and display, and another in different size variants for headings.
  - This means, for example, that you will not print out your dissertation in 18 pt Comic Sans or Klingon Warrior Bold, and that you have not used furry animals or autumn leaves as fancy borders or rows of smiley faces to mark section breaks or chapters.
- Beware of coloured text, unless you have a good reason to use it. It can look jokey and amateurish. Some built-in word-processor styles now use colours for text, so be careful.

Academic writing is based on a fairly sober register, so even if you like bright and breezy designs for other kinds of work and want to make the world a cheerier place, don't use your dissertation to launch your campaign.

---

[2] I mean, spacey in the sense of a more open design and plenty of interline space, etc., rather than something visualized during experiments with hallucinogens.

Navigation

- Have you organized the whole dissertation in a way that enables readers to find their way through easily and locate specific sections or elements with ease?
  - This means having a single sequence of page numbers.
  - And are the page numbers correct? You haven't accidentally turned on some section-based scheme, for example, that restarts from 1 every now and again.

- Use your word-processor's page numbering system so that when you move things around, add pages, etc., the whole thing renumbers automatically.

- Learn the finer points of your word-processor's page numbering facilities so that, for example, you can choose where page 1 falls and avoid page numbers on title pages, etc.

- If you want appendices and other endmatter to be useful and accessible, consider ways of numbering those pages too, either as part of the main sequence or in a separate one (such as page A1, A2, etc.).

Naturally, you have included a contents list and you put that as near the front of your dissertation as possible, so that readers can find it without having to wade through prefaces and other material first.

- It's useful to include the main subheads ('A heads') as well as the chapter heads in your contents list. How much you include in the contents depends on your overall structure, though. The key question is whether your readers can find things relatively quickly.

- Be sure to update your contents list whenever you change anything in the dissertation. Even if the headings don't change, the page numbers will – as they will if you redesign everything after the draft with a different font or font size.

- Or you can use your word-processor's contents list generating facility so that it updates automatically, whenever you make changes.

- Will you include an index? It's uncommon but a nice touch. Remember that it is time-consuming and can't really be finalized until you have your confirmed printed draft with all of the page numbers in place.

- As with the contents, you can use your word-processor's index generating facility, flagging up words for the index as you go through the text

- If you have a lot of other elements, such as figures and tables, you could consider having a contents list for those too (often headed, unsurprisingly, List of Figures or List of Tables). Take advice if you're unsure.

- If you are working in a law discipline make sure you have followed the precise requirements for any table of statutes or table of cases you have to include. That means observing the details too (whether to italicize parties, etc.), as outlined in the next section.

Style and detail

- Did you set up a list of key spellings, capitalization and hyphenations to follow throughout, and also decide to use 'single' or "double" quotation marks?
  - That means you'll have opted for UK or US English (you may have no choice), and have made a choice between alternative spellings – particularly for words that can be spelled with either '-ize' or '-ise' endings.
  - You will also decide to use a particular capitalization scheme in your headings and subheadings.
- Are you able to add nice 'professional' touches so that for example your parenthetical dashes look like this – rather than employ hyphens like this - which looks less convincing (these uses are spaced). Have a look at published materials to see how this works.
  - And can you add an additional refinement by using the same 'en rule' between number pairs, such as 'pp. 234–56' or in the sense of 'from . . . to' or 'between . . . and', such as in 'the north–south road between London and Scotland' (neither of these uses are spaced)?
- Um, have you checked to make sure that no horrendous errors like 'could of' and 'would of' have slipped through?

Consistency

- Have you been careful to be consistent in all matters of detail, including spellings, etc., such that you treat all similar items in the same way?

Emerson may have said (cliché alert) that 'a foolish consistency is the hobgoblin of little minds, adored by little statesmen and philosophers and divines', but this advice to be consistent in your dissertation does not represent a pettifogging or oppressive campaign against freedom of student expression. It is a routine aspect of the management of text in published work that helps to add polish to your work; it creates the impression that you have taken care rather than simply thrown the thing together.

Consistency is not just about spellings and hyphens, etc., but applies to all choices between alternatives affecting detail and design. You could say that all questions of style come down to decisions between possible alternatives. For example, you should use the same font for a feature wherever it appears, so a main (top-level) subhead should have the same appearance in every chapter instead of varying from one place to the next and, potentially, confusing readers about your structure.

Spellcheckers, grammar checkers, style checkers . . .?

I am sure you will use at least a spellchecker on your dissertation, probably as you create it and also afterwards as a kind of proofread (except that a spellcheck isn't a proofread – see below). As for grammar or style checkers I think they are rather more of a mixed blessing than spellcheckers, so if you choose to have them turned on I suggest you keep them under control by enabling them at a minimal level. They can make misleading and just plain wrong suggestions. Anyway, it's your choice: if you find them all useful then turn them on. But use them with care.

I'll just look briefly at spellcheckers, because their use raises two points. I'm not referring here to the claims that spellcheckers have stopped people thinking about spelling and are thus a Bad Thing. This may have happened, and may be a bad thing if we are concerned that everybody should have a basic competence at spelling. The worry is that they remove the thinking in the same way that GPS-based satellite navigation has taken the thinking out of route planning for car drivers. In the days of paper maps you planned a journey and checked it along the way using landmarks, road signs and so on. You had to keep thinking about where you were in relation to where you were going, and be aware of north, south, east and west. You would certainly not end up in the middle of a field or a river, as those people have done who blindly followed their navigation system's instructions.

The two points I want to raise are different: first, the dangers of undermining your spellchecker by careless use, and second, the question of when in the sequence you should use a spellchecker for a full document check.

How can you 'undermine' a spellchecker? There are two main ways, both of them connected with the facility to add words to the dictionary for the document or spellchecker. One way is deliberate, and the other accidental or careless. The deliberate way happens when people whose spelling is less than brilliant are confronted by the spellchecker stopping on a mis-spelled word in the usual way – for example, they intend 'tractor' but key 'tracter', which will probably not be in their dictionary (unless they want to use it to refer to somebody who distributes tracts or similar). The problem arises when the bad speller says 'But "tracter" is the right spelling', so adds it to their dictionary. From that point on, every instance of 'tracter' will be allowed through. This example is a bit obvious but you can see what I mean. Some kinds of bad speller can be so convinced the spellchecker is wrong that they 'correct' it by putting in their own 'special' spellings.

The accidental variant of undermining the spellchecker comes when people casually press 'Add' or 'Ignore' buttons because their concentration has dipped or their eyes have glazed over after spellchecking page upon page of their document. But the effect is the same as the deliberate version, and after a while the spellchecker becomes progressively less useful. It doesn't catch those words that people habitually spell badly, and unfortunately those are precisely the ones that it ought to catch.

So to the second point: when should you use a spellchecker during your dissertation quality-checking sequence? At the very end, just before you print everything out and take it to the binder? Students often think so, but no. It might be very tempting to do that, but spellcheckers sometimes do strange things, and not just when they've been compromised by bad spellers. Also, the users of spellcheckers can do strange things, mainly by agreeing unwanted changes without thinking or when not concentrating. All of this can leave unwanted changes and mistakes in the text, so *always do your spellchecking pass before you do your proofread*. That way, you can pick up any pieces of spellcheckerese and put them right before you print.

Don't become too reliant on a spellchecker. There are many things they can't do, and if you've used the wrong word but it's legitimate in that context the spellchecker won't show it – such as the very common (for some reason) mis-spelling of 'public' as 'pubic', which also finds its way past proofreaders into publications too. A grammar or style checker won't find this either because 'public' and 'pubic' can both be used in the same way as adjectives. Hence if you are unwittingly talking about pubic service in your dissertation it may not be flagged as an error.[3] It won't check your proper nouns either, and when these are also legitimate words in the spellchecker's dictionary you'll receive no warning. Imagine you are writing about Spenser but that occasionally your finger slips to an adjacent key and you produce Spender instead (rather a different figure). 'Spender' won't show up because it's an ordinary noun (as in 'big spender') and will be in the dictionary. The same applies to 'Spencer', if your finger slips to the next line. The spellchecker won't flag up either of these. Only you can find them by rereading your text carefully.

---

[3] Except that recent ones now do. When I keyed this sentence my word-processor politely asked if I mean 'public', so I may have to retire this example in future. Style and grammar checkers are much better than they used to be, but I still recommend caution and keeping them under tight control.

Make sure you have a good chunky dictionary such as the Chambers (my favourite) or Oxford variants, and use that instead. This is not a piece of anti-digital reactionary thinking. By all means use a spell-checker. I do. But look up all of your problem or unfamiliar words in a dictionary and get used to reading it. It will lead you astray and take you on all sorts of interesting journeys.

Reading the proof

With all of these details and features you will have made choices along the way and tried to impose them as your research progressed and dissertation took shape, but:

- Are you now going to do a thorough proofread of the whole dissertation, or at least schedule one in to your plans to be undertaken when you think the draft has had its last polish and is ready to go?

Yes? Of course you are. That's good. In fact most students routinely expect to proofread their dissertations at least once, and/or perhaps get others to do that too. They may say something like 'And then I'll do a quick proofread and get it printed.' But many of these 'proofreads' can fall very far short of the ideal. I'd go so far as to make this claim:

- Many people imagine that they can undertake a reasonably good proofread . . .
- But many people, based on my experience to date, are entirely wrong about this.

It also depends what people understand proofreading to be. Some seem to regard it as a kind of quick check based on a scan read, but that isn't proofreading. It's a quick check based on a scan read. You'll find some things and miss a lot of others. Proofreading involves a very close and detailed check, based on reading the entire piece with a methodical thoroughness. Besides, authors (and for your dissertation that means you) are notoriously bad proofreaders because they tend to read what they expect to find rather than what is actually there. So what is to be done?

I think you must proofread your dissertation regardless – and it would be hard to find anybody to disagree with that, even if they say you should hire a professional proofreader to do it too. And we've already seen that having others read your dissertation may need clearance or clarification for your regulations and supervisor, and also will cost money that you probably don't have. On the other hand, a non-threatening 'mum read' could find some problems that you might not have found yourself. However, as far as possible you should try to improve your own proofreading so that you do it at least carefully and methodically, rather than by scan reading and hence missing a lot. As you are going to do it, then do it as well as you can.

To help you with some techniques and tips I've provided some hints on 'How to proofread'. This very brief set of hints won't turn you into a professional proofreader overnight but it should help you do a far better job.[4] One clear consequence of doing the job properly is that it will take far longer than a quick scan for errors, so that means you should build in enough time for a proper proofread (no, not one hour) before you go into final production.

How to proofread

We can't read proofs in the same way that we read novels, newspapers, textbooks, etc., because we are not simply trying to gain information or reading for pleasure. Also, our sophisticated adult reading practice is complex and not simply a matter of decoding letter shapes one after another. In a sense, we frequently read what we expect to find rather than what's actually there, which is one reason why authors often make bad proofreaders. Naturally, this has implications for proofreading your own dissertation.

Your final proofread in particular must be a systematic, deliberate and thorough check of the whole document, not just a last-minute scan read. What follows is a suggested approach together with a list of techniques that will help you do this. Many of the suggestions are common sense, though some may be less obvious. Practice and experience are essential characteristics of a good proofreader too, but these take years to develop and you don't have time for that.

The basics

This set of techniques is intended to maximize your concentration and also slow down those sophisticated reading habits – but not too much, because the text must still make sense as you read and not just disintegrate into a collection of individual letters and words.

- Allow enough time for a proper proofread.

---

[4] Achieving a high standard needs a lot of practice too. I used to tell trainee editors and proofreaders that they need to do the equivalent of at least 50 substantial books in their chosen calling before they could be confident that they both knew what they were doing and had achieved a high degree of accuracy. This is in part because it takes time to become alive to some of the problems that arise and you need to see them 'in action', as it were. You can't possibly do this, but you can employ some basic techniques that will help you find more problems.

An hour on the day you submit is not going to be enough. If that's all the time you have, you will only be able to do a quick scan read, which will be almost worthless as a quality-control check. Set aside at least a day for it, and with enough time afterwards for you to make further changes if necessary (though if you're working directly on the text on screen you'll probably make changes as you go).

- Decide whether you're going to work directly on screen, or instead mark up a printout.

- Adopt a comfortable sitting position, desk height, etc., and arrange good task lighting
  - discomfort and poor light are enemies of concentration and accuracy.

If you're working on screen, then it's a good idea to follow some equivalent 'best practice' pointers:

- Position the screen carefully, making sure that it is clean and free from glare, reflections, etc.

- Check your display settings (brightness, contrast, etc.), screen colours and figure–ground contrasts, and choice of screen fonts and zoom ratio (how much of the page you see on screen at a time).

Remember that you should take regular breaks from the screen and do eye 'exercises'. It's very easy to work for long hours at the screen and exhaust yourself and your eyes in the process.

And now for one more 'common sense' technique that is designed to slow up your reading habits:

- Use a device (e.g. ruler, straight edge, pencil, pointer) to read each line in turn, making sure you read right to the end of one line before going right to the start of the next.

If you're working on screen rather than on paper, then you need to adopt an equivalent technique on screen, perhaps using a border or edge on your word-processor or methodically feeding the lines one by one. As on paper, read right to the end of one line before going right to the start of the next.

Some important techniques

Now here is a set of important practices that will improve your accuracy – finding problems – when used with the above methodical approach.

- Always reread lines/sentences after encountering and marking errors.

Why? There are two reasons. One is to make sure that the passage reads properly after it has been changed – it's easy to change something imperfectly or introduce a new error. The other reason is that your eye may jump to one error but miss another less obvious one that was right next to it. If you reread you stand a very good chance of finding the other error.

▨ Always reread lines/sentences after turning over pages or reading across other breaks.

Why? Because these are classic blind spots when we read normally. It's worth rereading over such breaks to make sure that you haven't missed something.

▨ Always mark your position when taking a break . . .
  – and when you resume, start reading some lines before that point.

Why? Well, you do need to take breaks – your concentration will flag and your eyes will get tired – and quite obviously you need to make some kind of mark to show where you stopped (something that you can rub out later if on paper, or a clear mark such as [BREAK] if you're reading on text, which you can then easily search for and remove before you print out).

What about restarting before the place where you stopped? Your concentration declines as you come to a stop, so it's more possible you will miss something at that stage. Also, when you've just started your concentration takes a little while to get going again. Hence, if you overlap the stopping and restarting you give yourself a better chance of finding any problems caught in the concentration dip.

Hints

Always read the whole document methodically, from the very first line on each page to the very last. Don't allow your eye to dash through headings to the text below, for example, as that's a good way to miss errors in the headings. Don't forget to include things like headers and footers, and page numbers. Above all, don't rush, and don't allow your normal everyday reading habits to take over.

You will almost certainly need to perform some secondary passes through the text before or after you've done the main read. Check the contents page against the chapter titles, etc., and cross-check text citations with reference lists, as well as things like the links between the text mentions of tables and figures and the corresponding objects.

And then, when the proofreading and the other checks are done, you can permit yourself the luxury of a scan read – one more fairly rapid run through the whole thing to make sure it's all there and in the right order.

▶

And spellchecks and grammar checks? Make sure you do these or any other automated or software based checking before you do your main proofread, not after it. That way you will catch any unintended problems the electronic checks may throw up.

Function

Does it all work, then? A rather general question, but it's what this section of the checking process covers. It refers not so much to the key functions within the dissertation, such as your core argument or supporting pieces of reasoning 'working', which is to do with the content being right and is covered in the first set of questions earlier in this chapter. By 'does it work?' in this section I'm referring to the 'mechanics' of the dissertation itself, so here are some questions about that, and you may think of others that apply to your particular dissertation or project. Many of the checks here can catch problems that arise when you amend and update your dissertation: for example, cross-references and other links break when you change things around. Let's start with a couple of basic questions about your terminology:

- Have you checked the proper nouns in your dissertation – place names, any people being described in the narrative or interviewed, author names, etc.?

- Are they the names you want? In the case of place names, are they in line with any specifications you are required to follow, such as recognized lists issued by learned bodies or publishers or your department? Note that atlases and online map sites differ from one another and over time with regard to place names, which can also invoke political sensitivities. More generally, news media vary widely in their spelling of people and place names. Be consistent.

Referencing and cross-referencing

- Do the reference and note systems work, in the sense that all note cues and all text citations for references lead to the right notes or references and nowhere else? Are you sure? Have you checked them? It's tedious but that's the only way to be sure.

- In reporting materials like interviews, etc., have you clearly distinguished your glosses of what people say from verbatim quotation of their actual words (see the *Procedures and ethics* notes below)?

- Do your text mentions of other elements work – such as table mentions and discussions link to the right tables and so on?

- Do your tables and figures work correctly, for example with the right captions, sources and notes, and with columns of numbers adding up properly?

- Do your tables, figures and other ancillary material all show what you say they show? Will the reader be able to work that out instantly when they come to use them?

- Have you checked all hyperlinks and URLs in your text and references to make sure they are all still live and point to the right places?

- Is all content from other authors, or from your other writings, clearly identified as such?

- Is everything properly referenced that needs to be referenced, including in non-text items like tables and figures? Are you sure? Have you done a check of the whole dissertation just for this factor alone?

- Do any cross-references to other parts of your dissertation ('see Chapter 4' and the like) actually link to the right items or parts of the text? Check them all before printing because they're prime examples of things that are vulnerable to changes in your dissertation (for example, if you switch things around and Chapter 4 becomes Chapter 5).

Some if not all of the above functional checks benefit from being performed in separate passes – that is, not at the same time you're (proof) reading for spellings, punctuation and other detail. Of course, you may still notice some of these problems when you're proofreading for problems of detail.

Formalities

Here is a short section that simply lists a few implications of RTFMing, or that are part of the overall regulations for your dissertation without actually appearing in the course handbook. They may be presented during your research methods course, for example.

- Check that all required chapters, sections, etc., appear in your dissertation, using the prescribed titles if your dissertation rules require you to use certain forms.

■ If you are free to create your own chapter structure and headings but must still include formal elements such as a lit review or methodology (both of these are highly likely), make sure that your reader (marker) can find them and recognize them for what they are.

  – It is too late to say afterwards 'But I did have a methodology! It was under the subheading "Ways and means" in the chapter "The evolution of the carrot as a ritual object". Isn't that obvious?'

■ Check that you understand all of the presentation and submission rules (see the next section), and seek them out if you don't (ask your supervisor, etc.).

Procedures and ethics

Make sure that you have followed prescribed or appropriate procedures, particularly in your dealings with people you have contacted in the course of your research.

■ This responsibility does not only apply to the start of your dissertation work, when you may sign an ethics declaration, for example, or obtain ethical clearance for any people-based work that you may do.

■ Think always 'Am I treating this person fairly and openly, respecting their possibly different views, and is there any way they could object to how I will use their contribution to, or appearance in, my dissertation?' (See the guide on 'Treating people properly')

Treating people properly

Here are some basic checks on your handling of what people say and do, their rights to privacy and proper representation of their sayings and views in your text:

■ Always obtain all required ethical clearance before you start, but don't assume that your responsibility stops there.

■ When inviting people to participate in your research in whatever way, tell them what you are doing and why, and what your approach will be.

If your research in, say, social science or medicine involves not giving people the whole truth or misdirecting them because of the experimental design, check very carefully with your supervisor and tutors beforehand to make sure that you follow standard acceptable practice for such research. Afterwards, you should tell your subjects what you have done, otherwise you have obtained information by lying to people (I'm sure you have covered this in research methods if it applies in your subject).

Be courteous at all times

▪ Never be resentful or angry if people decline to work with you, or change their mind after initially saying they would.
  - say thank you and smile and – yes – *move on*. Never, ever, send rude emails, tweets, etc., or make angry phone calls if somebody refuses you.

▪ Thank everybody who has given their time to help you with your dissertation, including interview subjects and those who have, say, given you permission or access.

▪ You are an academic researcher, not an investigative journalist
  - so when interviewing people don't browbeat or be aggressive, or try to catch them out by deceitful, dishonest or illegal means.

▪ Always respect confidences and preserve the security of what you have been told and/or have recorded
  - so don't chat about it to others, or share it with friends, feature it in gossip, or use it for any purpose other than the one you agreed with them . . .

Don't make assumptions

You must ask people what they want, or will be happy to do or see included in your dissertation. Don't just assume they won't mind because they have made a general agreement to talk to you.

▪ Always get explicit permission from people before recording them
  - and put the recording device(s) in plain view.

▪ On the rare occasions where such practices may be appropriate, two-way mirrors, hidden cameras, etc., will require special and explicit clearance from your supervisors and tutors.

▪ Whether you are transcribing an interview from an audio-recording or taking it down longhand or shorthand as they speak, the subject is entitled to see what you say they said
  - so offer them a copy of the transcript, and don't wait for them to ask; agree this kind of thing at the outset.

▪ People should also know how you intend to use what they say, so that means offering them the context too
  - offer them the whole chapter, ideally, or at least a long passage
  - a few lines either side is not enough.

- Check that people are happy for you to incorporate quotations from what they say in your dissertation.

- Make sure that you have their explicit permission to mention them by name.

- If they want to be anonymous, take care that you remove anything that could identify them
  - it's usually not enough just to remove their names.

- Your paraphrases and summaries of what people say are potentially dangerous too – it's not just direct quotations of what they say that are risky. This is one of the reasons why people should be able to see all parts of the dissertation in which they are mentioned or where their views and statements are used.

Practicalities

If you set up a good schedule early on, planned your dissertation progress with some care, and made allowances for appropriate contingencies – and if you stuck to your plans most of the time, of course – then you should be well placed to hand in the right materials at the right time. However, it's still worth reviewing some factors that are easy to overlook, or that can conspire to trip you up at the last minute.

One background aspect of these practicalities is that you should keep direct control over as many of them as possible, so don't ask others to do them for you – 'Hey, can you take this to the binder's for me?' or 'Can you hand my dissertation in for me?' could spell disaster for your dissertation and your friendships. I'm sure you wouldn't subcontract either of these key tasks. But people do.

Printing

- Check all of the RTFM stuff about bindings, cover sheets, declarations, submission dates and places and any online deliveries you may need to make.

- Have you allowed time in your plans for all of the stages needed to produce the final versions of your dissertation?
  - Fairly obvious, perhaps, but things like specialist printing can take longer than you expect.

- Check the printing requirements carefully. If they demand, say, double spacing, 12 pt Times New Roman for body text, 50 mm margins and printing on one side only, then do precisely that.

- How many copies?
  - If some of your printing will be very expensive, are you allowed to do that for just one copy and present the rest using cheaper printing? Don't assume you are – find out.
  - Are you printing extra copies or part-copies for any other people? Do them at the same time as the others. If those other copies are in confidence or not for circulation, etc., then put that on special cover sheets for them.

Binding

- Have you decided where you are getting it bound, if you have a choice?
  - Is that choice acceptable to your university?
  - You may have a choice between on-campus and commercial services, in which case make sure that the commercial binder can follow your – and your university's – instructions.
- If the nature of the binding is precisely specified (such as slotted comb binding), then do exactly that and not, say, some fancy leather-bound thing with a clasp – keep that for your 'directors' cut' version if you're going to do one (see Chapter 8).
- Do you need to book in the job or can you just turn up?
  - A booked-in service, where it exists, may be easier to plan for and schedule. If you turn up at a while-you-wait service near the deadline day don't be surprised to encounter a queue and delays.
- Do you have a contingency plan if there are problems with that bindery? What happens if they have a high workload and will take three days instead of the one day you had planned?
  - In other words, binding on the last possible day is as risky as leaving anything else to the last minute.

Complete and correct?

- Before you take the printed materials to the binder, have you checked that it is all complete?
- Are all the right pages there, in the right order (page numbers?), with additional elements such as colour printed pages in the right place?
  - Are all pages the right way up? (You may laugh, but these things happen.)
  - Are all pages, if printed on one side only, correctly face-up?

- Have you included all the official pages, cover sheets, etc., that you are required to bind in?
- Are there any special or unusual elements in your dissertation that the binder should know about?
  - For example, is there fragile artwork in a non-standard format that nevertheless must be bound in?
- If the binder dropped your carefully collated printout on the floor, could they put it all back together in the right order? (Think about it: this links to contents pages and accurate page numbering and other navigational aids.)
- When you get your bound copies back, do another check on them to make sure all is well inside – right pages, right order and so on. Are the cover pages in there too?

Backups and security

Keep your backup regime working rigorously, right up to the very last set of materials (see Chapters 5 and 8).

- Never have just one copy of anything.
- It is easy to become complacent as time goes on and start to get a bit careless about backups and security.
- But that is precisely when complacency becomes a danger – everything has gone fine up to now, so everything will continue to be all right (a piece of very human inductive reasoning). And then, crash!

Versions

- Make doubly, triply sure that you are handing in the right version of your dissertation.
  - It would be dreadful to hand in an earlier draft by mistake.
- Keep all materials and backups 'for ever' – i.e. at least beyond the end of your course, in case there are any comebacks or queries later (don't worry – there probably won't be – but be prepared). It's also for your benefit, though, as you can look back on it and perhaps even draw on it (legitimately, with due acknowledgement) in some future research you do.
  - This presupposes good version management and identification on your part.

- If you also have to submit an electronic version – for example, to a system like Turnitin – make doubly, triply sure that it is exactly the same version as the printed one you have submitted.
  - If your printed and electronic documents are even slightly different this may make people suspicious (because some wicked cheats do this kind of thing).

Submission specifications

- Be very precise about delivery details and observe them to the letter.
- If it says two (or three, etc.) identical versions, then do precisely that.
- If it says include specific cover sheets and signed declarations, get the right documents and do precisely that.
- If the regulations require you to submit anonymously, or in a way that allows your dissertation to be separate from identifiable covering materials for blind marking, then follow those instructions precisely.

Recorded delivery!

- If you have to give your dissertation to a named person when submitting it, and not just drop it into a box or office, then be sure you do that.
  - Get a signature and/or receipt if that is part of the system.
  - Make sure the receiver date-marks your dissertation if that is also part of the system – it would be galling to hand it in on time but not have that recorded.
- Consider the pros and cons of submitting your dissertation before the due date (if that is permissible) rather than on the last day.
- If you are away from your university at submission time – for example, if you are an international student and have gone home for good – make sure that you have the official instructions for your delivery procedures so that you know exactly how to submit.
  - Postal or courier systems can be slow or experience delays – for example, because of volcanic activity – so it's a good idea to submit an identical digital version online (or email a PDF, etc.), if your rules allow it, to show that you did submit your material by the due date. Needless to say, you must discuss this kind of arrangement with your supervisor or course leaders.

And finally

- RTFM one more tedious time.

Further reading

I have mentioned many times throughout this book that its focus is the dissertation itself – how to turn all that careful thinking, reading and research into a document that does it justice. I have assumed that you are also taking a research methods course, either in the same year as your dissertation or in a preceding year, and that you have a reading list of recommended research methods texts and other material to guide you.

In case you don't have any suggested reading, or want to look at other options, here is a brief list of research-related titles that I think you may find useful.

It's a personal thing, though – people's assessments of research methods texts and study guides vary widely, and whereas one student may find a particular book essential and sleep with it under their pillow, their friend on the same course may simply hate it. I can only list a few that I know have been useful to students I have worked with, and hope that you agree. If not, that's fine. There are a lot of research methods texts out there.

By their nature, these texts go through regular edition upgrades so you should check for the latest ones, but usually the previous editions are almost as useful and are available second-hand. Many of the new editions from more innovative publishers are now available in ebook form and/or with a companion website, so check this in your library.

You will come across many other sources during your dissertation, and I am sure your supervisor will suggest helpful titles and websites too. If you search the internet for 'research methods' or 'dissertation guides' you will find much useful material, especially on other university and college websites. When you consider this material do remember to keep your critical faculties finely tuned to make sure that it is both suitable and of good quality. Here are some questions you should ask:

- Does it apply to the right kind of course at the right level (the one you're doing)?
- Are the information and advice based on a different approach or educational system (for example, in another country)?
- Is it something that is designed very specifically for one particular course but not applicable to yours?
- Who created it, and for what reasons?

Most importantly, *never* use anything from sites claiming to sell dissertations, offer 'specimens' or 'examples' of dissertations for 'research' or 'study', or anything that sounds remotely like that. If you find yourself at one of these sites as a result of your searching, leave it immediately. These are cheat sites, the places from which fraudsters and plagiarizers obtain their raw materials. As I mentioned in Chapter 9, using anything like this is to admit a desire to deceive. Increasingly, cheat sites try to put a plausible gloss on what they do, hence the talk of 'research' and various disingenuous 'disclaimers' on their front pages. But you are a researcher, able to examine sources and raw materials *critically*, so you should find it easy to see through this.

Research methods reading

Lorraine Blaxter, Christina Hughes and Malcolm Tight, *How to Research*, 4th edn, Open University Press, 2010. A good, easy to follow introduction to research with a focus on the social sciences. I have known both undergraduate and postgraduate students use this as their main guide throughout their dissertation.

Martin Brett Davies, *Doing a Successful Research Project: Using Qualitative or Quantitative Methods*, Palgrave Macmillan, 2007. The book has a companion website. I have regularly recommended this book as a course text to undergraduate dissertation students because of both its content and structure. It covers qualitative and quantitative methods, and deals with starting your research all the way through to writing up; it's a book that students can read in its entirety or simply dip into. (See Gordon Rugg and Marian Petre, *A Gentle Guide to Research Methods*, below, for an example of alternative approach.)

Bill Gillham, *Research Interviewing: The Range of Techniques*, Open University Press, 2005. This book, with its single focus, provides a really thorough introduction to the principles and practice of interviewing for research projects. It is an extremely useful reference if your research makes extensive use of interviewing, though most general books cover the topic to a limited extent.

Jonathan Grix, *The Foundations of Research*, Palgrave Macmillan, 2nd edn, 2010. If you are interested in some of the terminology and underlying theories that characterize research and research methods, then you should find this book interesting. It is aimed primarily at postgraduates, though there is much of interest for advanced undergraduate students.

Kjell Erik Rudestam and Rae R. Newton, *Surviving Your Dissertation: A Comprehensive Guide to Content and Process*, 3rd edn, Sage, 2007. A guide biased towards graduate students and the social sciences.

Gordon Rugg and Marian Petre, *A Gentle Guide to Research Methods*, Open University Press, 2007. This is another introduction to research in general; it is more discursive and 'wordy' than Martin Brett Davies's *Doing a Successful Research Project* (see above), and hence a little harder to use as a quick 'dip in' reference, but you may prefer this approach.

Mark Saunders et al., *Research Methods for Business Students*, 5th edn, Financial Times / Prentice Hall, 2009, though earlier editions are still useful and of course cheaper. This is a comprehensive and thorough general guide to research with a particular bias towards research for business students. Since the 4th edition it has had a new large format and high production values as well as linked online resources. It covers all of the main theoretical and practical issues and you may find it a useful reference during your studies, though be warned that it is expensive.

Subject-specific reading

There is a large and growing list of research guides aimed at specific disciplines or subject groups. If there isn't one for your own study area, it may still be worth looking early in your research at those for related fields – they can contain different ideas that could inform or occasionally transform your research. Here are two examples of what I mean, one for media and one for politics:

Ina Bertrand and Peter Hughes, *Media Research Methods: Audiences, Institutions, Texts*, Palgrave, 2004.

Peter Burnham et al., *Research Methods in Politics*, 2nd edn, Palgrave, 2008.

Other useful publications

There are many other reference and self-help titles that could be useful for both your research and for writing up. Here are just three examples, and you will be able to find more:

R. W. Burchfield, ed., *The New Fowler's Modern English Usage*, revised 3rd edn, Oxford University Press, 2004. This is a classic work that manages to advise on current usage without being fanatical, reactionary or beset by the moral panic approach.

Richard Pears and Graham Shields, *Cite Them Right: The Essential Referencing Guide*, Palgrave Study Guides, 8th edn, 2010. Nearly all academic libraries will have copies of this.

Sally Rumsey, *How to Find Information: A Guide for Researchers*, 2nd edn, Open University Press, 2008. As its name suggests, it concentrates on finding the information itself, including from online sources. Certainly well worth a look if you're unsure about where to start looking or only have a general idea.

Index